JOEL C. ROSENBERG

* *

IMPLOSION

CAN AMERICA RECOVER FROM ITS ECONOMIC
& SPIRITUAL CHALLENGES IN TIME?

Tyndale House Publishers, Inc.
Carol Stream, Illinois

Visit Tyndale online at www.tyndale.com.

Visit Joel C. Rosenberg's website at www.joelrosenberg.com.

TYNDALE and Tyndale's quill logo are registered trademarks of Tyndale House Publishers, Inc.

Implosion: Can America Recover from Its Economic and Spiritual Challenges in Time?

Copyright © 2012 by Joel C. Rosenberg. All rights reserved.

Cover photograph of flag copyright © Jacob Termansen and Pia Marie Molbech/Getty Images. All rights reserved.

Author photo copyright © 2005 by Joel C. Rosenberg. All rights reserved.

Designed by Dean H. Renninger

Unless otherwise indicated, all Scripture quotations are taken from the New American Standard Bible,® copyright © 1960, 1962, 1963, 1968, 1971, 1972, 1973, 1975, 1977, 1995 by The Lockman Foundation. Used by permission.

Scripture quotations marked NIV are taken from the Holy Bible, *New International Version,*® *NIV.*® Copyright © 1973, 1978, 1984, 2011 by Biblica, Inc.™ Used by permission of Zondervan. All rights reserved worldwide. www.zondervan.com.

Scripture quotations marked NLT are taken from the *Holy Bible*, New Living Translation, copyright © 1996, 2004, 2007 by Tyndale House Foundation. Used by permission of Tyndale House Publishers, Inc., Carol Stream, Illinois 60188. All rights reserved.

Scripture quotations marked NKJV are taken from the New King James Version.® Copyright © 1982 by Thomas Nelson, Inc. Used by permission. All rights reserved. *NKJV* is a trademark of Thomas Nelson, Inc.

Scripture quotations marked KJV are taken from the *Holy Bible*, King James Version.

Library of Congress Cataloging-in-Publication Data

Rosenberg, Joel C., date.
   Implosion : can America recover from its economic and spiritual challenges in time? / Joel C. Rosenberg.
     p. cm.
   Includes bibliographical references and index.
   ISBN 978-1-4143-1967-4 (hc)
1. Forecasting—Religious aspects—Christianity.   2. United States—Forecasting.   3. End of the world.   4. Prophecy—Christianity.   5. United States—Social conditions—21st century.
6. United States—Economic conditions—2009- I. Title.
   BT877.R67 2012
   277.3'083—dc23   2012003017

Printed in the United States of America

18   17   16   15   14   13   12

7   6   5   4   3   2   1

To Caleb, our firstborn and our first to head off to college:
I'm very proud of you, son, and I can't wait to see how
God will use you to help to save this great country of ours.
America is worth fighting for. Never surrender.

Table of Contents

CHAPTER ONE

A COMING IMPLOSION?

im·plode—*to collapse inward as if from external pressure;*
to break down or fall apart from within; to self-destruct
MERRIAM-WEBSTER'S DICTIONARY

IS IT POSSIBLE THAT THE AMERICAN ECONOMY—and, more broadly, American society in general—is not simply facing serious challenges or a season of decline? Could America actually collapse in the not-too-distant future if serious, fundamental, and sweeping changes are not made soon? Once, such a question would have struck most Americans as ludicrous—even offensive. But times have changed.

The first time I noticed any serious public discussion of the possibility of the American economy imploding was in September 2010. Senator Judd Gregg, the New Hampshire Republican and onetime chairman of the Senate Budget Committee, was being interviewed live from the U.S. Capitol by Fox News host Greta Van Susteren. They were discussing the massive increases in federal spending, astronomically large U.S. deficits, and unprecedented and unsustainable levels of national debt being racked up by an out-of-control political culture in Washington and the grave dangers these challenges posed to U.S. economic and national security.

"I don't want to be an alarmist," Van Susteren said, "but based on what you say, if Congress can't do a very good job, and if spending is a very effective tool for politicians, and if they add every year, and if the national debt is creating national-security problems as the secretary of state has said, at some point, it seems, we're going to implode."

"That's right," Senator Gregg replied. "That's exactly what's going to happen."

At that moment in the interview, Van Susteren struck me as being taken aback by the fact that the senator had so quickly agreed with her. Perhaps she was expecting, as I was when I saw the interview, that the senator would dismiss the concept of an "implosion" as going a bit far. Yet that was not the case.

"So do you have any idea when that's going to happen and what that's going to mean?" Van Susteren asked.

"Sooner rather than later," Gregg replied matter-of-factly.[1]

Implosion? It's an awfully strong term. Van Susteren knew it. That's why she prefaced her comment by saying she didn't want to be an "alarmist." Still, to her the evidence Senator Gregg was laying out suggested the United States might not simply be headed down an increasingly dangerous path but rather a cataclysmic one.

Yet as startling as the question was, it was the answer, not the question, that was news. A respected U.S. senator was suggesting on national television that he believed America was on the path toward "implosion" unless dramatic, historic steps were taken to change course. It was a sobering moment, made all the more troubling by the fact that Gregg had never been known in Washington for fiery, wild-eyed, hyperbolic rhetoric. What's more, few in Washington, or in the country, were at that time in a better position than he was to truly understand the magnitude of the fiscal crisis we were—and still are—facing as a nation.

Over time, however, awareness of those troubles began to spread.

A few months later, a headline out of New York City—the financial epicenter of the American economy—caught my attention: "Rubin Warns of Bond Market 'Implosion': U.S. in 'Terribly Dangerous Territory.'" The article began:

> Warning of the risk of an "implosion" in the bond market, former Treasury Secretary Robert Rubin says the soaring federal budget deficit and the Fed's quantitative easing [the printing and pumping of more money into the American economy by the Federal Reserve] are putting the U.S. in "terribly dangerous territory."[2]

Rubin, a loyal Democrat who served as the country's chief financial officer in President Clinton's administration, had never been known for fiery, wild-eyed, hyperbolic rhetoric any more than Senator Gregg had been. He wasn't running for political office. He wasn't pontificating before a left-wing special-interest group. He was speaking at an event for business executives, financial professionals, and federal budget experts organized by the Concord Coalition, a "nonpartisan, grassroots organization dedicated to balanced federal budgets and generationally responsible fiscal policy." Also speaking at the event was former U.S. comptroller general David Walker, who has long argued that America "suffer[s] from a fiscal cancer" that is "growing within us," which if left untreated "could have catastrophic consequences" for our country.[3]

Senator Kent Conrad, the North Dakota Democrat and chairman of the Senate Budget Committee at the time, also spoke at the event. He agreed with Secretary Rubin's assessment, saying the U.S. was facing a "defining moment" in terms of our fiscal crisis and noting, "If we fail [to act], our nation will be condemned to second-class status."[4]

Not long after this, Congressman Paul Ryan, the Wisconsin Republican and chairman of the House Budget Committee, began briefing fellow members of Congress and speaking at forums in Washington and around the country on the grave danger facing the American economy in view of the skyrocketing federal debt. While Ryan didn't use the term *implosion*, he might as well have; his message was just as sobering.

"We're on a path where our debt goes from about 68 percent of GDP [Gross Domestic Product] to 800 percent of GDP over the three-generation window," Congressman Ryan said. "I asked CBO [the Congressional Budget Office] to run the model going out, and they told me that their computer simulation crashes in 2037 because CBO can't conceive of any way in which the economy can continue past the year 2037 because of debt burdens."[5]

Ryan has noted that by the time his young children reach forty years of age, "just . . . three programs—Social Security, Medicaid, and Medicare—will consume all federal revenues. There will be no room for anything else in the federal budget." He has also warned that "every year we delay fixing the debt problem, we go about $10 trillion deeper in the hole . . . adding to unfunded promises that we are making to Americans."[6]

The *St. Petersburg Times* ran an article on its website, PolitiFact.com, analyzing Congressman Ryan's case. "Paul Van de Water, a senior fellow at the liberal Center for Budget and Policy Priorities, said it's plausible that the [Congressional Budget Office] model could implode as early as the 2030s, though he added that other models analyzed by the CBO do not predict an implosion that soon," PolitiFact reported.[7]

Slowly but surely, the concept of the "implosion" of the American economy was entering the national conversation.

An Unexpected Question

It was during that period that I happened to be invited to the United States Capitol for a private meeting with a group of congressmen.

The purpose was to discuss the future of Israel in light of the rising Iranian nuclear threat and the future of the U.S.–Israel relationship given recent partisan political tensions in Washington. Because of the subject matter, I decided to accept and a few days later arrived at the meeting just off the floor of the House of Representatives.

During a break, I began chatting with the congressman sitting next to me. Soon the discussion shifted from the challenges facing Israel to the challenges facing the United States. We compared notes for a few minutes on the federal government's runaway spending, the exploding national deficit, the out-of-control debt, and our stagnant economy. Then the congressman leaned over to me and whispered, "This city doesn't get it, Joel. If we don't make major changes—and I mean sweeping reforms—really quickly, I'm not sure how much longer as a nation we can actually survive."

I certainly agreed the situation was bad, but in two decades of living and working in Washington, I had rarely heard a lawmaker speak in such an apocalyptic tone. "You really believe it's that serious?" I asked.

"I've never seen it worse than it is right now," he replied. "And most of Congress is absolutely asleep. They're arguing over cosmetic changes, but few people around here seem to realize just how much trouble we're really in."

Then he asked me the question I wasn't expecting.

"Joel, what does the Bible say happens to America in the last days?"

I have to admit, I was startled. It's not that I'd never been asked the question before. I just had never been asked it by a sitting member of Congress, inside the U.S. Capitol.

A few weeks later, I was on the phone with the governor of a large American state. We were discussing the revolutions under way in the Arab world, smoldering turmoil inside Iran, and the growing threats to the nation of Israel from radical Islam. Before long, however, the conversation turned back to the United States. We began talking about the enormous economic and spiritual threats facing our own country and the daunting prospects of how to turn things around. We also wondered who—if any—of the emerging crop of presidential candidates might have the vision, strength, and wherewithal to get this country back on track.

Then the governor surprised me by asking me a question very similar to one the congressman had asked a few weeks before.

"Joel, I'm curious; does the Bible give us any indication as to what will happen to the United States in the future?"

Soul Searching

Though it doesn't typically make news because it doesn't happen in the public eye, many world leaders through the years have asked deeply personal and profoundly important questions of Christian pastors, ministry leaders, and authors, as long as they have been confident that while they were still alive, those sensitive conversations would be kept private and their names would be kept confidential in connection to those discussions. Billy Graham is an example of a prominent Christian in whom many world leaders have confided.

In May 1954, for example, Winston Churchill, the prime minister of the United Kingdom, said to Graham, "I am a man without hope. Do you have any real hope?" In reply, Graham asked, "Are you without hope for your own soul's salvation?" Churchill answered, "Frankly, I think about that a great deal." The pastor gently opened the New Testament and took the great British wartime hero through the gospel's plan of salvation from the teachings of Jesus Christ.[8]

In the summer of 1955, Dwight Eisenhower, the former supreme Allied commander of all Western military forces in the European theater, who had recently been elected president of the United States, asked Billy Graham, "Could you explain to me how a person can be sure when he dies he's going to heaven?" Grateful for Eisenhower's sincere question, Graham shared with the president some key passages from the words of Jesus Christ explaining how a person can be absolutely certain that his sins are forgiven and that he will spend eternity in heaven with the Lord.[9]

In January 1961, John F. Kennedy, the first Catholic to be elected president of the United States, took the Protestant Christian minister aside for a discreet conversation and asked, "Do you believe in the second coming of Jesus Christ?" Graham was surprised by the question but responded, "I sure do." The president-elect asked, "Why doesn't my church teach it?" Graham told Kennedy that the Second Coming was written about in the creeds of the Catholic church. "They don't tell us much about it," Kennedy replied. "I'd like to know what you think." The minister then shared from the Bible prophecies about the last days, including some of the teachings of Jesus Christ's promise to return to earth in the End Times.[10]

We didn't learn that these powerful men had asked these specific questions until after each of those leaders had passed away. Yet these brief conversations give us a fascinating glimpse into their hearts and minds. Churchill, having helped defeat Adolf Hitler and the evil Third Reich, was serving in his second term as British prime minister. Now he faced a new threat. As he stated ominously just after the war at a college in the American Midwest, "From Stettin in the Baltic to Trieste in the Adriatic, an iron curtain has descended across the Continent" of Europe, controlled by the Soviet Empire. Churchill warned that if the Western democracies were not unified and steadfast in their resistance to Communism, "then indeed catastrophe may overwhelm us all."[11] He saw a terrible new war was looming with the Soviet bloc powers, a war he feared could prove far more horrific than the one the West had just survived and won. Eisenhower and Kennedy, too, saw a nuclear-armed Soviet Empire rising, horrible wars engulfing the Korean peninsula and Vietnam, and the risk of apocalyptic new wars erupting in Europe and Asia. The future of their nations and the world looked very grim from their vantage points. No wonder they were looking to the Bible to see if the Scriptures held any answers, any hope at all.

It is one thing, however, for leaders to discreetly ask soul-searching questions about how to know Jesus Christ personally, how to walk with God more closely, how to better understand the relevance of the second coming of Christ and other personal matters related to the Bible. We would hope and expect that they would ask such questions, and it's heartening to know—even years after the fact—that some do. But it is quite another thing for leaders to privately ask whether the Bible offers clues to the possible decline or even implosion of their own country.

There is nothing wrong with doing so. To the contrary, all leaders should feel comfortable asking honest, genuine questions about what the Bible says on any subject, including their nation's future. Most of us, however, simply would not expect such questions from our national leaders. In many ways, this is new, uncharted territory. Yet given the state of our economic and cultural troubles, these are the questions people are asking these days.

And it's not just politicians. In my experience, people at all levels of business, media, the arts, sports, ministry, education, and elsewhere are asking as well.

The Most Frequently Asked Question

Until recently, the question I was asked most frequently when I spoke and did interviews in the U.S. and around the world was, "Joel, how can you be Jewish and believe that Jesus is the Messiah?" Within the last few years, however, that important question has been significantly eclipsed by another one. These days, the question I am most frequently asked is this: "What happens to America in the last days?"

I also get plenty of variations on the theme:

- Is America simply in decline, or are we like the Roman Empire, stumbling toward collapse?
- Do you believe America's days are numbered?
- Are we approaching the end of America as we have known it?
- Are we living in the last days?
- What does the Bible say about the future of the United States?
- Is America even mentioned in End Times Bible prophecy?
- Is America mentioned, described, or hinted at in the Bible at all?

Christians are certainly wrestling with such questions. But I find that Americans from a variety of religious backgrounds—including Jews, Muslims, and others—are asking these and similar questions as well. Indeed, often when I am on a secular talk radio show, I'm invited to talk about geopolitical issues related to Israel, the broader Middle East, and radical Islam. The conversation tends to come around to my views of how Israel and the nations of the epicenter fit into Bible prophecy, and then it's not uncommon for the radio host to ask me, "So what about America? What does the Bible say about our future?"

Some people ask because they are certain America *is*, in fact, described in the Scriptures as a significant or even major player in the End Times, and they want to know more. They are looking for hope that we are going to weather the economic, political, moral, spiritual, and other storms now battering us so intensely. Others, however, ask because they are fearful the U.S. is *not* described in the Bible, and they are wondering, "Why not? And if not, what will happen to us, and how much time do we have left?"

My wife, Lynn, and I have lived in and around Washington, DC, since 1990, and neither of us recalls hearing such questions—much less being asked them ourselves—during our first decade in Washington.

During those years, my professional life was immersed in researching and advocating various economic/social/cultural/educational reforms and working on political campaigns for a variety of U.S. and Israeli leaders, not teaching Bible prophecy. I'm not saying such questions weren't being asked and answered by others during this time. I'm just saying that I, apparently, wasn't tuned in to such conversations.

Over the course of the last decade, however—and even more so in the last few years—as such questions have come up more and more, I'm increasingly aware of and focused on this conversation, more so than at any other time in my life, ever since I left the campaign trail, went through what I call "political detox," and began writing books about the growing geopolitical, religious, and economic threats facing America, Israel, and the church in light of Bible prophecy. My sense is that more people are asking these questions more often—and more openly—than ever before. A growing number of Americans fear that this period of our history is different and the crises we face today—and those coming up over the horizon—may be far worse than anything we have experienced in the past.

Why Are People Asking?

Indeed, Americans are asking such questions, in my experience, with growing frequency and urgency because of a gnawing and steadily intensifying anxiety they and their families and their neighbors have that, as challenging as things are in our country today, they very well could get catastrophically worse. Many Americans genuinely fear that God is preparing to remove his hand of protection and blessing from our country—or perhaps already has. They fear that unlike previous dark times in our national history, God may not intend to help us turn things around and get us back on the right track.

Understandably, such thoughts can be both unnerving and perplexing. The more optimistic among us ask questions like "Surely,

God *must* have a plan and purpose for America going forward, and it must be a good and wonderful plan, right?" Yet even these are signaling their doubts by asking the question.

When people in other countries ask what the future of America holds and whether America will continue to lead the world in the twenty-first century—and they do ask, with ever more frequency—they tend to do so, I believe, for one of two reasons: Either they honestly fear what the world will look like without an economically, militarily, and socially vibrant United States of America playing a central and starring role in shaping the future of the globe. Or they secretly long for a day when the U.S. is humbled, weakened, and even neutralized so that other nations can take the lead and reshape the future of the globe.

Such are the times in which we live.

Some Context

Before we go any further, let me just say it has been difficult for me to write this book. To be perfectly honest, there were many times when I simply didn't want to finish it. I didn't want to study the data or examine the trends, much less draw any conclusions about the future of our country. The process was, at times, depressing, and if I'm not careful, I can still find myself becoming anxious or gloomy.

I dearly love my country. I was born here and grew up here, and I don't want anything bad to happen to America. I don't want to imagine worst-case scenarios, much less write about them. I don't want to suffer through such times if they come. Nor do I want Lynn or our four sons—Caleb, Jacob, Jonah, and Noah—to suffer through such times. I don't want our extended family and friends, spread out all over this beautiful land, to go through such times, either. Maybe none of us will. Maybe the worst-case scenarios will be avoided. I certainly hope so.

Yet I live and work in the nation's capital. I regularly and extensively travel this country. I see what's happening all around me, and it is deeply disturbing. Marriages and families are imploding. Our federal debt is exploding. The tide of cultural pollution is rising. Our educational system is collapsing. Friends and neighbors are abandoning God and the church. The list of horrifying trends seems to grow longer each and every year. At this point, even a blind man can see the handwriting on the wall. The question is, what does the handwriting say, and what does it portend for the future of America?

The apostle Paul once said that God "made from one man every nation of mankind to live on all the face of the earth, having determined their appointed times and the boundaries of their habitation" (Acts 17:26). In other words, God decides precisely where on the planet and precisely in which period of history each man and woman is going to be born.

Centuries before Paul, David—the Jewish shepherd boy from Bethlehem who unexpectedly rose to become the beloved king of Israel from whom the Messiah would humanly descend—wrote that God "formed my inward parts" and "wove me in my mother's womb." In a remarkable prayer of gratitude to the Lord, David wrote, "I will give thanks to You, for I am fearfully and wonderfully made . . . Your eyes have seen my unformed substance; and in Your book were all written the days that were ordained for me, when as yet there was not one of them" (Psalm 139:13-16). David, too, understood the sovereign will and power of God. He understood that God is the creator who fashions each one of us with a plan and a purpose. He understood that God both knows and decides exactly where and when each one of us will be born, and he makes these decisions for a reason.

Such truths point us to another truth. God could have chosen you to live in another time and another place. You could have lived in the times of Moses or the times of David or the times of Jesus and Paul. But in his sovereign will, God decided you and I would live in these times. What's more, he chose the very family and language and country into which you and I would be born. It wasn't an accident. It was part of a plan. Most of those reading this book are likely to be American citizens. Have you ever taken time to consider why God chose you to be an American? What purpose are you to serve in this country? What role in the future of this country has God planned for you to play? Given the high stakes of this moment, I would encourage you to take some time to give these questions serious thought. Discuss them with your family and friends.

For those who are living in the United States but are not American citizens, I would encourage you to take some time as well to consider why the Lord has brought you to this country. What action does he want you to take at this critical hour? For those of you who are reading this someplace else, as citizens of another country, it is probably fair to say you would not have picked up this book unless you had an interest in the future of America. Take some time to consider why you care, what you're hoping to learn, and what role God has for you to play in the future of America as well as in your own country's future.

Jews, Gentiles, and the American Dream

Every American citizen has his or her own "American story," a heritage to be treasured and celebrated. My family is no different.

My family on my father's side was made up of Orthodox Jews who escaped from the "old country"—anti-Semitic, totalitarian, czarist Russia—during the pogroms against the Jews in the early 1900s. They made their way to America searching for religious freedom, freedom from persecution, and the opportunity for a better way of life.

Given that both of my paternal grandparents died before I was three years old, I never had the chance to talk to them and ask them their stories. Sadly, neither of my grandparents told my father or his brother many stories from the old country. They passed down few documents to us. So it's been challenging to piece together their journey. About the only story that has been passed down through our family is that when our Orthodox Jewish relatives wanted to leave Russia, some of them had to escape in a hay wagon that was crossing out of Russia into a neighboring country. (The best we can surmise is that they went into Poland.) Czarist soldiers plunged their swords into the hay to see if there was anyone hiding in there. By God's grace, no one was injured. By God's grace, my relatives weren't discovered. And by God's grace, having gotten out of Russia, they didn't decide to settle in Poland or Germany or anywhere else in central Europe. Many Russian Jews did settle there, of course, escaping the horrors of the Russian pogroms only to experience the horrors of the Third Reich and the Holocaust.

Called by freedom and the promise of a new world, my family kept moving across the continent of Europe until they got to a port, scrounged up enough money to pay for passage on a steamship, made their way to America, and settled in Brooklyn.

A few years ago, my wife and I found an actual copy of a 1930 U.S. census record showing that my great-grandfather Maximilian "Max" Jaffe lived in Brooklyn and that he was a tailor, from Russia, Jewish, with no formal education but could read and write. The records also indicated that Max arrived in the United States in 1903 and that his wife and his daughter, Selma—my father's mother— arrived in the U.S. five years after him in 1908.

What my Jewish grandparents and great-grandparents found here was more than they could have hoped for, dreamed of, or imagined. They were finally free to go to a synagogue and celebrate the Jewish holidays in peace, establish and raise a family in safety, and seek to give their children and grandchildren better lives than they had. Selma Jaffe would later marry Herman Rosenberg, also of Russian Jewish heritage. Together they had two sons, Jerome (my uncle Jerry), and Leonard, my father. Both brothers are first-generation American citizens. My father was born in Brooklyn in 1939 at a time when Adolf Hitler was on the move in Europe, seeking to take over the world and preparing to exterminate 6 million Jews, including more than a million Jewish children. My father was the first on his side of the family to ever graduate from college, and he was the first to become a licensed professional—in his case, an architect.

My family on my mother's side were Gentiles—white, Anglo-Saxon, Protestant Christians who came to the New World fleeing religious persecution from the state-controlled churches of Europe and seeking more economic opportunity. My maternal grandmother, Esther Cagwin, was a member of the Daughters of the American Revolution, her family having come to the colonies from England before the Revolution began. The ancestors of my maternal grandfather, Walter Copia, were Germans. His grandparents, Joseph and Elizabeth Copia, were from Baden and Berlin, Germany, respectively. Unfortunately, I know very little about them, their history, or their dreams and aspirations. My maternal grandfather abandoned the family and filed for divorce, leaving my grandmother, Esther, all alone to raise my mother, Mary, an only child, in a small city called Rome, New York—not far from Utica and Syracuse. My grandmother (Grammie), a public school teacher, was a heroic woman and one of the kindest and most generous people I have ever met. Since her husband had left her long before I came along, and since my Jewish grandparents passed away when I was just a toddler, Grammie Copia was the only grandparent I ever knew, and I loved her dearly and missed her terribly after she passed away in 1982.

Even with painful and at times tragic chapters, my family's story is an *American* story. We have truly had the opportunity to live the American dream. My forebears chose to leave the countries of their birth and travel to the New World despite many hardships. They wanted to be Americans, pure and simple. In God's sovereignty and by his grace, that's exactly what they became. For our family, America has truly proven to be a home for both Jews and Gentiles. For us, the verse at the base of the Statue of Liberty is not trite. It has real and personal meaning. *"Give me your tired, your poor, your huddled masses yearning to breathe free, the wretched refuse of your teeming shore. Send these, the homeless, tempest-tost to me, I lift my lamp beside the golden door!"* Members of my family were once part of the "huddled masses yearning to breathe free." America opened her "golden door" to us, and we will forever be grateful. But now, I am deeply concerned about the future of this country that has been so good to us.

Why I Wrote This Book

These are not normal times.

Americans have been gripped by a widespread and deeply rooted pessimism in recent years. They are openly asking whether our nation can survive. In the pages ahead, we'll consider whether such pessimism is reasonable or an unwarranted overreaction to current economic and spiritual trends. Americans have, after all, faced dark times before and overcome them. Then we'll look at recent events and trends in the light of Bible prophecy. We'll consider whether we are in the period of history the Bible calls the "last days" and look at which nations and regions of the world are specifically mentioned as key players in End Times prophecies. We'll then look directly at a central question people are asking—"What happens to America in the last days?"—and examine a range of scenarios Americans could face in the months and years ahead.

Then we'll take a look back at two remarkable periods in American history. We'll see how God has blessed this nation in the past with two tremendous spiritual revivals, and we'll quickly study some of the key human players God used to bring about these periods, known as the First Great Awakening and the Second Great Awakening. And then we will ask two other crucial questions: Given that God has blessed America with such amazing revivals in the past, might he choose to do so once again? Instead of allowing America to implode, might the Lord in his grace and mercy allow us to experience a Third Great Awakening in the years to come?

After some observations and interpretations, we'll begin to consider some applications. In light of where we are and where we are heading as a country, how should we then live? How should our relationship with God be different from what it is now, if at all? How should our relationships with our parents, our spouses, our children, and our neighbors change? How should our involvement in our churches change? Are we content with the church's involvement in our society? If so, why? If not, why not? To what extent, if at all, should we be involved in the political process? And how can we keep from losing hope if our nation continues to be shaken and loses her way?

My hope is that you will not only find this book helpful for yourself but that perhaps you'll share it with a friend and discuss it over a cup of coffee or a pot of tea. Perhaps you'll decide to study it with your book club or with your small-group Bible study or home fellowship group. Whatever you do, please don't keep your thoughts to yourself. Engage someone else in this conversation. Listen to what they think. Compare notes. Discuss practical steps you intend to take going forward and how you might encourage one another on the journey.

The stakes are very high. Our nation has come to a critical crossroads. We face the potential implosion of our economy and society. Let us, therefore, engage each other in discussing how we got here, where we are going, and most importantly what the Lord is telling us in his Word to do next.

Time is of the essence.

CHAPTER TWO

AMERICA'S RISING ANXIETY

MOST OF MY FOCUS in the past decade has been on the Middle East.

Given the enormous volatility of the region, its importance to global economic and national security, and its central role in Bible prophecy, I have crisscrossed the region from Morocco and Egypt, to Israel and Jordan, to Iraq and Afghanistan, analyzing and writing about geopolitical, economic, and spiritual trends. In researching and writing my 2009 book, *Inside the Revolution*, I was struck afresh by how deeply radical Islamic leaders—and particularly the leaders of Iran—believe the United States is destined for the ash heap of history and by how often they declare that America's demise is coming quickly. Recall for a moment a few examples:

- "We now predict a black day for America—and the end of the United States as the United States, God willing," Osama bin Laden famously declared in 1998, a prediction radical Muslims in al Qaeda still work and pray for despite bin Laden's demise.[1]

- "God willing, with the force of God behind it, we shall soon experience a world without the United States and Zionism," Iranian president Mahmoud Ahmadinejad predicted in a highly publicized speech in 2005.[2]
- "The end of the U.S. will begin in Iraq," Iran's Ayatollah Ali Khamenei confidently asserted that same year. "One day the U.S. will be history."[3]
- "Today, the time for the fall of the satanic power of the United States has come, and the countdown to the annihilation of the emperor of power and wealth has started," Ahmadinejad said in 2008. "Get ready for a world minus the U.S."[4]
- "Not only corrupted and despotic rulers, but the United States and other world powers with an aggressive nature will finally suffer a defeat by nations, and God's promises will come true," the Ayatollah Khamenei reiterated in 2011.[5]
- "I am certain that the region will soon witness the collapse of Israel and the U.S.," Ahmadinejad echoed the same year.[6]

On and on it goes. By now such sentiments and predictions should not be surprising. The jihadists believed their prayers and efforts led to the collapse of the Soviet Union in the late 1980s and early 1990s. Now they believe the "godless" American empire is next to fall.

What is surprising, however—stunning, really—is that large segments of American society have also come to believe that the United States is in severe trouble. Not just run-of-the-mill, garden-variety trouble, but real peril. Grave danger. And not just from threats without, such as radical Islam, but from threats within, such as financial ruin and moral decay. Vast numbers of Americans have come to believe we have entered a period of severe and potentially irreversible decline. What's more, many Americans go even further, fearing that the United States is in serious risk of economic and social collapse, not mere decline. Some fear America is following the path of the Roman Empire and wonder if their country is destined for destruction. Their reasoning may have little or nothing to do with that of the Islamic Radicals, but their conclusions seem unnervingly similar.

What's more striking is that these Americans are not limited to a particular political party, religion, socioeconomic status, or region of the country. They don't represent just one sliver or slice of the country. Rather, they increasingly span the full spectrum of partisan, ideological, racial, cultural, and spiritual backgrounds. Were one somehow able to put them all in the same place, they would surely have more disagreements than agreements on how best to solve our country's problems. But they would agree on at least one thing: they all genuinely wonder if we are in jeopardy of witnessing the end of America as we have known her for so long.

What the Polls Are Saying

Public opinion surveys are, to be sure, imperfect barometers of the American mood. Even the most carefully designed and trustworthy polls can provide only momentary glimpses into people's hearts and minds. They represent mere snapshots in time. Still, a review of polling trends over the last decade or so paints a sobering picture of rising American anxiety about the future of our country.

The Gallup organization, for example, routinely asks Americans, "In general, are you satisfied or dissatisfied with the way things are going in the United States at this time?"

In January 2000, at the dawn of a new millennium, we were brimming with optimism. Only 28 percent of Americans said they were dissatisfied with the way things were going in America, while 69 percent of Americans said they were satisfied.[7]

Eight years later, however, everything had changed. Amid the historic financial crisis on Wall Street in the fall of 2008, the loss of trillions of dollars of personal wealth, millions of layoffs, surging unemployment, soaring home foreclosures, an alarming number of bank failures, and skyrocketing national deficits and federal debt, such optimism had evaporated. By October of that year, a stunning 90 percent of Americans said they were dissatisfied with the situation in America, while a mere 9 percent said they were satisfied. This proved to be the lowest such reading to that point in Gallup's history, the organization noted, adding that "the previous low point for Gallup's measure of satisfaction had been 12 percent, recorded back in 1979, in the midst of rising prices and gas shortages when Jimmy Carter was president."[8]

Other polls taken during that period similarly captured the magnitude of Americans' anxiety about the condition of their country and their increasingly deep-rooted pessimism about the future. A remarkable 73 percent of Americans at the time told pollsters they believed the U.S. was in a state of decline, according to an NBC News/*Wall Street Journal* poll.[9] What's more, according to an ABC News/*Washington Post* poll, 82 percent of Americans said the country was on the wrong track.[10]

Over the next several years, those poll numbers ebbed and flowed, but overall the nation remained deeply pessimistic. As businesses continued to shut their doors or lay off employees, more homes were foreclosed, more banks failed, federal spending continued to skyrocket, and the federal deficit and debt exploded to levels never before seen in the entirety of our nation's history, Americans remained deeply anxious about the country's short-term future, to say nothing of our long-term prospects. It was as if Americans felt they were standing in the middle of a frozen lake, far away from the safety of the shore, and they were beginning to hear the ice cracking under their feet. They had not plunged into the bone-chilling waters below—not yet—but they feared a wrong step, a wrong move, could prove fatal.

Consider the following numbers:

- In the spring of 2010, nearly eight in ten Americans said they feared the U.S. economy could collapse entirely.[11]
- A year later, the same number said they were dissatisfied with what's happening in our country, while only two in ten Americans said they were satisfied.[12]
- Four in ten Americans in the summer of 2011 said that "the current economic downturn is part of a long-term permanent decline, and the economy will never fully recover."[13]
- Nearly half of all Americans feared the U.S. was heading for another Great Depression.[14]
- At the end of 2011, more than seven in ten Americans said they believed the country was on the wrong track.[15]

Permanent decline? Economic collapse? Another Great Depression? Do Americans really believe such catastrophic events could happen here? Not all Americans do, of course, but yes, clearly tens of millions of people believe this. And while it's probable that these polls are partly picking up the views of perennial pessimists and congenital hypochondriacs, the data suggest that such fear about the future of our country has become both widespread and mainstream.

What the Pundits Are Saying

Consider, too, what a wide range of political analysts, columnists, social scientists, historians, and other commentators are saying. Not only are Americans across the political spectrum privately contemplating the possibility that the United States may be in a tailspin from which we may not be able to recover, but they are also increasingly feeling compelled to say such things aloud.

- Keith Olbermann, a liberal political commentator, told viewers on MSNBC that we are witnessing "the beginning of the end of America."[16]
- Glenn Beck, a conservative political commentator, told his nationwide radio audience that "this is the end of America as you know it."[17]
- Al Gore, former vice president of the United States and the Democratic nominee for president in the 2000 campaign, has said he believes that America is in "grave danger" and that the world faces a "planetary emergency."[18]
- Charles Krauthammer, a Pulitzer Prize–winning conservative columnist, told Fox News viewers that "it's midnight in America."[19]
- Paul Krugman, a liberal *New York Times* columnist, believes "the American dream is not totally dead, but it's . . . dying pretty fast."[20]
- Peggy Noonan, a conservative *Wall Street Journal* columnist, says there is across America "a sense that the wheels are coming off the trolley and the trolley off the tracks. That in some deep and fundamental way things have broken down and can't be fixed, or won't be fixed anytime soon. That our pollsters are preoccupied with 'right track' and 'wrong track' but missing the number of people who think the answer to 'How are things going in America?' is 'Off the tracks and hurtling forward, toward an unknown destination.'"[21]
- Chalmers Johnson, a late liberal professor emeritus at the University of California, San Diego, wrote before his death in 2010 that "the capacity for things [in America] to get worse

is limitless" and that "Roman history suggests that the short, happy life of the American republic may be coming to its end."[22]

- Thomas Sowell, a conservative professor and economist, observes that "the collapse of a civilization is not just the replacement of rulers or institutions with new rulers and new institutions. It is the destruction of a whole way of life and the painful, and sometimes pathetic, attempts to begin rebuilding amid the ruins. Is that where America is headed? I believe it is. Our only saving grace is that we are not there yet."[23]

- Cullen Murphy, the liberal editor of *Vanity Fair* and former editor of *The Atlantic*, asks, "Are we Rome? In a thousand specific ways, the answer is obviously no [but] in a handful of important ways, the answer is certainly yes."[24]

- Pat Buchanan, a conservative columnist and former advisor to Presidents Nixon and Reagan, believes that "The United States is strategically overextended worldwide. . . . It is an empire, and the empire is coming down."[25]

- David Murrin, an international market strategist and author of a book on the future of the markets, warned viewers on CNBC's *Squawk Box Europe* that the enormous deficit and debt crisis facing the United States was causing him to become very doubtful about America's ability to turn things around. "It's the beginning of the end," he said, assessing the whole of the American economic and political system.[26]

- Tom Friedman, a liberal *New York Times* columnist, surmises, "You really do have to wonder whether a few years from now we'll look back at the first decade of the twenty-first century—when food prices spiked, energy prices soared, world population surged, tornadoes plowed through cities, floods and droughts set records, populations were displaced, and governments were threatened by the confluence of it all—and ask ourselves: What were we thinking? How did we not panic when the evidence was so obvious . . . ?"[27]

Yet it is not merely partisans on the Left or Right who are deeply worried about where America is headed. The so-called mainstream media sees the decline of America as mainstream thinking as well.

- A 2009 headline in *U.S. News & World Report* declared: "Nine Signs of America in Decline."[28]
- In 2010, Salon.com published a story titled "How America Will Collapse (by 2025): Four Scenarios That Could Spell the End of the United States As We Know It—In the Very Near Future."[29]
- In 2011, *Time* published a cover story with the headline "Are America's Best Days Behind Us?"[30]
- In 2011, an article in *Psychology Today* was titled "Why America Is in Decline."[31]
- Also in 2011, *Newsweek* reported that, aboard the Pentagon jet on his last foreign trip as secretary of defense, Robert Gates—a bipartisan veteran of the administrations of Ronald Reagan, George H. W. Bush, George W. Bush, and Barack Obama—took a moment to peer across the American horizon and explain that "the view is dire" because "the U.S. is in danger of losing its supremacy on the global stage."[32]

What the Publishers Are Selling

Consider, too, what kinds of books editors in American publishing houses are signing contracts for, marketing, and finding widespread audiences and significant sales for. Given the enormous economic and social challenges America is presently facing, it would not be surprising to find a range of successful books on ways to reform, fix, and improve our country, and there are plenty of those on the market, many written by the nation's political leaders. What is surprising is to find a remarkable number of influential, thought-provoking, and often bestselling books on the market suggesting that an apocalyptic moment may be fast approaching and that America's days may be numbered. Among them:

- *Colossus: The Rise and Fall of the American Empire* by Niall Ferguson (Penguin: 2004, 2005)
- *The End of America: Letter of Warning to a Young Patriot* by Naomi Wolf (Chelsea Green: 2007)
- *Nemesis: The Last Days of the American Republic* by Chalmers Johnson (Metropolitan: 2006)
- *Are We Rome? The Fall of an Empire and the Fate of America* by Cullen Murphy (Mariner: 2007)
- *The Post-American World* by Fareed Zakaria (Norton: 2009, 2011)
- *Dismantling America* by Thomas Sowell (Basic: 2010)
- *After America: Get Ready for Armageddon* by Mark Steyn (Regnery: 2011)
- *Suicide of a Superpower: Will America Survive to 2025?* by Patrick J. Buchanan (Thomas Dunne: 2011)

Not long ago, it would have been inconceivable to the vast majority of Americans to read a book about the possible imminent demise of their country. Today, such books are becoming national bestsellers on a fairly frequent basis. To better understand the phenomenon, let us take a closer look at three such recent titles.

Are We Really Hurtling toward "The End of America"?
Perhaps the quintessential book capturing the depth of anxiety on the American political Left in recent years is *The End of America:*

Letter of Warning to a Young Patriot. Published in 2007, it was written by Naomi Wolf, the noted liberal author, feminist, and political activist who writes for *The New Republic*, the *New York Times*, and *Glamour* magazine.

"To U.S. citizens in the year 2007, the very title of this book should be absurd," Wolf concedes[33] before going on to lay out her central thesis that because of our fear of radical Islam, the American federal government is steadily taking away Americans' civil liberties and creating conditions for tyranny. She continues:

> I am writing because we have an emergency. . . . My sense
> of alarm comes from the clear lessons of history that, once
> certain checks and balances are destroyed, and once certain
> institutions have been intimidated, the pressures that can
> turn an open society into a closed one turn into direct
> assaults; at that point events tend to occur very rapidly, and
> a point comes at which there is no easy turning back to
> the way it used to be. The fascist shift . . . progresses in a
> buildup of many acts assaulting democracy simultaneously,
> which then form a critical mass. . . . If fascist Germany—
> a medium-sized modern European state—could destabilize
> the globe in a matter of a few years, and it took a world war
> to overcome the threat, what force on earth might restrain
> an America that may have abandoned the rule of law—
> an America with its vastly greater population, wealth, and
> land mass; its far more sophisticated technology; its weapons
> systems; its already fully established global network of
> black-site secret prisons; and its imperial reach?[34]

My point here is not to critique the validity of Wolf's thesis or research. Rather, it is to note that a prominent American thinker on the Left—one who lost relatives on both sides of her family in the Holocaust—wrote a book arguing that if we don't make major course corrections—and soon—the United States as we have known her for more than two hundred years will cease to exist. Is that true? Are we really hurtling toward "the end of America"? There was a time not long ago when suggesting such things would cast a writer so far out of the mainstream he or she might never be heard from again. Remarkably, Wolf and her book weren't laughed at, dismissed, or casually ignored by fellow liberals or the media elites. Rather, her title and theme so resonated with a segment of American society that her book became a *New York Times* bestseller.

Are We Really Preparing for Life "After America"?

Naomi Wolf's perspective received little interest, much less sympathy, from American conservatives. But as we have seen, the Left is not alone in harboring—and increasingly being willing to publicly express—dark fears about the future of our country. One recent book capturing the depth of anxiety on the American political Right is titled *After America: Get Ready for Armageddon*, released by Regnery Publishing, the foremost conservative publishing house in the U.S. The book's author, Mark Steyn, who was born in Toronto but now lives in New Hampshire, is a popular conservative who is regularly published by center-right publications such as *National Review* and the *Washington Times* and who has guest-hosted Rush Limbaugh's and Sean Hannity's highly rated conservative radio and TV programs.

"*America Alone: The End of the World As We Know It* was about the impending collapse of all of the Western world *except* America," Steyn writes in his prologue, referring to his previous book. "The good news is that the end of the rest of the West is still on schedule. The bad news is that America shows alarming signs of embracing the same fate, and then some."[35]

A few pages later, Steyn cites Douglas Elmendorf, the director of the Congressional Budget Office (CBO), who in 2010 described current U.S. deficits as "unsustainable." Steyn then quotes President Obama, who said in 2011, "We've got a big hole that we're digging ourselves out of." Quips Steyn, "Usually, when you're in a hole, it's a good idea to stop digging. But, seemingly, to get out of the Bush hole, we needed to dig a hole twice as deep."[36] Analyzing the CBO projections for net interest payments on U.S. federal debt, Steyn writes that by 2050, "if that trajectory holds, we'll be spending more than the planet's entire military budget on debt interest."[37]

Steyn does hold out a shred of hope throughout the book that Americans can still make the changes necessary to prevent an implosion, but he argues strenuously that time is rapidly running out.

> The existential questions for America loom not decades hence, but right now. It is not that we are on a luge ride to oblivion but that the prevailing political realities of the United States do not allow for any meaningful course correction. And, without meaningful course correction, America is doomed. . . . Look around you. From now on, it gets worse. In ten years' time, there will be no American Dream, any more than there's a Greek or Portuguese Dream. In twenty, you'll be living the American Nightmare. . . . "After America"? Yes. It will linger awhile in a twilight existence, arthritic and ineffectual, declining into a kind of societal dementia, unable to keep pace with what's happening and with an ever more tenuous grip on its own past. For a while, there may still be an entity called the "United States," but it will have fewer stars in the flag, there will be nothing to "unite" it, and it will bear no relation to the republic of limited government the first generation of Americans fought for. And life, liberty, and the pursuit of happiness will be conspicuous by their absence.[38]

Again, my intention here is not to critique the validity of Steyn's research or every point he makes in the book. Rather, it is to show that a noted thinker on the Right wrote a book arguing that if we don't make major course corrections—and soon—the United States will soon cease to exist as we have known her. Is that true? Are we really preparing for life "after America"? Like Wolf, Steyn wasn't ridiculed or dismissed for such a stark and essentially apocalyptic analysis of the American condition. To the contrary, his book also became a *New York Times* bestseller, and conservatives not only bought it but also discussed it widely.

Are We Really Entering a "Post-American World"?

Profound pessimism about the future of America is not isolated to intensive analysis and spirited discussions on the political Left and Right. Moderates and the politically unaligned are deeply engaged in the conversation as well. Thus, in 2008, when Fareed Zakaria released a provocative, intriguing, and much-talked-about book titled *The Post-American World*, it immediately became a *Time* cover story and went on to become a *New York Times* bestseller. When the 2.0 version of *The Post-American World* was released in paperback in 2011, it, too, became a national bestseller.

One of the reasons for this particular book's influence and success is that Zakaria was not making his case as an ideologue or a partisan. He was writing as an ostensibly mainstream journalist who grew up halfway around the world, chose to make America his home, and over time became deeply concerned about his adopted nation's future. A nominal Muslim who emigrated from India to the U.S. in the 1980s and went on to earn degrees from Yale and Harvard, Zakaria rose to become the host of an influential Sunday interview program on CNN and editor-at-large for *Time* magazine. He describes himself as neither a liberal nor a conservative but as a political Independent.

"There have been three tectonic power shifts over the last five hundred years, fundamental changes in the distribution of power that have reshaped international life—its politics, economics, and culture," Zakaria writes. The first, he argues, was the rise of the Western world. The second was the rise of the United States, which, soon after it industrialized, became "the most powerful nation since imperial Rome, and the only one that was stronger than any likely combination of other nations." But Zakaria believes that "we are now living through the third great power shift of the modern era," which he calls "the rise of the rest." America, for example, is struggling to stay out of recession, while countries like India and China are growing economically at upwards of 9 percent every year with no signs of slowing down.[39]

"We are moving into a post-American world," Zakaria writes, and thus the central question of our time is, "What will it mean to live in a post-American world?"[40]

Put simply, Zakaria believes the United States is not only struggling *not* to collapse, but with many other countries rapidly rising, we are in growing danger of being left in the dust. He notes:

> The tallest building in the world is now in Dubai. The world's richest man is Mexican, and its largest publicly traded company is Chinese. The world's biggest plane is built in Russia and Ukraine, its leading refinery is in India, and its largest factories are all in China. By many measures, Hong Kong now rivals London and New York as the leading financial center, and the United Arab Emirates is home to the most richly endowed investment fund. Once quintessentially American icons have been appropriated by foreigners. The world's largest Ferris wheel is in Singapore. Its number one casino is not in Las Vegas but in Macao, which has also overtaken Vegas in annual gambling revenues. The biggest movie industry, in terms of both movies made and tickets

sold, is Bollywood, not Hollywood. Even shopping, America's greatest sporting activity, has gone global. Of the top ten malls in the world, only one is in the United States; the world's biggest is in Dongguan, China.* Such lists are arbitrary, but it is striking that twenty years ago, America was at the top of many, if not most, of these categories."[41]

America today remains the global superpower, Zakaria concedes, but he says we are an "enfeebled" one. The U.S. economy is "troubled, its currency is sliding, and it faces long-term problems with its soaring entitlements and low savings." What's more, he notes, "anti-American sentiment is at an all-time high everywhere from Great Britain to Malaysia." He goes on to argue:

> The most striking shift between the 1990s and now has to do not with America but rather with the world at large. In the 1990s, Russia was completely dependent on American aid and loans. Now, it has its own multibillion-dollar fund, financed by oil revenues, to reinvigorate its economy during slowdowns. Then, East Asian nations desperately needed the IMF [International Monetary Fund] to bail them out of their crises. Now, they have massive foreign-exchange reserves, which they are using to finance America's debt. Then, China's economic growth was driven almost entirely by American demand. In 2007, China contributed more to global growth than the United States did—the first time any nation has done so since at least the 1930s—and surpassed it as the world's largest consumer market in several key categories. In the long run this secular trend—the rise of the rest—will only gather strength.[42]

---

*Zakaria noted in the original edition of his book that "the Mall of America in Minnesota once boasted that it was the largest shopping mall in the world" but "today it wouldn't make the top ten."

"How did the United States blow it?" Zakaria asks. "The United States has had an extraordinary hand to play in global politics—the best of any country in history. Yet, by almost any measure—problems solved, success achieved, institutions built, reputation enhanced—Washington has played this hand badly. America has had a period of unparalleled influence. What does it have to show for it?"[43]

Bottom Line

Unfortunately, there is a compelling case for such deep and rising anxiety. As we'll see as we move deeper into this book and examine more specific data, the leading economic and cultural indicators do not bode well for America. The evidence, I believe, strongly suggests an implosion is possible.

But as we end this chapter, we must draw an important distinction right up front. Do the authors and analysts I have cited in this chapter believe America is predetermined to implode? Do they believe our fate is sealed and there is no longer any hope? No, most do not. Most believe there is still a chance for Americans to turn things around. The point is that most of these observers—and many Americans like them—see our situation as more precarious than perhaps at any other point in our nation's history, and they have become steadily more pessimistic over time. They believe time is running out, and most are not encouraged by the leadership being shown in politics, business, media, or education, much less the church.

That said, theirs is not the only view.

CHAPTER THREE

THE CASE
OF THE OPTIMISTS

TO BE CLEAR, not all Americans fear we're in decline.

Nor do all Americans believe we are facing an implosion. Indeed, many Americans believe the magnitude of the challenges we face is being overstated. They argue that the "doomsday" talk by some in the media, academia, the financial sector, the pulpits, the political sphere, and around the watercooler is just a vastly overblown and dangerous overreaction. What's more, they fiercely maintain their belief that America is poised for a historic renaissance.

These people are determined optimists. Yes, the threats Americans face from within and without are real and serious, the optimists readily concede, but this doesn't necessarily mean our challenges are insurmountable. To the contrary, they argue, our greatest days are still ahead.

We have faced dark times before in our nation's history. We have faced moments when it truly seemed like the American experiment was destined to fail. Yet by the grace of God and the wisdom of some extraordinary leaders in government, business, and the church, we have repeatedly made the critical course corrections that were necessary. We have gotten our country back on the right track numerous times and have subsequently soared to heights never really dreamed possible by Americans or by anyone else in the world, and these optimists are certain we can do it again.

Barack Obama has certainly sought to position himself politically as America's "optimist in chief." As a candidate, he inspired tens of millions of Americans with his message of hope and change. As president, he has engendered enormous criticism from the Right, Center, and even some from the Left. Many commentators have accused him of (wittingly or unwittingly) leading the U.S. to the brink of outright collapse by accelerating the fiscal bankruptcy of the country and undermining the moral authority of American foreign policy with his approach of "leading from behind," as one of his advisors so memorably described Obama's approach to world affairs.[1]

President Obama has steadfastly refused to be labeled a pessimist, arguing that America has a hopeful future and that one of the things that makes our country great is "an enduring faith, even in the darkest hours, that brighter days lie ahead."[2] President Obama epitomized his views in an essay titled "Why I'm Optimistic," published in the fortieth-anniversary issue of *Smithsonian* magazine:

> There is, of course, no way of knowing what new challenges and new possibilities will emerge over the next forty years. There is no way of knowing how life will be different in 2050. But if we do what's required in our own time, I am confident the future will be brighter for our people, and our country. Such confidence stems largely from the genius of America. From our earliest days, we have reimagined and remade ourselves again and again.[3]

Even many strong critics of the president and his devout ideological liberalism join him in describing themselves as fundamentally optimistic regarding the future of America, though they would hasten to add that their policy prescriptions for getting us out of the severe mess we are in differ dramatically from President Obama's.

Bullish on America

One example is William J. Bennett, the conservative former secretary of education under President Ronald Reagan and "drug czar" for President George H. W. Bush. Bennett, who now hosts a nationally syndicated talk radio show called *Morning in America*, remains convinced that Americans can and will turn things around in time, despite having chronicled the enormous surges in violent crime, out-of-wedlock births, and other social pathologies rampant in the United States over the past four decades. In his 1999 book, *The Index of Leading Cultural Indicators: American Society at the End of the Twentieth Century*, Bennett wrote, "To those who believe our decline is inevitable because social trends are irreversible, our answer should be: no, it need not be so, and we will not allow it to happen. Restoring civilization's social and moral order—making it more humane, civil, responsible, and just—is no simple task. But America remains what it has always been: an exceptional nation. Our capacity for self-renewal is rare, and real. We have relied on it in the past [and] we must call on it again."[4]

Ten years later, in his book *A Century Turns: New Hopes, New Fears*, Bennett passionately continued to make the case that Americans have risen to the occasion of social and economic renewal before in tough times and said that he saw no reason why we could not do so again. "Today, the levels of both hope and fear are at a high point. Whether or not we can expand the former and reduce the latter, continuing to 'have the freedoms we have known up until now,' will depend precisely on what we do with the challenges before us today. Will people one hundred years from now say, 'Thank God for those people in 2009'? As an American, as an optimist, as a true believer in the uniquely American capacity for self-renewal, I hope and believe the answer is 'Yes!'"[5]

Larry Kudlow, the CNBC host and *National Review* columnist, is similarly bullish on America's future, despite being a sharp critic of President Obama and his policies. "The pessimists are now talking about the end of capitalism or a permanent decline of America. I don't believe that for one moment," Kudlow wrote in September 2008, just as the economic meltdown was beginning. "Specific regulatory reforms can get us out of this fix. And most of all, policymakers must maintain the low-tax, low-inflation, open-trade formula that has propelled this nation's economy and produced so much prosperity for so long. I say, never sell America short."[6]

The upheavals of the next few years rattled many, but not Kudlow. While he wrote repeatedly about the severe challenges to the nation and its economy and spoke out strongly about the damage he believed the Obama team was doing to America's fiscal health, he remained remarkably positive about the future. "There's a lot of pessimism in the air right now," he wrote in the spring of 2011. "It's rooted in themes I've been discussing for weeks and weeks—namely, lower profit margins from spiking energy, food, and raw-material prices; supply-chain disruptions from the Japanese disaster that cuts into top-line sales revenue; and gasoline price hikes that are depressing the consumer. . . . This is not the end of the world. . . . I still believe in longer-term optimism."[7]

Editorial Optimism

The contributors to the *Wall Street Journal*'s editorial page likewise remain fundamentally optimistic about America's future. Like

Bennett and Kudlow, they don't fail to point out the serious challenges facing the country, nor do they hesitate to advocate specific
reform proposals. Yet the *Journal*'s editors regularly publish essays by
those who specifically push back at the notion of America in decline.
In February 2011, for example, the *Journal* published an essay titled
"The Misleading Metaphor of Decline" by Joseph Nye, distin-
guished professor at Harvard University's John F. Kennedy School
of Government. "Is the United States in decline? Many Americans
think so, and they are not alone. A recent Pew poll showed that
pluralities in thirteen of twenty-five countries believe that China
will replace the U.S. as the world's leading superpower," Nye wrote.
However, he argued, "America is likely to remain more powerful than
any single state in the coming decades." Nye also noted that even
"Rome remained dominant for more than three centuries after the
apogee of Roman power. . . . Rather than succumb to self-fulfilling
prophecies of inevitable decline, we need a vision that combines
domestic reforms with smart strategies for the international deploy-
ment of our power in an information age."[8]

Two months later, the *Journal* published an essay called "The Facts
about American 'Decline,'" written by Charles Wolf Jr., a corporate
fellow in international economics at the RAND Corporation and a
senior research fellow at Stanford University's Hoover Institution.

It's fashionable among academics and pundits to proclaim
that the U.S. is in decline and no longer No. 1 in the world.
The declinists say they are realists. In fact, their alarm is
unrealistic. . . . In absolute terms, the U.S. enjoyed an
incline this past decade. Between 2000 and 2010, U.S.
GDP increased 21 percent in constant dollars, despite the
shattering setbacks of the Great Recession in 2008–09 and
the bursting of the dot-com bubble in 2001. In 2010, U.S.
military spending ($697 billion) was 55 percent higher than

in 2000. And in 2010, the U.S. population was 310 million, an increase of 10 percent since 2000. . . . Some numbers show inclines, some show declines, and some numbers are mixed. . . . The overall picture is far more complex than the simple one portrayed by declinists. The real world is complicated, so a portrait in one dimension distorts rather than reflects reality.[9]

Three months after Wolf's op-ed ran, the *Journal* published "The Future Still Belongs to America" by Walter Russell Mead, professor of foreign affairs and humanities at Bard College and editor-at-large of *American Interest*:

It is, the pundits keep telling us, a time of American decline, of a post-American world. The twenty-first century will belong to someone else. Crippled by debt at home, hammered by the aftermath of a financial crisis, bloodied by long wars in the Middle East, the American Atlas can no longer hold up the sky. Like Britain before us, America is headed into an assisted-living facility for retired global powers. This fashionable chatter could not be more wrong. . . . Every major country in the world today faces extraordinary challenges—and the twenty-first century will throw more at us. Yet looking toward the tumultuous century ahead, no country is better positioned to take advantage of the opportunities or manage the dangers than the United States."[10]

These are but a few of many examples of the pushback from both the Left and the Right against the real and increasingly widespread notion that America is rapidly approaching—or even has passed—the point of no return.

Trials and Triumphs

What's more, the case the optimists are making is historically valid. Americans have faced very dark times before and overcome them.

"A Long Train of Abuses and Usurpations"

The American Revolution itself was one such dark time.

As Thomas Jefferson wrote so eloquently in the Declaration of Independence, the citizens of the thirteen colonies were suffering from "a long train of abuses and usurpations" designed "to reduce them under absolute despotism" by a "tyrant" who was "unfit to be the ruler of a free people." After many humble—and rebuffed—attempts at gaining redress for their grievances, and after much prayer and soul-searching and much discussion and debate, the people concluded it was their right and their duty "to throw off such government, and to provide new guards for their future security." They appealed in the process to the God of the Bible, "the Supreme Judge of the world," knowing as they did that the task of establishing a free and independent country would require them to go to war with the British Empire, the most powerful military entity on the planet. The undertaking seemed nearly impossible.[11]

To war they did go, of course, and a painful, bloody, and often gloomy war it was at that. At times, no small number within the American military forces—both officers and enlisted men—were so utterly demoralized that they were more inclined to give up than to fight on, to simply return home to their families and friends. Some soldiers didn't have shoes to wear or blankets to keep them warm or enough rations to keep them fed and energized. They were young and homesick and convinced neither they nor those for whom they were supposedly fighting had any hope for the future.

Historian Washington Irving noted that at one point during the conflict, "half of the officers of the rank of captain were inclined to retire, and it was probable their example would influence their men," who would not reenlist unless they saw their leaders making the same commitment.[12] At that point, an utterly depressed George Washington, commander of the American forces, wrote a letter to the president of the Congress, saying, "I am sorry to be necessitated to mention to you the egregious want of public spirit which prevails here. . . . I find we are most likely to be deserted in a most critical time."[13] In a letter to his secretary, Washington wrote, "Could I have foreseen what I have experienced and am likely to experience, no consideration upon earth should have induced me to accept this command."[14]

Yet George Washington did not abandon the cause or his responsibilities. Despite how dark the situation often seemed to be, the military commander chose to believe that the impossible was only impossible if they gave up and stopped trying. Thus he rallied himself and his men to commit their lives, their fortunes, and their sacred honor to the cause of liberty, as stated in the immortal words of the Declaration of Independence. He encouraged his distraught and downtrodden men to press on despite the enormous challenges and seemingly overwhelming odds against them, and they chose to follow his lead.

In the end, the cost was brutally high. More than twenty-two thousand Americans lost their lives fighting for liberty, out of a population of merely 2.5 million. Yet the enterprise was a stunning success. By God's grace, the Revolution succeeded. Washington and his men and the Founding Fathers who had asked them to go into battle not only established a new country but also helped create a remarkable new model of freedom and democracy for the rest of the world.

A "Volcanic Upheaval"

The Civil War posed an even greater existential threat to the republic.

Henry Clay, Speaker of the House and secretary of state during the earlier years of the nineteenth century, had long warned the people of the North and the South that the dissolution of the union would lead to a war "so furious, so bloody, so implacable, and so exterminating" that few would be able to bear the results. Indeed, he feared his own heart wouldn't be able to take such an apocalypse within the country he loved and had worked so hard to build. "If the direful and sad event of the dissolution of the union shall happen, I may not survive to behold the sad and heartrending spectacle."[15]

Yet the war did come, though Clay did not survive to see it and witness whether the republic would stand. Americans were suddenly and viciously pitted not against a foreign empire but against one another. Their irreconcilable differences led to a willingness to use deadly force to accomplish their objectives and defend their principles. The mood of the country turned darker than at any previous point in her brief history. President Abraham Lincoln "understood that his country faced a perilous situation, perhaps the most perilous in its history," wrote Pulitzer Prize–winning historian Doris Kearns Goodwin in her masterful biography of Lincoln, *Team of Rivals*.[16] And Lincoln was far from alone.

"Clouds and darkness are upon us at present," Ohio governor Salmon Chase observed as he perceived the bitter, brutal fighting on the horizon.[17]

"The sun rises, but shines not," poet Walt Whitman wrote.[18] Americans, he said, were witnessing a "volcanic upheaval."[19]

"We are in the midst of the most terrible battle of the age," General George McClellan, commander of the Union Army, observed.[20]

"The fate of the nation hung in doubt and gloom," U.S. attorney general Edward Bates wrote.[21]

Many wondered openly whether America could survive, and pessimism was rampant. The Battle of Gettysburg was surely the turning point of the war, but it was also one of the bloodiest. At Gettysburg alone, the Union Army suffered some twenty-three thousand casualties and the Confederacy twenty-eight thousand.[22] President Lincoln was by no means understating the severity of the situation when on the afternoon of Thursday, November 19, 1863, he spoke at the dedication of the Soldiers' National Cemetery at Gettysburg and suggested that the very fate of the American nation and the premise of her founding were at stake.

Fourscore and seven years ago our fathers brought forth on this continent a new nation, conceived in liberty and dedicated to the proposition that all men are created equal. Now we are engaged in a great civil war, testing whether that nation or any nation so conceived and so dedicated can long endure. We are met on a great battlefield of that war. We have come to dedicate a portion of that field as a final resting place for those who here gave their lives that that nation might live. It is altogether fitting and proper that we should do this. But in a larger sense, we cannot dedicate, we cannot consecrate, we cannot hallow this ground. The brave men, living and dead, who struggled here, have consecrated it far above our poor power to add or detract. The world will little note nor long remember what we say here, but it can never forget what they did here. It is for us the living rather to be dedicated here to the unfinished work which they who fought here have thus far so nobly advanced. It is rather for us to be here dedicated to the great task remaining before us—that from these honored dead we take increased devotion to that cause for which they gave the last full measure of devotion—that we here highly resolve that these dead shall not have died in vain, that this nation under God shall have a new birth of freedom, and that government of the people, by the people, for the people shall not perish from the earth.[23]

In the end, the pessimists were wrong. Lincoln and his forces won a great victory. The union was preserved. The American democracy did experience "a new birth of freedom" and soared to heights few could have foreseen during the war's most difficult days. But the costs were catastrophic. The conflict "that no one imagined would last four years," Goodwin observed, had "cost greater than six hundred thousand lives—more than the cumulative total of all our other wars, from the Revolution to Iraq. The devastation and sacrifice would reach into every community, into almost every family, in a nation of 31.5 million. In proportion to today's population, the number of deaths would exceed 5 million."[24]

Travails of the Twentieth Century

America went on to face other dark times.

In the last century alone, we endured World War I, the Great Depression, World War II, the Korean and Vietnam conflicts, the American cultural revolution of the 1960s (complete with an explosion in violent crime, a precipitous rise in the use of drugs among young people, widespread rebellion against authority and the traditional family, and a sharp turning away from God), and the national malaise that defined much of the 1970s, to name some of the worst. These violent storms posed a real and severe threat to our security, economy, and moral and spiritual well-being. During each, there were some who feared we might not survive, much less thrive. Yet time after time, Americans weathered the storms, often to the surprise (and at times the chagrin) of the rest of the world.

To keep our current troubles in context, let's briefly consider two examples: the Great Depression during Herbert Hoover's and Franklin Delano Roosevelt's administrations and the malaise that occurred during Jimmy Carter's.

FROM THE ROARING TWENTIES TO THE GREAT DEPRESSION

The 1920s in America were known as the Roaring Twenties. The economy was booming. The stock market was climbing ever higher.

Factories were operating at full tilt, and jobs were plentiful. In 1927, the unemployment rate in the United States was a mere 3.3 percent.[25] Then came the unprecedented crash on Wall Street in the fall of 1929, the implosion of the nation's industrial production, a rapidly spreading global economic meltdown, and the beginning of the era known as the Great Depression.

On September 3, 1929, the Dow Jones Industrial Average reached a record high of 381. But just eight weeks later, the market collapsed. By the end of Black Tuesday, October 29, 1929, the Dow closed at a mere 230.07. This represented a collapse of nearly 40 percent. Hundreds of billions of dollars in American wealth simply vanished into thin air.[26]

Over the course of the next year, Americans witnessed the failure of more than 1,300 banks.[27]

By July 8, 1932, the Dow Jones Industrial Average had sunk to just 41.22, an apocalyptic loss of 89 percent of the market's value from its high in 1929.[28]

By 1933, more than nine thousand American banks—half of all the banks in the country at the time—had failed.[29] That same year, nearly a third of all workers in the United States found themselves without jobs.[30]

Americans were terrified. Many saw the United States imploding and believed there was no way to turn things around. Many lost the will to go on. Between 1929 and 1933, the number of suicides in America tragically shot up by nearly 23 percent, the biggest surge in the suicide rate in the history of the country.[31]

Upon entering office, however, President Franklin Delano Roosevelt resisted the skyrocketing national pessimism and challenged Americans not to succumb to fear. He was, after all, a congenital optimist. He had valiantly faced enormous adversity in his own personal life, including physical paralysis, and he was certain America would overcome as well. He believed the nation would emerge from the most severe economic and social crisis in her history stronger than ever.

"I am certain that my fellow Americans expect that on my induction into the presidency I will address them with a candor and a decision which the present situation of our nation impels," Roosevelt said as he began his inaugural address on Saturday, March 4, 1933. "This is preeminently the time to speak the truth, the whole truth, frankly and boldly. Nor need we shrink from honestly facing conditions in our country today. This great nation will endure as it has endured, will revive and will prosper. So, first of all, let me assert my firm belief that the only thing we have to fear is fear itself—nameless, unreasoning, unjustified terror which paralyzes needed efforts to convert retreat into advance." He readily conceded that "only a foolish optimist can deny the dark realities of the moment," but he insisted that "compared with the perils which our forefathers conquered because they believed and were not afraid, we have still much to be thankful for. . . . In this dedication of a nation we humbly ask the blessing of God. May he protect each and every one of us. May he guide me in the days to come."[32]

America did, of course, eventually emerge from the Great Depression. How the recovery was achieved is a matter of intense debate among historians and politicians, including whether FDR's New Deal policies were a net positive for the country or whether they exacerbated the country's structural problems and prolonged the depression. The point here is not to enter that debate but to focus on the obvious: we made it through one of the most difficult periods in our history when many feared we would not. By 1936, industrial production in the United States had finally regained 1929 levels and later would surge dramatically further with the outbreak of World War II and the need for enormous production to defeat the fascists in Europe and the imperialists in Asia.[33] The Dow Jones Industrial Average, on the other hand, wouldn't reach its 1929 record high of 381 until November 1954, but recover it eventually did and went on to hit stunning new heights in the decades beyond.[34]

A NATIONAL MALAISE

As we turn the pages of history, we see that Americans faced another round of storms in the 1970s. Among them: widespread anger—especially among young people—over our role in Vietnam, deep disillusionment over Watergate and other scandals of the Nixon administration, rising unemployment, paltry economic growth, soaring inflation, towering interest rates, mushrooming energy prices, severe energy shortages, and ever-growing lines at gas pumps.

Few authors better captured the pessimism of the times—and particularly the gloomy views of the liberal elites who believed ordinary Americans were primarily to blame for their troubles—than Christopher Lasch, a history professor at the University of Rochester. In 1979, Lasch published what became a highly influential book titled *The Culture of Narcissism: American Life in an Age of Diminishing Expectations*. Describing "postwar America as a society of dangerously self-absorbed individuals, fixated on personal goals, fearful of their impulses, and easily controlled by power elites," according to a summary in the *New York Times*, the book quickly became a national bestseller, spent seven weeks on the *Times* bestseller list, and generated much discussion around the country, including inside the White House and even in the Oval Office.[35]

"Hardly more than a quarter century after Henry Luce proclaimed 'the American century,' American confidence has fallen to a low ebb," Lasch began on the first page of his preface. "Those who recently dreamed of world power now despair of governing the city of New York. Defeat in Vietnam, economic stagnation, and the impending exhaustion of natural resources have produced a mood of pessimism in higher circles, which spreads through the rest of society as people lose faith in their leaders."[36]

Lasch went on to argue that "as the twentieth century approaches its end, the conviction grows that many other things are ending too. Storm warnings, portents, hints of catastrophe haunt our times. The 'sense of an ending,' which has given shape to so much of twentieth-century literature, now pervades the popular imagination, as well. . . . The question of whether the world will end in fire or in ice, with a bang or a whimper, no longer interests artists alone. Impending disaster has become an everyday concern, so commonplace and familiar that nobody any longer gives much thought to how disaster might be averted."[37]

The book quickly caught the attention and the imagination of Pat Caddell, a young pollster for—and key advisor to—President Jimmy Carter, as Caddell was beginning to map out Carter's reelection plan for the 1980 campaign. Caddell not only read the book and agreed with it but drew heavily upon Lasch's gloomy end-of-the-world observations in a long memo for the president. In the memo, Caddell essentially argued that it was not Carter's fault that the economy was in the toilet, that American prestige around the world was evaporating, and that the American people were deserting the president and the Democratic Party. Rather, Caddell claimed, the American people were a bunch of narcissists, in a funk that couldn't be fixed, and this was simply the zeitgeist of the times.

Caddell specifically picked up two key phrases used by Lasch, suggesting the American people were suffering from a "crisis of confidence" and a national "malaise." He recommended that the president deliver a speech to explain to the American people what their problem was and to encourage them to lower their standards and do things like wear sweaters inside when it got cold and they couldn't afford to sufficiently heat their homes.

Caddell's memo sparked a firestorm of controversy within Carter's inner circle. Vice President Mondale, for one, thought the young pollster was out of his mind and under no circumstances should the president scold the country on its national malaise. Carter, however, loved the memo and Lasch's book. Indeed, he invited Lasch to meet with him and discuss the book. When the meeting was over, Carter decided to proceed with the nationally televised address.[38]

On July 15, 1979, President Carter spoke to an estimated one hundred million Americans in a televised address from the Oval Office. Among his remarks were these words:

> I want to speak to you first tonight about a subject even more serious than energy or inflation. I want to talk to you right now about a fundamental threat to American democracy. . . . The threat is nearly invisible in ordinary ways. It is a crisis of confidence. It is a crisis that strikes at the very heart and soul and spirit of our national will. We can see this crisis in the growing doubt about the meaning of our own lives and in the loss of a unity of purpose for our nation. The erosion of our confidence in the future is threatening to destroy the social and the political fabric of America. . . . The symptoms of this crisis of the American spirit are all around us. For the first time in the history of our country, a majority of our people believe that the next five years will be worse than the past five years. Two-thirds of our people do not even vote. The productivity of American workers is actually dropping, and the willingness of Americans to save for the future has fallen below that of all other people in the Western world.[39]

Later in the speech, Carter bemoaned the nation's energy crisis and set forth several ideas to enact legislation to force Americans to use less energy in the coming years. This continued the dismal theme Carter had set forth from the beginning of his administration, when he stated bluntly in a speech on February 2, 1977, "We must face the fact that the energy shortage is permanent. There is no way we can solve it quickly. . . . We will ask private companies to sacrifice, just as private citizens must do."[40]

Two days after the "crisis of confidence" speech, the president asked his entire cabinet to resign, hoping this would be a message to the country that he was hitting the reset button, as it were, and making a fresh start of his administration. Instead, the move was widely seen throughout the country as evidence that the president had run out of ideas for fixing the nation's structural problems—the energy crisis, in particular—and was himself suffering from a crisis of confidence and a malaise.

While Carter didn't actually use the word *malaise* in the address, his advisors used it in private discussions with reporters and columnists, and journalists recognized the language from Lasch's bestselling book. Soon, the address was being dubbed the "malaise speech," and Carter was pilloried for it. California governor Ronald Reagan, the front-runner in the race among Republican candidates to replace Carter, led the way, saying he deeply disagreed with Carter's analysis and using the speech to help frame the differences between himself and the president. "Does history still have a place for America, for her people, for her great ideals?" Reagan asked. "There are some who answer no, that our energy is spent, our days of greatness at an end, that a great national malaise is upon us. . . . I find no national malaise. I find nothing wrong with the American people."[41]

Reagan argued, in particular, that the energy shortage and sky-high energy prices and ever-longer lines at gas stations were neither permanent nor the result of Americans' greed or narcissism. Yes, we can all do a better job of conserving energy, he agreed, but he went on to argue that shortages and high prices were the result of too much government regulation and could be easily and quickly remedied with a new approach—a conservative and free-market approach. Carter and his senior aides sneered at such talk and dismissed the Californian as a foolish B-movie actor who didn't understand the complexities of real life.

"MORNING IN AMERICA"

Ronald Reagan, of course, won the 1980 election in a landslide. On the day of his inauguration, moments after being sworn in, Reagan stepped into a room in the Capitol and signed an executive order removing price controls on oil and gasoline, his first official act as president.[42] "Critics of Reagan's action . . . warned that gas prices would rise to two dollars a gallon. Reagan predicted that oil and gas prices would fall dramatically, and he proved to be right," noted one Reagan biographer.[43]

When Reagan took office in 1981, the average price of a gallon of leaded regular gasoline in the United States was $1.31. Rather than climb when Reagan removed price controls and began reducing regulations on the gas industry, prices dropped immediately to $1.22 in 1982 and fell to just eighty-six cents by 1986.[44]

Simultaneously, oil prices fell as well. In April 1980, oil had hit a record high of $103.76 per barrel (in 2008-inflation-adjusted dollars). But by 1985, the price of a barrel of oil had dropped to a mere $20 (in 2008 dollars).[45] Indeed, Reagan's policies worked so well and so quickly that barely six months into his first term, the media were already talking about an "oil glut," with too much oil on the market. On June 21, 1981, for example, the *New York Times* actually published this headline: "How the Oil Glut Is Changing Business." Reporter Robert Hershey wrote, "Oil glut! . . . Suddenly, oil is so plentiful that prices are falling by amounts that impress even big-time corporate decision makers."[46]

By 1984, the economy was humming, Americans' confidence in the future had largely been restored, and Reagan was running for reelection. His most famous television campaign ad proclaimed, "It's morning again in America. Today, more men and women will go to work than ever before in our country's history. With interest rates at about half the record highs of 1980, nearly two thousand families today will buy new homes, more than at any time in the past four years. This afternoon, sixty-five hundred young men and women will be married, and with inflation at less than half of what it was just four years ago, they can look forward with confidence to the future. It's morning again in America, and under the leadership of President Reagan, our country is prouder and stronger and better. Why would we ever want to return to where we were less than four short years ago?"[47]

Reagan defeated Walter Mondale in the biggest electoral landslide in American political history, winning forty-nine of the nation's fifty states. By the time Reagan left office in 1989, he had racked up many remarkable accomplishments, including rebuilding America's military, reestablishing credibility with both our allies and our enemies, helping bring down the Berlin Wall and the "evil empire" of the Soviet bloc, and helping liberate the American economy from high taxes and overregulation. Under his leadership, some 18 million new jobs were created,[48] millions of new small businesses were developed and expanded,[49] the Dow Jones Industrial Average grew to more than twice what it had been when he took office,[50] a dazzling high-tech revolution was set into motion, and Silicon Valley emerged as the computing capital of the world.

For Reagan, however, one of the accomplishments he was most proud of was liberating Americans from gas lines, energy inflation, and the prevailing sense of doom, gloom, and failure of the late 1970s. "Many of you, I'm sure, recall the howls that went up when we acted to deregulate oil prices two years ago," Reagan said in a 1983 radio address to the nation. "Remember how you were told that deregulation would lead to skyrocketing prices for the gasoline that fuels millions of American cars or the oil that heats millions of American homes? Well, the evidence is in, and the doomsayers were dead wrong. You don't have to go any further than the nearest filling station to see that prices have gone down, not up, since decontrol, just as we promised they would."[51]

Bottom Line

To be sure, then, the optimists have a compelling case. When they argue that Americans have faced very dark times in our history and have made the fundamental changes and reforms needed to avert a full-fledged implosion of the country, they are absolutely right. When they say that given this encouraging track record, they feel confident that we can do so again, they say it with conviction. So who is right—the optimists or those who are more pessimistic? Before we can draw any conclusions, we first need to look at events through the "third lens."

CHAPTER FOUR

THE THIRD LENS

IT WOULD BE A SERIOUS MISTAKE to look at events and trends in the United States merely through the lenses of economics and politics. It might seem normal, even tempting, to do so. But to truly understand the significance of global events and trends, we must not limit ourselves to a conventional worldview. We must also analyze events through what I call the "third lens"—the lens of Scripture. Only when we have a biblical worldview can the full picture become clearer. Only then can we begin to see in three dimensions.

I first wrote about the importance of taking this approach in my 2006 book, *Epicenter*, with regards to understanding the future of Israel and the Middle East from a biblical perspective. But looking through the third lens is an equally valid and important approach in understanding the future of other nations, including the United States. For while it is interesting to read what the pessimists and the optimists say about the future of any country, what matters most is what God says in his holy Word.

The third lens is essential in addressing whether the Bible describes the future of America and what clues it can provide as to whether we will survive the severe threats facing us today. More precisely, does the Bible actually answer the question so many people are asking: "What happens to America in the last days?"

Truly and effectively answering that question requires a step-by-step process of addressing several other matters first:

- Does the Bible really claim to know and describe the future?
- On what basis can we trust the prophecies found in the Bible?
- What does the Bible say will happen in the last days?
- Are we living in the last days?
- Is America mentioned specifically in Bible prophecy?

Let us, therefore, consider these five critical questions one by one. The rest of this chapter will address the first two; we will look at the following three in subsequent chapters.

Does the Bible Really Claim to Know and Describe the Future?

Make no mistake: the Bible is not shy about describing itself as a supernatural book. Yes, it was written down on tablets and parchments and scrolls of various kinds across the span of several thousand years by a wide variety of mere men, including Jewish shepherds, kings, warriors, fishermen, and rabbis, as well as a Gentile medical doctor. But though the Scriptures were written *down* by men, they were not written by men. To the contrary, the Bible states clearly and unequivocally that it is the inspired Word of God himself.

In the first chapter of the first book of the Bible, for example, we read again and again, "Then God said . . ." (Genesis 1:3, 6, 9, 11, 14, 20, 24, 26, 29).

In the second book of the Bible, we learn that Moses didn't write the Ten Commandments. Rather, Moses wrote down the words of the Lord, as the Lord commanded. The Bible tells us, "Then God spoke all these words. . . ." (Exodus 20:1).

As we work our way through the Hebrew Scriptures, we continue to read verses like: "the word of the LORD came to Abram in a vision, saying . . ." (Genesis 15:1); "the word of the LORD came to Samuel, saying . . ." (1 Samuel 15:10); "the word of the LORD came to Elijah in the third year, saying . . ." (1 Kings 18:1); "the word of the LORD came to me [Jeremiah] saying . . ." (Jeremiah 1:4); "the word of the LORD came expressly to Ezekiel . . ." (Ezekiel 1:3); and so forth.

The longest chapter of the Bible—Psalm 119—is about how powerful and helpful and wise and life-changing the Scriptures are because they are the very words of the living God. "Your commandments make me wiser than my enemies, for they are ever mine," the psalmist wrote. "I have more insight than all my teachers, for Your testimonies are my meditation. . . . Your word is a lamp to my feet and a light to my path" (Psalm 119:98-99, 105).

When we get to the New Testament, we continue to learn that the words of the Scriptures are the very words of God. "In the beginning was the Word, and the Word was with God, and the Word was God," the apostle John wrote of the Lord Jesus Christ. "And the Word became flesh, and dwelt among us, and we saw His glory, glory as of the only begotten from the Father, full of grace and truth" (John 1:1, 14).

The apostle Paul put it as clearly as anyone could in his second letter to his young disciple Timothy: "All Scripture is inspired by God and profitable for teaching, for reproof, for correction, for training in righteousness" (2 Timothy 3:16).

What's more, the Bible states that the prophecies contained within it were inspired by the all-seeing, all-knowing, all-powerful God, who chooses to give his people advance warning of the future events he deems of utmost importance.

Through the Hebrew prophet Isaiah, the Lord said, "I am God, and there is no other; I am God, and there is none like me. I make known the end from the beginning, from ancient times, what is still to come" (Isaiah 46:9-10, NIV).

Through the prophet Amos, the Lord said, "The Lord GOD does nothing unless He reveals His secret counsel to His servants the prophets" (Amos 3:7).

Through the prophet Jeremiah, the Lord told his people, "Call to Me and I will answer you, and I will tell you great and mighty things, which you do not know" (Jeremiah 33:3).

Referring to the Holy Spirit, the Lord Jesus told his disciples, "When He, the Spirit of truth, comes, He will guide you into all the truth; for He will not speak on His own initiative, but whatever He hears, He will speak; and He will disclose to you what is to come" (John 16:13).

Bible prophecies are, if you will, intercepts from the mind of God. They tell us God's secrets. They tell us "great and mighty things" we do not know about the future. They tell us "what is to come." Often, biblical prophecies are "storm warnings" for the future, warnings of wars or natural disasters or other catastrophic events that God has decided he is going to allow to happen or cause to happen. Yet in his love and mercy, he wants us to be aware of—and thereby fully prepared for—these events before they come to pass.

On What Basis Can We Trust the Prophecies Found in the Bible?

Couldn't any book claim to be written by God? Yes.

Haven't other books in history claimed to predict the future? Yes.

On what basis, then, can we trust the prophecies found in the Bible about the last days in general and about the future of specific countries in particular? This is an important question, and the answer is simple: we can trust the Bible's prophecies about the future because the Bible's prophecies about the past have all come true.

Think about it for a moment. The prophets in the Bible told mankind about hundreds of specific events that would happen—and made those predictions *before* they happened. And then those events actually happened just as they were foretold. That fact provides proof that these men in the Bible truly spoke from God. After all, only God knows "the end from the beginning." Therefore, only God could give his servants advance knowledge of the things to come, not just in a few instances, but in hundreds and hundreds of specific cases, and with 100 percent accuracy. Indeed, fulfilled prophecy is one of the distinctive elements that give us confidence that the Bible is the very Word of God, not the scribblings of mere mortals.

The Prophecies about the Captivity of Jerusalem Came True
The Hebrew prophet Jeremiah once prophesied that God was going to enact judgment on an unrepentant nation of Israel by sending the Babylonians to conquer the Holy Land and take her inhabitants captive. "And the LORD has sent to you all His servants the prophets again and again, but you have not listened nor inclined your ear to hear . . . Therefore thus says the LORD of hosts, 'Because you have not obeyed My words, behold, I will send and take all the families of the north . . . and I will send to Nebuchadnezzar king of Babylon, My servant, and will bring them against this land and against its inhabitants and against all these nations round about . . . This whole land will be a desolation and a horror, and these nations will serve the king of Babylon'" (Jeremiah 25:4-11). Scholars indicate that Jeremiah began his prophetic ministry around 626 BC. And sure enough, the

Babylonians, under the leadership of King Nebuchadnezzar, conquered Jerusalem in 586 BC, just as prophesied.

Jeremiah also prophesied that the captivity of the Jewish people in Babylon would last for seventy years, at which point the prophet said the Jewish people would be set free to return to Jerusalem and the Holy Land. "'Then it will be when seventy years are completed I will punish the king of Babylon and that nation . . . For behold, days are coming,' declares the LORD, 'when I will restore the fortunes of My people Israel and Judah.' The LORD says, 'I will also bring them back to the land that I gave to their forefathers and they shall possess it'" (Jeremiah 25:12; 30:3).

The prophet Daniel was one of the exiles living in the Babylonian Empire during this time. He had been taken captive at a young age and had grown up and been educated in the capital of Babylon. Yet while he had a powerful and intimate relationship with the God of Israel, he did not realize that the captivity was prophesied to last for a specific period of time. One day, however, as he was having his daily Bible study and poring over the prophecies of Jeremiah, he was startled by what he found. "I, Daniel, observed in the books the number of the years which was revealed as the word of the LORD to Jeremiah the prophet for the completion of the desolations of Jerusalem, namely, seventy years," Daniel would later write. "So I gave my attention to the Lord God to seek Him by prayer and supplications, with fasting, sackcloth, and ashes" (Daniel 9:2-3). Daniel confessed his sins and the sins of his people and asked the Lord to have mercy and to forgive the Jewish people for turning their backs on the Lord. What's more, he asked the Lord to keep his promise and release the Jewish people from captivity at the end of seventy years. This, of course, is precisely what happened. The Babylonian Empire was conquered by the neighboring Medo-Persian Empire, and the Jewish people were eventually set free to return to Israel and Jerusalem by order of the Persian king, right on the prophetic schedule.

The Prophecies about Four World Empires Came True

Among the most fascinating examples of Bible prophecies coming to pass is the dramatic dream of the Babylonian king Nebuchadnezzar.

One night, the king had an unusually vivid dream about future events. The dream was so troubling that he could not sleep, and he called together the wise men of his kingdom to seek their counsel. In chapter 2 of the book of Daniel, we learn that the king's most senior advisors anxiously waited for the king to tell them the dream so they could interpret it, but the king refused. "If you do not make known to me the dream and its interpretation, you will be torn limb from limb and your houses will be made a rubbish heap," he said (v. 5). The magicians and conjurers and sorcerers again insisted that the king first share the dream and then they would explain it to him, but Nebuchadnezzar became enraged. "I know for certain that you are bargaining for time, inasmuch as you have seen that the command from me is firm, that if you do not make the dream known to me, there is only one decree for you. For you have agreed together to speak lying and corrupt words before me until the situation is changed; therefore tell me the dream, that I may know that you can declare to me its interpretation" (v. 8).

The king's advisors were incredulous—and terrified. They had just been threatened with death. Yet they were in an impossible situation. They were fully prepared to analyze future events for their monarch, using all the worldly knowledge and experience they possessed. But how could they possibly tell the king what his dream meant until they knew what his dream was? And how could they know what his private dream was unless he told them? "There is not a man on earth who could declare the matter for the king, inasmuch as no great king or ruler has ever asked anything like this of any magician, conjurer, or Chaldean," they replied. "The thing which the king demands is difficult, and there is no one else who could declare it to the king except gods, whose dwelling place is not with mortal flesh" (vv. 10-11).

The furious Nebuchadnezzar then ordered that all the wise men of Babylon be put to death. Daniel, a young man at the time, was among this group. He had a reputation for having a relationship with a God who interpreted dreams and provided extraordinary wisdom. When Daniel heard about the death sentence, he went to the king and requested some time to respond to the king's demands. Nebuchadnezzar agreed. "Then," the Bible tells us, "Daniel went to his house and informed his friends . . . about the matter" and asked them to pray for "compassion from the God of heaven" (vv. 17-18) so that the Lord would reveal the dream and its interpretation, and so their lives would be saved. "Then the mystery was revealed to Daniel in a night vision," the Scriptures explain (v. 19). Daniel thanked the Lord profusely for being a prayer-hearing and prayer-answering God, a wonder-working God. Then Daniel humbly went before the king.

"Are you able to make known to me the dream which I have seen and its interpretation?" King Nebuchadnezzar asked (v. 26).

"As for the mystery about which the king has inquired, neither wise men, conjurers, magicians, nor diviners are able to declare it to the king," Daniel replied. "However, there is a God in heaven who reveals mysteries, and He has made known to King Nebuchadnezzar what will take place in the latter days" (vv. 27-28).

Daniel understood that only God "removes kings and establishes kings" and that "it is He who reveals the profound and hidden things" (vv. 21-22). Daniel, therefore, took no credit for what he did that day. Instead, he gave all the credit to the Lord as he explained that the king had dreamed about a great statue with a head of gold, a body and arms of silver, a belly and thighs of bronze, legs of iron, and feet partly made of iron and partly made of clay. Daniel then described how all the different elements were crushed by a stone "cut out without hands" (v. 34). Nebuchadnezzar was stunned. Daniel had his full attention, for that was *exactly* what he had dreamed. Now, what did it mean?

Daniel explained that the head of gold represented Nebuchadnezzar, overseeing the Babylonian Empire. "After you there will arise another kingdom [of silver] inferior to you, then another third kingdom of bronze . . . Then there will be a fourth kingdom as strong as iron." But that, Daniel said, would be "a divided kingdom" (vv. 39-41).

Remarkably, Daniel had not simply told the king the substance of his private dreams. He had also explained that this dream was given by God to describe future events, namely the coming destruction of the Babylonian Empire and the rise and fall of three other great world empires, one after another.

The accuracy of Daniel's analysis is startling. Just as he said, the Babylonians were overtaken by the Medo-Persian Empire, which was symbolized by silver, a metal precious to the Persians to this day. The Medo-Persian Empire was then overtaken by the Greek Empire, represented in the dream by bronze. The Greek Empire was overtaken by the Roman Empire, with its iron-strong military might, so powerful it overwhelmed all others before it. The Roman Empire was, as Daniel foretold, a divided kingdom. It was ruled for a time by four coemperors. Later, it was divided into eastern and western empires, with its western seat of power in Rome and its eastern portion becoming known as the Byzantine Empire, whose seat of power was centered in the city known in antiquity as Byzantium—the city that was later called Constantinople and is known today as Istanbul.

The Prophecies about the First Coming of the Messiah Came True
One of the most compelling reasons we can trust that Bible prophecies related to the second coming of the Messiah will come to pass is because the prophecies related to the Messiah's first coming have already come to pass.

The Hebrew prophet Micah, for example, told us the Messiah would be born in Bethlehem Ephrathah, a town located south of Jerusalem in the area of Judea. "'But as for you, Bethlehem Ephrathah, too little to be among the clans of Judah, from you One will go forth for Me to be ruler in Israel. His goings forth are from long ago, from the days of eternity.' . . . And He will arise and shepherd His flock in the strength of the LORD" (Micah 5:2-4). Sure enough, some seven hundred years later, the Lord Jesus was born in Bethlehem Ephrathah, just as the prophecy foretold.

The prophet Isaiah, meanwhile, told us that the Messiah would be born as a male child, yet he would actually be God himself and would live and minister and bring divine light to the people of Israel. "The people who walk in darkness will see a great light," Isaiah wrote. "For a child will be born to us, a son will be given to us; and the government will rest on His shoulders; and His name will be called Wonderful Counselor, Mighty God, Eternal Father, Prince of Peace" (Isaiah 9:2, 6). Sure enough, God became flesh for a time by being born into the world as a baby boy named Jesus, who grew up to live, minister, and bring a great light to the people of the Galilee region, as well as to all of Israel and the world.

The prophet Daniel, writing nearly six hundred years before the time of Jesus, told us that while the Messiah would come to make atonement for our sins and bring mankind into everlasting righteousness, something tragic would happen to him, and at some time after that, Jerusalem and the holy Temple would be destroyed by an invading power. God declared in Daniel 9:24-26 that a certain period of human history had been "decreed for your people [the Jews] and your holy city [Jerusalem], to finish the transgression, to make an end of sin, to make atonement for iniquity, [and] to bring in everlasting righteousness," and then "the Messiah will be cut off and have nothing," and after that, "the people of the prince who is to come will destroy the city and the sanctuary." Sure enough, the Lord Jesus came early in the first century AD, he was "cut off" through a terrible torture and crucifixion at the hands of the Roman army around AD 32, and then in AD 70 the Romans destroyed the city of Jerusalem and the Temple, just as Daniel prophesied.

The Prophecies Spoken by Jesus Came True

Another reason we can trust the prophecies found in the Bible is that the prophecies uttered by the Lord Jesus himself have all come true, except for those that will be fulfilled in the Tribulation, by his second coming, and by events he spoke of that will occur after his second coming.

For example, Jesus once told his disciples, who had not caught any fish after fishing all night on the Sea of Galilee, that they would catch some fish by casting their nets on the other side of the boat, and his prediction came true immediately. He told them, "'Cast the net on the right-hand side of the boat and you will find a catch.' So they cast, and then they were not able to haul it in because of the great number of fish" (see John 21:1-6).

Another time Jesus pronounced that a fig tree that didn't have any fruit on it would never bear fruit again, and it happened within twenty-four hours. "May no one ever eat fruit from you again!" Jesus said. The next day, "as they were passing by in the morning, they saw the fig tree withered from the roots up. Being reminded, Peter said to Him, 'Rabbi, look, the fig tree which You cursed has withered'" (see Mark 11:11-21).

Jesus prophesied that the Second Temple in Jerusalem would be destroyed, and it came to pass about forty years later (see Matthew 24:1-2).

Jesus prophesied that he would "go to Jerusalem, and suffer many things from the elders and chief priests and scribes, and be killed, and be raised up on the third day," and his torture, execution, and resurrection dramatically and miraculously occurred less than three years later (see Matthew 16:21-23 and Matthew 26–28).

Shortly before his death, Jesus prophesied that Peter would deny knowing him three times before the rooster crowed the following morning, and it happened just as he said it would—despite Peter's intense promises to the contrary (see Matthew 26:31-35 and Matthew 26:69-75).

Jesus prophesied after his resurrection that his disciples would be "baptized with the Holy Spirit not many days from now," and it came to pass within a few days (see Acts 1:5 and Acts 2:1-4).

The fact that Jesus was both a great prophet and the Messiah should not come as a surprise. Centuries before, Moses had told the children of Israel to expect a prophet in the future who would be like himself in the sense that he would speak the words of God and demonstrate the power of God through great signs and wonders. Moses warned the people to listen to and obey the future prophet or face the judgment of God. "The LORD your God will raise up for you a prophet like me from among you, from your countrymen, [and] you shall listen to him," Moses explained. "The LORD said to me, '. . . I will raise up a prophet from among their countrymen like you, and I will put My words in his mouth, and he shall speak to them all that I command him. It shall come about that whoever will not listen to My words which he shall speak in My name, I Myself will require it of him" (Deuteronomy 18:15, 17-19).

In the early years of the first century AD, the rabbis and priests from Jerusalem heard about the things John the Baptist was doing, and they wondered whether he was the one Moses had foretold. "Are you the Prophet?" they asked him. John replied, "No. . . . I am a voice of one crying in the wilderness, 'Make straight the way of the Lord,' as Isaiah the prophet said" (John 1:21-23). Then John saw Jesus and declared, "Behold, the Lamb of God who takes away the sin of the world! . . . I myself have seen, and have testified that this is the Son of God" (John 1:29, 34). In other words, John the Baptist made it crystal clear to the people of Israel that he was not the prophet of whom Moses spoke, but Jesus was. Many Jewish people began to realize this for themselves after hearing Jesus teach with authority and seeing him perform miracles that could only be done by the power of God. "This is truly the Prophet who is to come into the world," they said in Galilee after Jesus supernaturally fed more than five thousand people with just five loaves of barley bread and two fish (see John 6:1-14).

The apostles eventually understood this and preached it as well. "Repent and return [to the Lord], so that your sins may be wiped away, in order that times of refreshing may come from the presence of the Lord; and that He may send Jesus, the Christ [or *Messiah*] appointed for you, whom heaven must receive until the period of restoration of all things about which God spoke by the mouth of His holy prophets from ancient time," the apostle Peter said to a crowd of very curious Jewish people at the Temple after a lame man had been healed at Peter's command. He continued, "Moses said, 'The Lord God will raise up for you a prophet like me from your brethren; to Him you shall give heed to everything He says to you. And it will be that every soul that does not heed that prophet shall be utterly destroyed from among the people'" (Acts 3:19-23).

Bottom Line

The Bible actually contains about one thousand prophecies, more than half of which have already been fulfilled.[1] Most of the prophecies that are yet to be fulfilled relate to the events of the last days of human history before the second coming of Jesus Christ. These include prophecies about the Rapture, the Tribulation, and the Day of the Lord, all of which we will examine in due course. Other major Bible prophecies will be fulfilled during the thousand-year reign of Christ on earth (known as the millennial kingdom), the final battle between God and Satan at the end of history, and the establishment of the new heavens and the new earth. While it is beyond the scope of this book to provide a survey of the more than five hundred Bible prophecies that have already come to pass, let me encourage you to carefully study and test the Bible and ask God to reveal to you the truths contained therein.

Now, with this foundation established, let's continue in our journey to examine the questions "Are we living in the last days?" and "Is America mentioned specifically in Bible prophecy?" Then, as we understand what the Bible says and how to examine events and trends in the United States and around the globe through the third lens of Scripture, we will be able to effectively answer our central questions, "What happens to America in the last days?" and "Is America heading for an implosion?"

CHAPTER FIVE

SIGNS OF THE TIMES

ARE WE LIVING IN THE LAST DAYS before the return of Jesus Christ? You might be surprised how many Americans say yes. To many in politics and the media, the idea may seem ridiculous. But millions of Americans from Maine to California have seen events in this country and around the world and have come to the conclusion that we are, in fact, living in the last days.

In 2006, when I was working on a nonfiction book called *Epicenter: Why the Current Rumblings in the Middle East Will Change Your Future*, I commissioned a national survey of American adults to better understand contemporary attitudes toward Bible prophecy. The poll was conducted by the respected firm of McLaughlin & Associates, founded by John McLaughlin, who over the years has worked with some of the world's leading business and political leaders, including Steve Forbes, Israeli prime minister Benjamin Netanyahu, Tennessee senator Fred Thompson, and Florida governor Jeb Bush.

The survey asked people if they agreed with the following statement:

Events such as the rebirth of the State of Israel, wars and instability in the Middle East, recent earthquakes, and the tsunami in Asia are evidence that we are living in what the Bible calls the last days.

Remarkably, more than four out of ten Americans (42 percent) said they agreed that yes, we are living in what the Bible calls the last days. Perhaps more remarkably, common stereotypes notwithstanding, it was not just white Anglo-Saxon Protestants or rural Southern men who said they agreed.[1]

- One in three Jews believe we are living in the last days.
- Four in ten Catholics believe we are living in the last days.
- Half of all women believe we are living in the last days.
- Nearly half of all senior citizens believe we are living in the last days.
- Nearly six in ten young people age eighteen to twenty-five believe we are living in the last days.
- A remarkable 75 percent of African Americans believe we are living in the last days.

To be sure, plenty of Americans disagree. More precisely, most Americans do not believe we are living in the last days. But when it comes to those who do believe these are the End Times, we are not talking about a tiny fringe minority. We are talking about 100 million Americans or more.

Ultimately, however, the important thing is not how many Americans believe we are living in the last days. The important thing is whether they are right.

Analyzing This Present Time

In Luke 12, we find thousands of people gathered to hear what Jesus had to say. His critics were growing in number and in the intensity of their opposition to the man from Galilee, but so were the number of those who wanted to learn more from the one who taught with such wisdom and authority. Then, to the surprise of many, Jesus sharply criticized the crowd for not analyzing current events through the third lens of Scripture.

> When you see a cloud rising in the west, immediately you
> say, "A shower is coming," and so it turns out. And when
> you see a south wind blowing, you say, "It will be a hot day,"
> and it turns out that way. You hypocrites! You know how
> to analyze the appearance of the earth and the sky, but why
> do you not analyze this present time?
>
> LUKE 12:54-56

Why such a strong rebuke? Because while those living in first-century Judea (as the Romans referred to the biblical land of Israel) certainly knew the many ancient Hebrew prophecies describing the coming Messiah (that he would be born in Bethlehem Ephrathah, live in Galilee, teach in parables, do miracles, care for the poor, etc.), they could not—or would not—connect the dots and accept that it was Jesus himself to whom the prophets were pointing. And the stakes were high. This was a matter of eternal life with the Father in heaven or eternal punishment in the lake of fire. As Jesus had said before, "For God so loved the world, that He gave His only begotten Son, that whoever believes in Him shall not perish, but have eternal life. . . . He who believes in the Son has eternal life; but he who does not obey the Son will not see life, but the wrath of God abides on him" (John 3:16, 36).

The situation isn't that different today. How many people living in the twenty-first century who are familiar with the many biblical prophecies concerning the second coming of the Messiah are able—or willing—to connect the dots and see what is coming? And the stakes are just as high today as they were in the first century.

Not all future events are described in advance in the Bible. Nor can the prophecies be used to determine the future of every country. But there are key events and trends that Jesus and the prophets and the apostles said would occur in the last days that would help us know Christ's return was drawing closer. It is imperative that we know what those are and understand what they mean if we are to properly analyze the signs of the times.

What Are the Last Days?

Let us begin by defining some terms.

Last days is a biblical term used in both the Old and New Testaments in reference to the time leading up to the second coming of Jesus Christ. It is described as a time of prophetic signs and wonders, the spread of the gospel, the growth and persecution of believers, and other dramatic events. Also variously referred to in the Scriptures as the "latter days," the "latter years," and by the prophet Daniel as "the time of the end," this period is sometimes known colloquially in the modern era as the "End Times" or the "end of days." This is not because this period leads up to the actual end of the world but because it constitutes the last days before the Day of the Lord, when the Messiah comes to earth to reign over all mankind in fulfillment of Bible prophecy.

It is beyond the scope of this book to deal in depth with all the other elements of the last days that the Bible tells us to expect. Many books have been written about topics like the Rapture and the Tribulation and the Millennium, and I will not get into those events here (though I will talk more about the Rapture in chapter 12). But I do want to look a little more closely at the Day of the Lord because that is the culmination of the last days—and arguably the most significant event in human history.

The Day of the Lord refers to the actual, physical, literal second coming of the Lord Jesus Christ to earth. This is the time when the Scriptures indicate that Christ's feet will touch down on the Mount of Olives, splitting the mountain in two. The Bible describes this as a time of darkness and judgment, during which no more salvations will be possible. At this time, Christ will cleanse the land of Israel from the horrors of war, oversee the building of a new Temple (the one described in Ezekiel 40–48), and begin his one-thousand-year reign in Jerusalem over all mankind, a period that believers commonly call the "millennial kingdom."

The Day of the Lord—including related biblical references to this unparalleled moment in human history such as "the day," "that day," and the like—is mentioned more than sixty times in the New American Standard translation of the Bible. The Day of the Lord is synonymous with the second coming of Christ, and the two phrases are often used interchangeably by scholars and commentators. The term *Second Coming* itself is not a phrase found in the Bible, though it is a powerful and pervasive concept in the Scriptures.

The prophet Malachi refers to "the great and terrible day of the LORD" (Malachi 4:5). The prophet Joel refers to "the great and dreadful day of the LORD" (Joel 2:31, NIV). Why does each prophecy use such divergent terms to describe the same event? Why would the coming of the Lord be "great" on the one hand and "terrible" or "dreadful" on the other? In one sense, the Second Coming will be great in terms of its enormous scope and magnitude. Yet in another sense, the Day of the Lord will be great for those who have received Jesus Christ as their Savior and Lord and thus are excited about his return and his loving and benevolent rule over the earth that will follow. However, the Scriptures also indicate that the Day of the Lord will be terrible and dreadful for those who have rejected Jesus as Messiah because the time for accepting him will have expired. Those who are not at that moment born again (as explained in John chapter 3) will go to hell. That's how high the stakes are. This is why the Scriptures put such a heavy emphasis on the importance of believers sharing the good news of Christ's love and forgiveness with the whole world and urging them to receive Christ as Savior before it is too late.

It should be noted here that all truly born-again followers of Jesus Christ believe that the second coming of Jesus Christ will occur at some point in the future. All the major Christian denominations around the world—and all independent Bible-believing and Bible-teaching congregations—hold the second coming of Christ as a fundamental, essential, and nonnegotiable element of orthodox Christian doctrine. To deny the second coming of Christ, which is taught clearly and unapologetically in the Bible, is heresy. The return of Jesus Christ to earth to be reunited with his followers is, therefore, an event that should unite all sincere Christians as something very much to look forward to.

That said, while all faithful Christians believe Jesus Christ is coming back, not all sincere Christians agree on all aspects of biblical eschatology, or End Times theology. There are differences of opinion on how to correctly interpret the Scriptures that describe what will happen in the last days and in what order these events will take place. These are important debates, and it is worth familiarizing yourself with these concepts from the Bible, but my purpose here is not to painstakingly go through every element of End Times prophecy. I do, however, recommend that you undertake your own study of these critical concepts. Why? Because these events are coming, and people need to know what's ahead and be prepared. This is why we were given these prophecies: to offer us advance warning of the storms that are approaching so we can be ready and prepare others to be safe and secure through faith in Christ Jesus.

As I have pointed out, my intention here is not to attempt to settle disputes among Christians with regard to the specifics of the last days. It is, rather, first to acknowledge to those who have never seriously studied Bible prophecy that there are disagreements among men and women of goodwill. And second, I want to encourage you to study the Scriptures very carefully for yourself, pray and ask the Lord to reveal the truth to you, discuss these prophecies with family and friends, and seek to honestly discover their meaning.

What Are the Signs of the Last Days?

The good news is that the Bible provides a list of geopolitical, spiritual, and environmental signs that will be visible in the last days as we get closer to the return of Christ. The most famous and detailed explanation of these signs was given by the Lord Jesus himself on the Mount of Olives, just outside the city of Jerusalem. Shortly before his arrest, trial, crucifixion, and resurrection, Jesus was asked by his disciples, "Tell us, when will these things happen, and what will be the sign of Your coming, and of the end of the age?" (Matthew 24:3). The disciples, eager to understand the future, were hoping Jesus would give them at least one sign that would help them know when the "end of the age" would occur and the reign of the Messiah on earth would begin.

The conversation that ensued, often referred to by Bible scholars as the Olivet discourse, was so important that it was recorded at length in three of the Gospel accounts. Jesus could have given a very political answer, like "No comment. Next question." Instead, he answered their questions. But rather than giving them just one sign of the last days, he described numerous signs.

Matthew 24, Mark 13, and Luke 21 give us three vantage points on Christ's teaching about the signs of the last days. When one carefully studies all three accounts of the Olivet discourse, along with the other passages in the Old and New Testaments that refer to the last days, a fascinating and sobering list emerges.

Here are twenty signs Bible prophecy tells us we will see in the last days:

1. Wars and rumors of wars
2. Uprisings and revolutions and kingdoms being shaken
3. Famines
4. Earthquakes
5. Pestilences and plagues
6. Terrors and growing fears
7. Great signs in the heavens and bloodred moons
8. The roaring of the sea and the waves
9. Persecution of the church
10. Apostasy of the church
11. Betrayal
12. Lawlessness
13. False prophets and false teachers
14. False messiahs
15. Increase in knowledge and travel
16. The State of Israel being reborn and increasingly becoming the epicenter of international attention
17. The gospel being preached to every nation
18. A spiritual awakening in Israel and among the Jewish people
19. A spiritual awakening in Iran
20. An increase in mockery of Bible prophecy

That's quite a list—yet these signs are just the beginning. "But all these things are merely the beginning of birth pangs," the Lord Jesus said in Matthew 24:8 (see also Mark 13:8). In other words, the Bible teaches that while all of these signs will be visible in the last days as we approach the Day of the Lord and the Second Coming, these and other events will radically accelerate and intensify as the time of Christ's return draws nearer.

Are We Seeing the Signs Come to Pass?

Is there any sign on that list we haven't seen come to pass over the course of the last century?

Let's briefly consider a few of these "birth pangs."

Wars and Revolutions

Jesus told his disciples that in the last days there would be "wars and rumors of wars" when "nation will rise against nation, and kingdom against kingdom" (Matthew 24:6-7). Surely there have been wars and rumors of wars throughout history, but have any been as widespread and destructive as the wars in the last century? They were, after all, called World War I and World War II for a reason—because they were unprecedented in their scope and devastation. The first led to at least 37 million casualties (injuries and deaths), including 200,000 American casualties.[2] The second led to at least 46 million deaths alone—including 6 million Jews exterminated by the Nazis—though some historians believe the number of worldwide military and civilian deaths tops 60 million.[3] Add to this all the other wars of the twentieth and twenty-first centuries, and a ghastly picture emerges unlike any other period in history, yet consistent with the prophecies.

Jesus also said there would be uprisings and revolutions and geopolitical disturbances in the last days (see Luke 21:9-10). Surely there have been uprisings and revolutions throughout history, but there has never been a span of history with more sweeping, bloody, and internationally game-changing revolutions as the last hundred years or so. One country after another has experienced unprecedented upheavals, from the Mexican Revolution of 1910, to the Russian

Revolution of 1917, to the Hungarian Revolution of 1956, to the Cultural Revolution in China from 1966 to 1976, to the Islamic Revolution in Iran in 1979, to the pro-democracy revolutions that brought down the Warsaw Pact countries and the Soviet Union in the late 1980s and early 1990s, to the multiple Palestinian uprisings, to the 2011 revolutions in Tunisia, Egypt, Yemen, and Libya that led to the downfall of each of those Arab countries' tyrannical yet long-serving dictators. The list goes on and on, including revolutions in Cuba, Nicaragua, Vietnam, Bosnia, Rwanda, Liberia, and beyond. These trends are all consistent with Bible prophecy.

Earthquakes

Jesus said in the last days there would be "earthquakes" and "great earthquakes" (Matthew 24:7; Luke 21:11). Can anyone reasonably deny that this has been happening in the past century or so?

The top five most intense earthquakes in all of recorded history have occurred since 1900, each 9.0 or higher on the Richter scale.[4] Three of the top five deadliest earthquakes in human history have occurred since 1900.[5] The 2011 earthquake in Haiti "only" registered 7.0 on the Richter scale, and thus isn't in the top five, or the top ten, or even the top hundred most intense earthquakes in history in terms of magnitude. It actually ranks number 352.[6] Yet it was the deadliest earthquake in nearly five hundred years and the second-deadliest earthquake in all of recorded history.[7]

Given increasing urbanization around the globe, an earthquake doesn't necessarily have to be a 9.0 magnitude or higher to cause apocalyptic levels of death and destruction. The 2005 earthquake in northern Pakistan, for example, measured "only" 7.6, yet tragically 86,000 people died, and some 4 million people were left homeless. Likewise, the 2008 earthquake in eastern China measured "only" 7.9 but killed more than 87,000 people and displaced more than 5 million people.[8] Again, such trends are consistent with Bible prophecy.

The Remarkable Advance of the Gospel

The good news, Jesus said, was that in the last days, "this gospel of the kingdom shall be preached in the whole world as a testimony to all the nations, and then the end will come" (Matthew 24:14). In other words, Jesus' return won't occur until every man, woman, and child in every nation on the planet has had the opportunity to hear the salvation message of Jesus Christ and has had the opportunity to either receive Christ or reject him. Church congregations, denominations, parachurch ministries, and missionaries around the globe have worked hard over the past several centuries to accomplish this task of giving everyone the opportunity to hear the gospel. With the advent of radio, broadcast television, satellite television, the Internet, and new developments in transportation and translation technology, the most dramatic advancements in the history of the gospel have been made over the past century. Some pastors and missions experts say we still have a ways to go to reach everyone on the planet. Others, however, believe we may actually be there already.

Consider, for example, the reach and impact of just two ministries: the Billy Graham Evangelistic Association and the *JESUS* film project. Two *Time* magazine reporters published a book in 2007 noting that "Billy Graham is believed to have spoken face-to-face with more people in more places than anyone in history, having preached the gospel to 210 million people in 185 countries in 417 crusades over the course of more than half a century. Not even Billy Sunday or Dwight L. Moody or any of the great evangelists going back to Saint Paul had spread their message so far; it was Billy Graham alone, inserted into history at just the right moment, who became the unrivaled global ambassador for Christ."[9]

At the same time, the *JESUS* film—produced in 1979 by Warner Brothers and Campus Crusade for Christ—has been translated into more than five hundred languages and dialects. It has been shown by Campus Crusade and more than 1,500 other Christian agencies in every country on the planet. According to the *JESUS* film project's website, the film "has had more than 6 billion viewings worldwide since 1979" and "as a result, more than 200 million people have indicated decisions to accept Christ as their personal Savior and Lord."[10] These trends too are consistent with the fulfillment of Bible prophecies.

Skeptics and Cynics

Are there skeptics out there, people who are cynical about the possibility that we may be living in the last days? Are there those who mock followers of Jesus Christ for believing in the Bible and in the prophecies of Christ's second coming? Of course. But that should come as no surprise. Indeed, Bible prophecy tells us there will be mockers in the last days. "Know this first of all," the apostle Peter wrote, "that in the last days mockers will come with their mocking, following after their own lusts, and saying, 'Where is the promise of His coming? For ever since the fathers fell asleep, all continues just as it was from the beginning of creation'" (2 Peter 3:3-4). Such mockers are all around us, and we should expect their numbers to grow.

One night in the spring of 2011, while I was taking a break from working on this book, I was scanning through the TV channels and saw MSNBC talk show host Lawrence O'Donnell mocking the Bible. "The book of Revelation is a work of fiction describing how a truly vicious God would bring about the end of the world," O'Donnell said. "No half-smart religious person believes the book of Revelation."[11]

In his 2000 book, *The End of Days*, Israeli journalist Gershom Gorenberg mocked belief in biblical prophecies of the End Times as a "fantasy" and "dangerous."[12]

Bill Moyers, the longtime PBS journalist and former White House press secretary for President Lyndon Johnson, mocked American Christians during a 2004 speech, saying that evangelicals care nothing for the environment because the last days are here. "Why care about the earth when the droughts, floods, famine, and pestilence brought by ecological collapse are signs of the apocalypse foretold in the Bible? Why care about global climate change when you and yours will be rescued in the Rapture? And why care about converting from oil to solar when the same God who performed the miracle of the loaves and fishes can whip up a few billion barrels of light crude with a word?" he sneered, quoting a left-wing journalist who had caught his attention. Calling End Times beliefs "bizarre," Moyers was incredulous that there are actually "people who believe the Bible is literally true" and that they are trying to shape the future of America.[13]

Kevin Phillips, the former Republican political strategist, wrote in his bestselling 2006 book, *American Theocracy*, that Americans who believe in Bible prophecy are "overimaginative" at best and "radical" at worst, asserting that "the rapture, end-times, and Armageddon hucksters in the United States rank with any Shiite ayatollahs."[14]

Over the years, I've met similar skeptics, cynics, and mockers. Occasionally they've challenged me during speaking events. Often they e-mail me. I have been interviewed by some of them on radio and television and for various newspaper and magazine articles and for books. Fox News Channel analyst Alan Colmes once asked me on his late-night radio show whether Jesus was coming back so soon that he needn't bother picking up his dry cleaning or buying green bananas.

A few years ago, I was interviewed by a Cambridge- and Princeton-educated professor of history from Great Britain named Nicholas Guyatt. He said he was writing a serious book about American evangelical Christianity and Americans' interest in Bible prophecy. I was happy to answer his questions, even knowing he was, at best, a skeptic. The final product, unfortunately, did not turn out to be a serious look at the beliefs of sincere Christians, as Guyatt suggested.

Guyatt's book, *Have a Nice Doomsday: Why Millions of Americans Are Looking Forward to the End of the World*, turned out to be part mockery, part incredulity that so many Americans could believe such ridiculous things. He wrote, "It's easy to imagine Bible prophecy as a playpen for lunatics" and that "the temptation, when considering these notorious cult leaders or the avid audience for the Left Behind novels, is to dismiss End Times thinking as deranged."[15] Yes, people have believed in Bible prophecy through the ages, he conceded, but he argued that it's worse now because "apocalyptic Christians" are trying to persuade officials in Washington to bring about the end of the world. He warned that Christian interest in the last days, and specifically in the reconstruction of the Jewish Temple in Jerusalem, is not only "kooky" but "lethal."[16]

Bottom Line

We are living at an extraordinary moment in human history. The Bible gives us a list of signs to be watching for that indicate when the return of Jesus Christ is increasingly close at hand. Remarkably, we have seen all of these signs come to pass over the past century or so, and we are continuing to see them come to pass in our lifetime, up to and including this present time. From this preliminary assessment, is it reasonable to conclude that we are living in what the Bible calls the last days? I believe it is. But let's go further.

CHAPTER SIX

THE SIGNIFICANCE
OF THE REBIRTH OF ISRAEL

THE MOST DEFINITIVE AND CONCLUSIVE SIGN that we are living in the era the Bible calls the last days was the miraculous rebirth of the State of Israel in 1948, the return of millions of Jews to the Holy Land after centuries of exile, the wars and rumors of wars that have engulfed the Jewish state for the last half century and more, the rebuilding of the ancient ruins in Israel, and the increasing international focus on the nation of Israel as the epicenter of the momentous events that are shaking our world and shaping our future. Some Bible scholars have described the rebirth of Israel as the "super sign," and I agree.

Many people did not see the modern resurrection of the Jewish state coming. Many thought it would never happen and shouldn't. For centuries, world leaders had cruelly scattered and persecuted the Jewish people and denied their right to return to their ancient homeland. Sadly, even many church leaders throughout history came to believe in a pernicious doctrine called "replacement theology," which denied the veracity and legitimacy of Bible prophecies that said Israel would be reborn in the last days. Such replacement theologians, and the pastors and laypeople who read and followed their conclusions, said God had rejected the Jewish people and would no longer honor the ancient covenants to give the Jewish people the heretofore "Promised Land." Unfortunately, many people in the United States and around the world also vigorously opposed the creation of the modern State of Israel. Indeed, most of the Arab and Islamic world was willing to use any means necessary, including war, to strangle the reborn infant nation in her cradle, as they demonstrated time and time again.

Yet those who were watching events through the third lens of Scripture knew Israel would one day be reborn. What's more, those who believed the ancient biblical prophecies were true and valid often did much to assist the young nation of Israel. In this chapter, we will take a look back at the early days of Israel's modern rebirth and see how the United States played a key role in the Jewish state's resurrection. We will also take a look at some of the Bible prophecies fulfilled by Israel's rebirth and what they might mean for the future of our own nation.

Showdown in the Oval Office

Over the past six decades, the United States has been Israel's best friend and chief ally. That warm and strategic relationship began with President Harry Truman's official and highly public decision to be the first world leader to recognize and support the newly declared State of Israel on May 14, 1948. Yet few Americans realize the tectonic struggle that took place at the highest levels of the U.S. government and almost prevented Truman from making or implementing that decision.

Until recently, despite decades of studying Jewish history, traveling to Israel, and working with various Israeli leaders, I had no idea just how close the Jewish state came to being denied early and critical recognition by the American government. Not long ago, however, an Israeli friend recommended that I read *Counsel to the President*, a book that takes readers inside the Oval Office and describes the political infighting against Israel in vivid detail. What I found absolutely fascinated me.

The book is the memoir of Clark Clifford, a highly respected Democrat who served as senior advisor for and special counsel to President Truman. Later, Clifford served as chairman of the President's Foreign Intelligence Advisory Board for President John F. Kennedy, as secretary of defense under President Lyndon Johnson, and as an informal but highly trusted advisor to President Jimmy Carter before retiring from government and later passing away in 1998 at the age of 91. Clifford's memoir explains his up-close-and-personal role in some of the most dramatic moments of American history in the post–World War II years, from advising Kennedy after the Bay of Pigs fiasco, to helping Johnson seek an exit strategy from the Vietnam War, to counseling Carter during the darkest days of his presidency, to playing poker with Winston Churchill on a train bound for Fulton, Missouri, where Churchill was set to deliver his "Iron Curtain" speech.

Yet Clifford didn't begin his 709-page tome with a description of any of these events. His first chapter, titled "Showdown in the Oval Office," begins like this:

> May 12, 1948—Of all the meetings I ever had with
> presidents, this one remains the most vivid. Not only did
> it pit me against a legendary war hero whom President
> Truman revered, but it did so over an issue of fundamental
> and enduring national security importance—Israel and
> the Mideast.[1]

Clifford noted that Truman regarded then–secretary of state (and decorated Army general) George C. Marshall as "the greatest living American," yet Truman and Marshall were on "a collision course" over Israel that "threatened to split and wreck the administration."[2] Simply put, "Marshall firmly opposed American recognition of the new Jewish state," opposition that was "shared by almost every member of the brilliant and now-legendary group of men, later referred to as 'the Wise Men,' who were then in the process of creating a postwar foreign policy that would endure for more than forty years."[3] President Truman, in contrast, was a strong supporter of Israel, in large part because of his belief in the Bible.

Among the secretary of state's allies in opposing recognition of Israel was James V. Forrestal, the secretary of defense. Some months before, Forrestal had told Clifford, "You fellows over at the White House are just not facing up to the realities in the Middle East. There are 30 million Arabs on one side and about six hundred thousand Jews on the other. It is clear that in any contest, the Arabs are going to overwhelm the Jews. Why don't you face up to the realities? Just look at the numbers!"

"Jim, the president knows just as well as you do what the numbers are . . . but he doesn't consider this to be a question of numbers," Clifford replied. "He has always supported the right of the Jews to have their own homeland, from the moment he became president. . . . He is sympathetic to their needs and their desires, and I assure you he is going to continue to lend our country's support to the creation of a Jewish state."

"Well, if he does that, then he's absolutely dead wrong," the secretary of defense shot back.[4]

Now the moment of truth had come. The British Mandate for oversight of the land then referred to as Palestine (a term that dated back to the Greeks' and Romans' descriptions of the Holy Land) was set to expire in forty-eight hours. David Ben-Gurion, the head of the Jewish Agency, was poised to announce the declaration of the Jewish state's independence on May 14. That action, the administration knew, would almost certainly trigger a war between Israel and the surrounding Arab nations. Interestingly, Clifford noted that Ben-Gurion and his advisors had not yet decided on a name for the Jewish state. "The name 'Israel' was as yet unknown," Clifford wrote, "and most of us assumed the new nation would be called 'Judaea.'"[5]

At four o'clock in the afternoon on Wednesday, May 12, Marshall, Clifford, and several other advisors entered the Oval Office to meet with the president. Secretary Marshall explained that the creation of a Jewish state would be "dangerous." He said he had told a representative of the Jewish Agency that if the Jews got into trouble and "came running to us for help . . . they were clearly on notice that there was no warrant to expect help from the United States, which had warned them of the grave risk they were running."[6]

When Marshall and his colleagues were finished making their case opposing a Jewish state, the president turned to Clifford and asked for the case in support. Clifford noted a war between Israel and its neighbors was going to begin any moment and that delaying support would be tantamount to denying support. He said that the more quickly the president supported the Jewish state, the more likely it was for the new state to become friendly with—and hopefully eventually an ally of—the United States. If the Soviet Union, however, were the first to recognize the state, perhaps the Jews would form closer ties to Moscow. He continued by stating that in the Balfour Declaration, the British government had long before promised a state to the Jews and that "the United States has a great moral obligation to oppose discrimination" against the Jews and to create a "safe haven" for Jews escaping the Holocaust and Eastern European Communism. Finally, he argued that the U.S. should support the creation of democracies, that the Middle East had long been unstable, and that helping establish a democracy in the Middle East would be consistent with American values.

At that point, Secretary Marshall exploded. "Mr. President . . . I don't even know why Clifford is here. He is a domestic advisor, and this is a foreign policy matter."

"Well, General," the president replied calmly, "he's here because I asked him to be here."

Marshall and his colleagues protested that Clifford was pressing for support in order to win Jewish votes in the next presidential election. Marshall then threatened that if Truman supported the Jewish state, he would lose Marshall's vote. The room grew silent. The president ended the meeting by saying he would consider both sides seriously and make his decision soon.[7]

American Jewish Opposition to Israel

Actually, Truman's support of the creation of the Jewish state was opposed by many American Jews, a fact unknown or forgotten by many friends of Israel.

"A significant number of Jewish Americans opposed Zionism," Clifford wrote in his memoir. "Some feared that the effort to create a Jewish state was so controversial that the plan would fail. In 1942 a number of prominent Reform rabbis had founded the American Council for Judaism to oppose the establishment of a Jewish state in Palestine. It grew into an organization of over fourteen thousand members, which collaborated closely with State Department officials." Clifford also noted that Arthur H. Sulzberger, the Jewish publisher of the *New York Times*, and Eugene Meyer, the Jewish publisher of the *Washington Post*, "opposed Zionism" as well.[8]

Nevertheless, Truman had spoken favorably of the creation of a Jewish national homeland since not long after taking office. In 1947, for example, Truman had publicly made it the policy of the

United States government to back passage of the United Nations Partition Plan, creating the legal framework for the rebirth of the State of Israel as well as an adjoining state for the Palestinian Arabs. To succeed, the Partition Plan needed a two-thirds majority vote of the U.N. General Assembly. With just days to go before that historic vote on November 29, 1947, however, supporters of the plan were still three votes short. Some have suggested that President Truman personally called leaders of other nations to encourage them to support the American position. Others say he didn't but that staff in his administration did; the record is not clear.[9] Either way, most historians—including David McCullough, who won the Pulitzer Prize for his extraordinary biography *Truman*[10]—acknowledge that Truman wanted the plan to pass and played a role behind the scenes.*

In the end, Truman got his way. The Partition Plan dramatically passed at the last moment, thirty-three to thirteen, with ten abstentions.[11]

Truman's Historic Decision

Given the president's backing of the Partition Plan, it would seem in retrospect that his decision to formally support the new state was a fait accompli. But the political crisis inside the White House and State Department was real and festering for the next two days. Tensions mounted, and time was running out. Reporters were asking what the president would do on the issue, and the advisors closest to the president had no clue. President Truman kept his cards close to

---

*McCullough wrote, "It was in late 1947, on Saturday, November 29, over the Thanksgiving weekend, that the United Nations, at the end of a dramatic two-and-a-half-hour session, voted for partition by a narrow margin, the United States taking a lead part behind the scenes to see the measure through. . . . Eddie Jacobson recorded in telegraphic style his own chronicle of the unfolding drama: 'Nov. 6th—Wash.—Pres. still going all out for Palestine. Nov. 17th—Again to White House. . . . Wed., 26—Received call from White House—everything O.K. Nov. 27—Thanksgiving. Sent two-page wire to Truman. Friday, received call from his secretary . . . not to worry. Nov. 29th—Mission accomplished.' Truman, Jacobson noted, had told him that 'he [Truman] and he alone was responsible for swinging the votes of several delegations'" (pp. 601–602).

his vest. Clifford later wrote that he thought "the chances for salvaging the situation were very small—but not quite zero."[12]

By May 14, neither the secretary of state nor the secretary of defense nor any of the Cabinet or senior advisors knew which side the president would come down on. Then, a few hours before Ben-Gurion's scheduled announcement, an aide to Secretary Marshall called Clifford at the White House to say that Marshall still did not support the creation of Israel but would not oppose the president publicly if he declared in favor. This was a significant breakthrough. With less than an hour to go, the State Department aide called back to suggest again that Secretary Marshall hoped the president would delay making any decision for more internal discussions, presumably over the next few days.

"Only thirty minutes . . . before the announcement would be made in Tel Aviv," Clifford recalled, "the American segment of the drama was now coming to a climax." Clifford told the aide he would check with President Truman and get back to the secretary. He waited three minutes, then called the aide back, saying delay was out of the question. Finally, at six o'clock, the president formally announced his final decision to Clifford. The United States would recognize and support the State of Israel. Truman handed his statement to Clifford, who immediately took it to the president's press secretary, Charlie Ross. At 6:11 p.m., Ross read the statement to the press, and thus to the world:

> Statement by the president. This government has been
> informed that a Jewish state has been proclaimed in
> Palestine. . . . The United States recognizes the provisional
> government as the de facto authority of the new State
> of Israel.[13]

History had been made. Bible prophecy had just been fulfilled. After a long and painful labor, the State of Israel had miraculously been born in a day. "Who has heard such a thing?" the prophet Isaiah wrote more than seven hundred years before Jesus' birth. "Who has ever seen things like this? Can a country be born in a day or a nation be brought forth in a moment? Yet no sooner is Zion in labor than she gives birth to her children" (Isaiah 66:8, NIV).

What's more, the first world leader officially to recognize Israel's legitimacy was a Christian who had been raised reading the Bible and believed it was true. Most of his senior advisors had vehemently opposed the creation of Israel. Much of the American Jewish community opposed it too. The Arab world would soon turn against the United States and move increasingly into the orbit of the Soviet Union. Yet Truman backed Israel anyway because he believed it was the right thing to do, the biblical thing to do.

"The fundamental basis of this nation's ideals was given to Moses on Mount Sinai," Truman once told an audience. "The fundamental basis of the Bill of Rights of our Constitution comes from the teachings which we get from Exodus, St. Matthew, Isaiah, and St. Paul. The Sermon on the Mount gives us a way of life, and maybe someday men will understand it as the real way of life. The basis of all great moral codes is 'Do unto others as you would have others do unto you.' Treat others as you would like to be treated."[14]

That is not to say that Truman made all his decisions based on Scripture. Truman was an intensely private man when it came to spiritual and religious matters, and he did not often discuss what he believed about the Bible and how he connected those beliefs to public policy. The 1940s were a different age. Presidents rarely discussed such matters with the public. Truman even felt reticent about discussing his beliefs with Billy Graham, as Graham described in his autobiography.[15] However, it is not conjecture to say that Bible prophecy was a critical element in Truman's decision-making process.

Clifford confirmed it in his memoir. "[Truman] was a student and believer in the Bible since his youth. From his reading of the Old Testament he felt the Jews derived a legitimate historical right to Palestine, and he sometimes cited such biblical lines as Deuteronomy 1:8, 'Behold, I have given up the land before you; go in and take possession of the land which the Lord hath sworn unto your fathers, to Abraham, to Isaac, and to Jacob.'"[16]

Bible Prophecies Foretelling the Rebirth of Israel

Are there really ancient prophecies in the Bible that point to the rebirth of Israel in the last days? There are.

The most famous of these, perhaps, are found in the book of Ezekiel, chapters 36 through 39. Here, the Hebrew prophet Ezekiel, writing more than 2,500 years ago, describes in great detail, in chapter after chapter, how "in the last days" (Ezekiel 38:16) the Lord will remember the Jewish people, resurrect the "dry bones" of the Jewish people who seemed left for dead (Ezekiel 37:1-14), remember the land of Israel, bring the Jewish people back to the land, cause the land of Israel to flourish again, and help the Jewish people rebuild the ancient ruins of Israel. The prophet also describes how the Lord would help the Jewish people survive and multiply and be blessed again in a resurrected land of Israel—which Ezekiel describes as "the center of the world" (Ezekiel 38:12)—even though their enemies would repeatedly seek to destroy them.

Consider a few excerpts from these important passages:

- **Ezekiel 36:8-10**—"But you, O mountains of Israel, you will put forth your branches and bear your fruit for My people Israel; for they will soon come. For, behold, I am for you, and I will turn to you, and you will be cultivated and sown. I will multiply men on you, all the house of Israel, all of it; and the cities will be inhabited and the waste places will be rebuilt."
- **Ezekiel 36:22-24**—"It is not for your sake, O house of Israel, that I am about to act, but for My holy name. . . . For I will

take you from the nations, gather you from all the lands, and bring you into your own land."

- **Ezekiel 37:1, 11-14**—"The hand of the LORD was upon me, and He brought me out by the Spirit of the LORD and set me down in the middle of the valley; and it was full of bones. . . . Then He said to me, 'Son of man, these bones are the whole house of Israel; behold, they say, "Our bones are dried up and our hope has perished. We are completely cut off." Therefore prophesy and say to them, "Thus says the Lord GOD, 'Behold, I will open your graves and cause you to come up out of your graves, My people; and I will bring you into the land of Israel. Then you will know that I am the LORD, when I have opened your graves and caused you to come up out of your graves, My people. I will put My Spirit within you and you will come to life, and I will place you on your own land. Then you will know that I, the LORD, have spoken and done it,' declares the LORD.""

- **Ezekiel 38:8, 12**—"After many days you [Gog, a key enemy of Israel] will be summoned; in the latter years you will come into the land that is restored from the sword, whose inhabitants have been gathered from many nations to the mountains of Israel which had been a continual waste; but its people were brought out from the nations, and they are living securely, all of them . . . the people who are gathered from the nations, who have acquired cattle and goods, who live at the center of the world."

Ezekiel and Auschwitz

In January 2010, my wife, Lynn, and I traveled to Edmonton, Alberta, Canada, where I was to address an evangelical Christian conference. I was teaching on the prophecies of Ezekiel 36–39, on the centrality of Israel in God's plan and purpose for mankind in the last days, the threat of radical Islam, and the importance of building a global movement of Christians committed to showing the people of the epicenter unconditional love and unwavering support. As I prepared to teach, I happened to read news coverage of Israeli prime minister Benjamin Netanyahu's address in Poland, commemorating the sixty-fifth anniversary of the liberation of Auschwitz. Speaking at the actual site of the Nazi death camp, the prime minister delivered a major address warning the world of new genocidal threats against the Jewish people and the importance of acting early enough to prevent such devastations. He also declared to the people of Europe and the world that the prophecies of Ezekiel had been fulfilled.

> The most important lesson of the Holocaust is that a murderous evil must be stopped early, when it is still in its infancy and before it can carry out its designs. The enlightened nations of the world must learn this lesson. We, the Jewish nation, who lost a third of our people on Europe's blood-soaked soil, have learned that the only guarantee for defending our people is a strong State of Israel and the army of Israel. We learned to warn the nations of the world of approaching danger but at the same time to prepare to defend ourselves. As the head of the Jewish state, I pledge to you today: we will never again permit evil to snuff out the life of our people and the life of our own country.
>
> [After the Holocaust,] the Jewish people rose from ashes and destruction, from a terrible pain that can never be healed. Armed with the Jewish spirit, the justice of man, and the vision of the prophets, we sprouted new branches and grew deep roots. Dry bones became covered with flesh, a spirit filled them, and they lived and stood on their own feet. As Ezekiel prophesied, "Then He said unto me, These bones are

the whole house of Israel. They say, 'Our bones are dried up, our hope is gone; we are doomed.' Prophesy, therefore, and say to them, Thus said the Lord God: I am going to open your graves and lift you out of your graves, O My people, and bring you to the land of Israel." I stand here today on the ground where so many of my people perished—and I am not alone. The State of Israel and all the Jewish people stand with me. We bow our heads to honor your memory and lift our heads as we raise our flag, a flag of blue and white with a Star of David in its center. And everyone sees. And everyone hears. And everyone knows—that our hope is not lost.[17]

It was an extraordinary moment. Rarely has any world leader given a major address on an international stage declaring that End Times prophecies from the Bible have come true. Yet that is exactly what Netanyahu did.

Other Hebrew Prophets Foretold Israel's Rebirth

Ezekiel was by no means the only Hebrew prophet who foretold Israel's miraculous rebirth and the Jews' return to the Holy Land after centuries of exile. Consider several other key passages of Scripture:

- **Isaiah 66:8-9**—"'Who has heard such a thing? Who has seen such things? Can a land be born in one day? Can a nation be brought forth all at once? As soon as Zion travailed, she also brought forth her sons. Shall I bring to the point of birth and not give delivery?' says the LORD. 'Or shall I who gives delivery shut the womb?' says your God."
- **Jeremiah 16:14-15**—"'Therefore behold, days are coming,' declares the LORD, 'when it will no longer be said, "As the LORD lives, who brought up the sons of Israel out of the land

of Egypt," but, "As the LORD lives, who brought up the sons of Israel from the land of the north and from all the countries where He had banished them." For I will restore them to their own land which I gave to their fathers.'"

- **Jeremiah 31:3-9**—"The LORD appeared to him from afar, saying, 'I have loved you with an everlasting love; therefore I have drawn you with lovingkindness. Again I will build you and you will be rebuilt, O virgin of Israel! Again you will take up your tambourines, and go forth to the dances of the merrymakers. Again you will plant vineyards on the hills of Samaria; the planters will plant and will enjoy them. For there will be a day when watchmen on the hills of Ephraim call out, "Arise, and let us go up to Zion, to the LORD our God." . . . Behold, I am bringing them from the north country, and I will gather them from the remote parts of the earth, among them the blind and the lame, the woman with child and she who is in labor with child, together; a great company, they will return here. With weeping they will come, and by supplication I will lead them; I will make them walk by streams of waters, on a straight path in which they will not stumble; for I am a father to Israel.'"

- **Amos 9:11-15**—"'In that day I will raise up the fallen booth of David, and wall up its breaches; I will also raise up its ruins and rebuild it as in the days of old; that they may possess the remnant of Edom and all the nations who are called by My name,' declares the LORD who does this. 'Behold, days are coming,' declares the LORD, 'when the plowman will overtake the reaper and the treader of grapes him who sows seed; when the mountains will drip sweet wine and all the hills will be dissolved. Also I will restore the captivity of My people Israel, and they will rebuild the ruined cities and live in them; they will also plant vineyards and drink their wine, and make gardens and eat their fruit. I will also plant them on their land, and they will not again be rooted out from their land which I have given them,' says the LORD your God."

Jesus and the Rebirth of Israel

The Lord Jesus himself repeatedly reaffirmed the teachings of the Hebrew prophets from the Old Testament. Indeed, he challenged people for not having read or understood the Scriptures.

- **Matthew 5:17**—"Do not think that I came to abolish the Law or the Prophets; I did not come to abolish but to fulfill."
- **Matthew 19:4 (NLT)**—"'Haven't you read the Scriptures?' Jesus replied."
- **Matthew 22:29 (NLT)**—"Jesus replied, 'Your mistake is that you don't know the Scriptures, and you don't know the power of God.'"

By reaffirming the truth and the value of the Old Testament Scriptures, the Lord Jesus reaffirmed the truth and the value of God's promises to resurrect the people and the land of Israel in the last days.

What's more, Christ specifically spoke of the rebirth of Israel in Matthew 24:32-33. "Now learn the parable from the fig tree," Jesus said. "When its branch has already become tender and puts forth its leaves, you know that summer is near; so, you too, when you see all these things, recognize that He is near, right at the door."

What is the "parable from the fig tree" to which Jesus referred? The fig tree repeatedly symbolizes the nation of Israel throughout the Old Testament. In Jeremiah 24, for example, the Lord referred to the Jewish people as figs—some good, some bad—as he promised to bring them back from captivity to the Promised Land. Hosea 9:10 says, "I found Israel like grapes in the wilderness; I saw your forefathers as the earliest fruit on the fig tree in its first season." In Micah 4, in a passage specifically about the last days and people coming to Jerusalem to visit the Lord's Temple, Micazh writes that when it comes to the Jewish people in the last days, "each of them will sit under his vine and under his fig tree."

When the Lord Jesus spoke of the "parable from the fig tree" in Matthew's Gospel, he was referencing these and similar passages. He was saying that when you see the State of Israel reborn, and Jews coming back to the Holy Land, and the land of Israel turning green and flourishing again—and when you see this happening in the context of all the other signs, all the other "birth pangs"—then you should know we are in a special and distinctive moment in history, a moment unlike any other. At that time, while we won't know the day or hour of Christ's return, the Lord Jesus told us to "recognize that He is near, right at the door" (Matthew 24:33).

The Apostles and the Rebirth of Israel

The apostles believed the prophecies about Israel would one day come to pass. In Acts 1:6, they asked the Lord Jesus after his resurrection if he was now going to bring the prophetic promises to fulfillment, end the Roman occupation, and rebuild the kingdom of Israel. It is reasonable to believe they expected Israel to be reborn as a politically independent state at any moment.

"Lord, is it at this time You are restoring the kingdom to Israel?" they asked. Jesus did not say that theirs was a stupid question. He did not say those prophecies about Israel's future rebirth were inaccurate or irrelevant or canceled by Jewish unfaithfulness to God, or that his followers were misinterpreting those passages. Rather, he said to them, "It is not for you to know times or epochs which the Father has fixed by His own authority" (Acts 1:7). For Christ and his apostles, it was not a matter of *if* the Father would fulfill his promises to Israel and the Jewish people, but *when*. And since the Lord Jesus knew the promises would not be fulfilled for more than 1,900 years, he mercifully chose not to give the disciples any details, for it may well have discouraged them.

The apostle Paul also repeatedly affirmed the truth and value of all the Hebrew prophecies in the Scriptures. In so doing he reaffirmed the rebirth of Israel and the regathering of the Jews in the last days. In 2 Timothy 3:16, for example, Paul wrote, "All Scripture is inspired by God and profitable for teaching." That certainly covers all the prophecies in the Old Testament, including those describing the future resurrection of Israel. In Romans 9:3-4, Paul writes about his deep love for "my brethren, my kinsmen according to the flesh, who are Israelites" and explains that to the children of Israel "belongs the adoption as sons, and the glory and the covenants and the giving of the Law and the temple service and the promises." When he speaks of "the covenants," Paul speaks of *all* the covenants. He does not exclude the Abrahamic covenant, in which the Lord unconditionally promised the land of Israel to the Jews, his chosen people according to Genesis 12 and 17, among other passages. What's more, when Paul speaks of "the promises," he speaks of *all* God's promises to the Jewish people. He does not exclude the promises of Ezekiel 36, 37, 38, or any of the other promises of resurrecting the nation of Israel or regathering the Jewish people to Israel.

Implications for the United States

There is another critically important passage of Scripture we must consider in this context of the prophetic rebirth of the State of Israel and its implications for the future of the United States.

> Now the LORD said to Abram, "Go forth from your country, and from your relatives and from your father's house, to

the land which I will show you; and I will make you a great
nation, and I will bless you, and make your name great; and
so you shall be a blessing; and I will bless those who bless
you, and the one who curses you I will curse. And in you all
the families of the earth will be blessed."

GENESIS 12:1-3

Later in the Bible, these promises to Abram were passed down to
his grandson Jacob, who was renamed Israel.

Then his father Isaac said to him . . . "Cursed be those who
curse you, and blessed be those who bless you."

GENESIS 27:26, 29

Still later in the Bible, the Lord again explicitly repeats these
promises. "Balaam saw that it pleased the LORD to bless Israel. . . .
Balaam lifted up his eyes and saw Israel camping tribe by tribe; and
the Spirit of God came upon him," we are told in Numbers 24:1-2.
Then the Lord spoke through Balaam:

The oracle of him who hears the words of God. . . . How
fair are your tents, O Jacob, your dwellings, O Israel! . . .
Blessed is everyone who blesses you, and cursed is everyone
who curses you.

NUMBERS 24:4-5, 9

The Bible's message is clear: God promises to bless individuals
and nations who bless the Jewish people and the State of Israel, and
he promises to curse those who curse Jews and Israel.

The good news is that America has been Israel's most faithful
friend and ally for the past six decades, since helping to bring about
the prophetic rebirth of the Jewish state. We have blessed the Jewish

people here at home and around the globe. And in so many ways, the Lord has, in fact, blessed the United States of America as a result. If we remain faithful allies of Israel and continue to bless the Jewish people in real and practical ways—while we increasingly turn our hearts back to the Lord, who made this promise in the first place— then I believe God will continue to bless America and help us recover from our many challenges and our many sins. God made this wonderful promise, and we can depend upon him to be true to his Word.

But let us make no mistake: if the United States stops blessing Israel and the Jewish people and either abandons them or begins actively working against them, then we will no longer be eligible for the blessings of God. Rather, we will face God's curse. This is a fate no nation can long endure. Certainly not ours. Indeed, given all the other enormous and existential economic, fiscal, spiritual, and moral challenges we face, I have no doubt that America will most certainly implode if we stop actively and consistently blessing Israel and the Jewish people.

God will not be mocked. One way or another, America will reap what she sows.

Bottom Line

Do there remain skeptics, cynics, opponents, and enemies of Israel here at home and around the world? Yes.

Will their numbers grow and their hatred of Israel and the Jewish people intensify as we go deeper into the last days? Unfortunately, yes.

But does their skepticism or cynicism or opposition nullify the truths of the Bible that Israel will be reborn and the Jews regathered to the Holy Land in the last days? Not at all.

Indeed, the rebirth of Israel is a remarkable development in our time. Some scholars have described it as the definitive sign—the "super sign," as it were—that we are not merely living in an interesting or extraordinary period of history but, in fact, living in what the Bible calls the last days before the return of Christ. I believe that. Furthermore, I believe God's promises that if we as Americans continue to bless Israel and the Jews—God's chosen people—then God will bless us. But if the U.S. abandons or works against Israel and the Jewish people, then God will curse us.

Given the unprecedented challenges we already face as a nation, the stakes could not be higher.

CHAPTER SEVEN

ARE WE LIVING
IN THE LAST DAYS?

SO FAR WE HAVE REVIEWED some of the different signs the Bible tells us to watch for in the last days.

We have examined events and trends that the Bible tells us will be increasingly visible and evident as we get closer to the second coming of Christ. It's important to be aware of such things if we are to accurately address the question of whether we are living in the last days at all and the issue of whether Bible prophecy has any bearing on the future health and stability of the United States of America.

Having examined the evidence, what do you believe? Are we living in the last days?

I believe we are. After decades of studying Bible prophecy, reading hundreds of books on these subjects, discussing prophecy with many Bible teachers and scholars in the U.S. and around the world, analyzing geopolitical events, global economic trends, and spiritual and cultural trends, and seeing so many prophetic signs come to pass, I have come to the conclusion that the Rapture of the church is increasingly close at hand.

In an upcoming chapter, I will explain what the Rapture is and why it is important to the future of the United States. For now, let me just say that I have no specific idea when the Rapture will occur. What's more, I am strongly opposed to speculating about dates and times.

Some may criticize me for denying the so-called doctrine of imminency, which states that Jesus could come back at any moment, without any advance warning. To be clear, however, I do believe in the doctrine of imminency. I do not deny it. But it is important that we are clear as to what this doctrine does and does not entail.

Tim LaHaye, one of the foremost teachers of Bible prophecy in the world today, has written that "*Imminency* is the word we use to refer to the doctrine that Christ could come at any moment to call His bride [the church] to be with Him in His Father's house. That is why Scripture has so many admonitions to watch, be ready, and to look for Him to come at any moment."[1]

I agree entirely with this statement, and I seek to be ready for the Lord to come at any time.

Thomas Ice, another leading Bible prophecy scholar, has written that "imminence in relation to the Rapture has been defined as consisting of three elements: 'the certainty that He [Christ] may come at any moment, the uncertainty of the time of that arrival, and the fact that no prophesied event stands between the believer and that hour.'"[2]

I agree entirely with Ice's statement as well. I am certain Jesus is coming back. I don't know when he is coming—he could come at any moment. And no prophesied event stands between us and Christ's return.

That said, let's be clear about something else: While all the signs of the last days have to happen before the second coming of Christ, no sign of the last days has to happen before the Rapture occurs. However, that does not mean that no sign *will* happen before the Rapture occurs. For example, the Rapture could have happened at any time from the first century to the present. No signs *had* to precede it—not the "birth pangs" of which Jesus spoke or any other. Even the rebirth of Israel as a nation didn't *have* to occur before the Rapture. Theoretically, Israel could have been reborn after the Rapture of the church. Nevertheless, Israel *was* re-created as a nation before the Rapture. Likewise, the apostle Peter—citing a sign foretold by the Hebrew prophet Joel—said the Holy Spirit would be poured out on all mankind around the world in a more dramatic fashion in the last days than ever before. This didn't have to happen before the Rapture either. Yet it did begin to happen in chapter 2 of the book of Acts, and it has dramatically accelerated in our times.

Again, while no prophetic sign *has to* precede the Rapture, that does not mean no sign *will* occur before the Rapture. This is a critical point. Indeed, as we look at the events of the past century or so—and specifically at events that are occurring here in the twenty-first century—we can see that so many of the prophetic signs related to the last days, the "birth pangs," have already come true.

That has significant implications for your life and mine and for the future of the United States.

How Long Will the Last Days Last?

The overall length of the period leading up to the second coming of Christ is never defined by the Bible. To the contrary, the Lord Jesus specifically said that "no one knows" when he will return (Matthew 24:36), and it is precisely because we don't know exactly when he is coming for us that we are to be constantly ready for him—living lives of holiness and purity, being faithful in daily prayer and Bible study, sharing the gospel with others, making disciples of all nations, and so forth. "Therefore be on the alert," Jesus told his disciples, "for you do not know which day your Lord is coming" (Matthew 24:42).

One thing we are not supposed to do is guess or set dates with regard to either the Rapture or the Second Coming. To do so is unbiblical, unwise, and evidence of false teaching, which is sternly forbidden in the Scriptures. The Lord Jesus said, "But of that day and hour no one knows, not even the angels of heaven, nor the Son, but the Father alone" (Matthew 24:36). The apostle John concluded the book of Revelation by warning that when it comes to "the words of the prophecy of this book: if anyone adds to them, God will add to him the plagues which are written in this book; and if anyone takes away from the words of the book of this prophecy, God will take away his part from the tree of life and from the holy city, which are written in this book" (Revelation 22:18-19).

Unfortunately, people throughout the centuries have disregarded the clear teaching of the Scriptures and have sought to convince others that they knew when Jesus was coming back. Perhaps some have set dates truly believing they were right. Others have surely been motivated by greed or pride. Either way, they have disobeyed the Bible, misled people, brought ridicule against the church, and caused some to doubt any teaching related to Bible prophecy and the second coming of Christ.

False Teaching about the Last Days

A radio host named Harold Camping made headlines in 2011 by publicly predicting that the Rapture would occur on May 21, 2011. The *San Francisco Chronicle* was the first to pick up the story in January 2010.

> Camping, 88, has scrutinized the Bible for almost 70 years
> and says he has developed a mathematical system to interpret

prophecies hidden within the Good Book. One night a few years ago, Camping, a civil engineer by trade, crunched the numbers and was stunned at what he'd found: The world will end May 21, 2011. . . . Employees at the Oakland office run printing presses that publish Camping's pamphlets and books, and some wear T-shirts that read, "May 21, 2011." They're happy to talk about the day they believe their souls will be retrieved by Christ. "I'm looking forward to it," said Ted Solomon, 60, who started listening to Camping in 1997.[3]

Camping then made his prediction even more specific, saying the Rapture would occur at or around 6 p.m. (though he didn't specify which time zone).[4] His radio network purchased billboards announcing the date all over the country and even some in other countries (I saw one in Israel). People printed all kinds of things with the date on them. The Internet was abuzz with speculation about the date, and as the date drew closer, media attention grew steadily.

Camping was wrong, of course. May 21 came and went, and the Rapture did not occur. Undaunted, the radio charlatan—whose Family Radio network has brought in more than $80 million in donations since 2005[5]—then said his calculations were flawed and that the real date of the Rapture would be October 21, 2011.[6] The following month, Camping suffered a stroke, and his show was taken off the air.[7] When October rolled around, the revised date turned out to be a false alarm as well.

These were not the first times that Harold Camping had misled people regarding the date of the Rapture. In 1992, he published a book titled *1994?* I actually have a copy in my personal library because I have started a collection of books and pamphlets of false teachings about Bible prophecy. Camping's book is over 550 pages long and concludes, "The results of this study teach that the month of September of the year 1994 is to be the time for the end of history."[8]

The radio host was wrong then, too, of course. Neither the Rapture nor the end of the world occurred in 1994.

Camping is not the only one who has spread false teaching about the last days. I own a copy of a now-infamous booklet titled *88 Reasons Why the Rapture Will Be in 1988.* "You only need one good solid reason why 1988 will be the church's Rapture," wrote Edgar C. Whisenant. "Here are 88 reasons why 1988 looks like the year."[9] Whisenant said he calculated that the Rapture would happen on either September 11, 12, or 13 of 1988 and that Christ's second coming would be in October of 1995.[10] What's more, he predicted the utter destruction of the United States before November 1988. "We will not see another national election," Whisenant wrote, "nor will we see the end of the 213th year of the Constitution (the end of 1988), before the war comes (World War III) which destroys us completely as a nation, before the election in November 1988."[11] Millions of copies of the booklet were sold or distributed throughout the United States in 1988, according to the publisher.[12]

Obviously, Whisenant was wrong. Neither the Rapture nor the end of the United States nor the end of the world occurred as he predicted. That, however, didn't dissuade him. I also have a copy of the sequel he published the following year, *The Final Shout: Rapture Report 1989.* In this one, he explained that he had miscalculated and there were actually eighty-nine reasons why Jesus was coming back in 1989! "Jesus is really coming, and I believe it is this year!" Whisenant wrote on page 1. "Last year I wrote the book *88 Reasons Why the Rapture Will Be in 1988* because I saw all the signs and believed the Rapture of the church would occur during Rosh Hashanah 1988. . . . My mistake was that my mathematical calculations were off by one year. The miscalculation was so simple, perhaps the reason I did not see my error was God's will, in order to issue the warning, or shout, to awaken a sleeping Bride or church."[13]

Yet again, Whisenant was wrong.

The Dangers of Overreaching about the Last Days

One of the most famous yet highly controversial writers about prophecy in recent memory is Hal Lindsey. His bestselling book *The Late Great Planet Earth* (with collaborator C. C. Carlson) was published in 1970 and in many ways helped popularize the idea that we are living in the last days. The book went on to sell more than 15 million copies. Unfortunately, Lindsey repeatedly overreached in his analyses.

For example, Lindsey wrote that since Israel was reborn in 1948 and since a generation—in his view—was forty years, the Rapture would likely take place by 1988. He began by citing Matthew 24:34, where Jesus said, "Truly I say to you, this generation will not pass away until all these things take place." Then Lindsey asked, "What generation? Obviously, in context, the generation that would see the signs—chief among them the rebirth of Israel. A generation in the Bible is something like forty years. If this is a correct deduction, then within forty years or so of 1948, all these things could take place. Many scholars who have studied Bible prophecy all their lives believe that this is so."[14]

Many Christians sincerely believed the Rapture would happen by 1988, in no small part because a popular author like Hal Lindsey had suggested it would. And Lindsey didn't back off of his convictions after the publication of *The Late Great Planet Earth*. Instead, he doubled down. In 1982, he published a book titled *The 1980s: Countdown to Armageddon*. On the very first page, he wrote, "I believe many people will be shocked by what is happening right now and by what will happen in the very near future. *The decade of the 1980s could very well be the last decade of history as we know it.*"[15]

When the Rapture didn't happen in 1988, many Christians who had listened to and believed Lindsey—and other pastors, teachers, and authors who were making a similar case—became disillusioned. They stopped studying Bible prophecy. They began doubting the validity of Bible prophecy. Some began doubting the inerrancy of Scripture.

Others turned away from Christ. I know pastors and Bible teachers who have told me they backed away from teaching Bible prophecy around this time precisely because they felt so many people had been burned by inaccurate, misguided, and overreaching teachers and authors. Some didn't want to be lumped in with teachers of "prophecy hype" and sensationalism or identified with what some were already describing as "doomsday chic."[16] Others were concerned that they, too, had perhaps been overreaching in their excitement about the possibility of Christ's sudden return and decided to cool things off a bit.

Lindsey then published a book in 1994 titled *Planet Earth 2000 A.D.: Will Mankind Survive?* He released a "revised updated edition" in 1996 as millennium fever was building. In the book, Lindsey conceded that many people believed he had predicted the Rapture would happen by 1988, but he defended himself by noting the caveats he had included in *The Late Great Planet Earth*. "I also said *'if'* a generation was 40 years and *'if'* the generation of the 'fig tree' (Matthew 24:32-34) started with the foundation of the State of Israel, then Jesus *'might* come back by 1988.' But I put a lot of ifs and maybes in because I knew that no one could be absolutely certain."[17]

Unfortunately, Lindsey overrreached again, this time by seeming to predict that the Rapture would happen by the year 2000. In his afterword, he described the world's biggest party being planned in Giza, Egypt, near the Great Pyramid on December 31, 1999. "Just for the record," Lindsey wrote, "I'm not planning to attend. In fact, looking at the state of the world today, I wouldn't make any long-term earthly plans. We may be caught to meet Christ in the clouds between now and then—just as I described in an earlier chapter. Could I be wrong? Of course. The Rapture may not occur between now and the year 2000. But never before in the history of the planet have events and conditions so coincided as to set the stage for this history-stopping event. Surely, this will be a show that surpasses any Great Pyramid millennium bash."[18]

Needless to say, the Rapture didn't happen in 2000 either.

This is not to say that all of Lindsey's research was flawed. To the contrary, some of it was useful. But his books are examples of the dangers—and ease—of overreaching in one's analysis and drawing conclusions that are premature. That's why I note that one must be extraordinarily careful when one writes or teaches about Bible prophecy. Prophecy teachers should be conservative in their analyses and avoid drawing quick conclusions. If one makes a mistake, one should own up to it and correct it, not double down and compound the error. People are watching and can be harmed by bad teaching. What's more, God is watching and will not bless poor, sloppy, or false teaching.

Additional Evidence

Overreachers, false teachers, poor teachers, cynics, and mockers notwithstanding, we *are* living in the last days. Of this we need have no doubt.

The apostle Peter told us back in the first century that the church began living in the "last days" on the Day of Pentecost, when the Holy Spirit enabled the apostles to begin preaching the gospel in languages they did not know. "This is what was spoken of through the prophet Joel," Peter explained. "'And it shall be in the last days,' God says, 'that I will pour forth of My Spirit on all mankind; and your sons and your daughters shall prophesy, and your young men shall see visions, and your old men shall dream dreams'" (Acts 2:16-17).

The apostle John, likewise, told us we were living in the "last hour" back in the days when he wrote his first epistle and so many false teachers and false prophets and opponents of Jesus Christ were appearing on the world scene. "Children, it is the last hour; and just as you heard that antichrist is coming, even now many antichrists have appeared; from this we know that it is the last hour" (1 John 2:18).

What's more, precisely because in recent decades we have seen so many other signs of the last days come true, we can be additionally certain that we are living in the last days. One by one we have seen the signs foretold by the Bible come to pass in our lifetimes. Events and trends that Jesus said would be the "birth pangs"—evidence that a dramatic delivery is increasingly close at hand—are being seen and felt all around us.

We don't know when the Rapture will happen or when the Tribulation will begin. Nor can we know precisely when the Second Coming will actually occur. Nor should we speculate. To do so is not biblical.

The Scriptures teach us that the Lord will only come when everyone on earth has had the opportunity to hear the gospel and choose to accept Christ or reject him. We are supposed to live with the sense that Jesus could come at any moment. But the Lord will delay until he is satisfied that everyone has had a chance to repent and be born again. Yes, "in the last days mockers will come with their mocking, following after their own lusts, and saying, 'Where is the promise of His coming?'" the apostle Peter told us well in advance. "But do not let this one fact escape your notice, beloved, that with the Lord one day is like a thousand years, and a thousand years like one day. The Lord is not slow about His promise, as some count slowness, but is patient toward you, not wishing for any to perish but for all to come to repentance" (2 Peter 3:3, 8-9).

Have you ever heard of the sons of Issachar? The Bible tells us that Issachar was one of the sons of the Hebrew patriarch Jacob. Issachar's descendants became one of the twelve tribes of Israel. At one point in the ancient history of the Hebrew people, the sons of Issachar were singled out in the Scriptures for being exceedingly observant and insightful about the dangerous and treacherous events that were unfolding all around them, and for being impressively wise about how their country should navigate through troubled waters. We read in 1 Chronicles 12:32 (NIV) that the sons of Issachar were "men who understood the times and knew what Israel should do." I pray that we find more sons (and daughters) of Issachar in our day, men and women who truly understand the times and know what the United States of America should do before it is too late.

Bottom Line

The Lord Jesus told us that rather than speculate on exactly when he is coming, we should analyze the times in which we live, be aware of the signs, and then be ready, be on the alert, be spiritually awake, be faithful and obedient when we see these signs of the last days coming to pass.

- Jesus said, "When you see all these things, recognize that He is near, right at the door" (Matthew 24:33).
- Jesus said, "Therefore, be on the alert, for you do not know which day your Lord is coming" (Matthew 24:42).
- Jesus said, "For this reason, you also must be ready; for the Son of Man is coming at an hour when you do not think He will" (Matthew 24:44).
- Jesus said, "Therefore, be on the alert—for you do not know when the master of the house is coming . . . in case he should come suddenly and find you asleep. What I say to you I say to all, 'Be on the alert!'" (Mark 13:35-37).
- Jesus said, "But when these things begin to take place, straighten up and lift up your heads, because your redemption is drawing near" (Luke 21:28).

Teachers of Bible prophecy need to be very careful, then. Our responsibility is not to predict when Christ will return but to help people understand the times and be ready for his return, whenever that occurs—especially since it could happen at any time. Likewise, students of Bible prophecy need to be very careful to discern the difference between solid Bible teaching and false teaching. We must carefully study what the entire Bible says—and what it does not say. We must meticulously and prayerfully study "the whole counsel of God" (Acts 20:27, NKJV) and, in so doing, avoid false teaching and the teaching of those who creatively use bits and scraps of the Bible in vain hopes of proving something the Bible never said while willfully or ignorantly turning a blind eye to other Scriptures that provide critically helpful details. We must, in other words, learn to discern the full, true, balanced teachings of God.

Which now brings us to the key question: If we really are living in the last days, what does the Bible say is going to happen to America during this time?

CHAPTER EIGHT

WHAT HAPPENS TO AMERICA IN THE LAST DAYS?

★ ★ ★ ★ ★ ★ ★ ★ ★ ★ ★ ★ ★ ★ ★ ★ ★

IS THE UNITED STATES OF AMERICA ever mentioned in the Bible? This is critical because if America is mentioned in Bible prophecy, then those prophecies would give us important clues about America's destiny.

Most Western, Asian, and sub-Saharan African countries are not mentioned in the Scriptures, but some nations are. Indeed, some nations are mentioned specifically in the context of End Times prophecies.

Israel, of course, is clearly and repeatedly mentioned in both the Old and New Testaments, and we learn many truths about her future since Israel is the central player in God's plan and purpose for the final years leading up to the second coming of Christ. Bible prophecies also provide us vital information about the future of a range of other Middle Eastern, North African, and European countries, including Egypt, Syria (Damascus and Assyria), Lebanon (Tyre),

Jordan (Ammon, Edom, and Moab), Iraq (Babylon), Greece, and a revived Roman Empire as described in the book of Daniel. There are also specific, detailed, and fascinating Bible prophecies that discuss the future of other key countries, notably Russia (Magog and Rosh) and a group of allies that will form an alliance against Israel in the last days, as described in Ezekiel 38–39 and Jeremiah 49. These include Iran (Persia and Elam), Turkey (Gomer), Sudan and Ethiopia (Cush), Libya and Algeria (Put), Central Asia (Beth-togarmah), and Saudi Arabia and the Gulf emirates (Sheba and Dedan).[1]

Countries like China, North Korea, Indonesia, and Pakistan are not specifically mentioned in the Bible. There is, however, an intriguing reference in Revelation 16:12 to "the kings from the east" who send their massive military forces through Iraq, up the Euphrates River, to the mountain of Megiddo, or Armageddon, to participate in the final, catastrophic, apocalyptic military showdown with Israel before the Day of the Lord.*

Conceptually, then, since other nations are specifically mentioned, it is not inconceivable that America should be found in Bible prophecy. For well over a century, authors and teachers from a wide range of religious beliefs and backgrounds have pondered and discussed this topic. Some have argued vehemently that America *is* mentioned in the Bible, insisting it was either patently obvious to everyone or simply obvious to them as uniquely enlightened observers. Others have concluded that America is not mentioned in the Bible. Over the years, I have developed a small library of books devoted to the topic.

More Than a Century of Books on America and Prophecy

In 1888, for example, Ellen G. White, the woman who helped found the Seventh-day Adventist church, published a 654-page book called

---

*The nation of India is also mentioned twice in the Bible (in Esther 1:1 and Esther 8:9, in defining the size and scope of the ancient Persian Empire under King Ahasuerus), though not in the context of Bible prophecy.

The Great Controversy between Christ and Satan, later retitled *America in Prophecy*. White cited a range of passages from the books of Daniel and Revelation in making her case that America was in fact referenced in Scripture. She specifically pointed to Revelation 13:11: "Then I saw another beast coming up out of the earth; and he had two horns like a lamb and he spoke as a dragon." White then argued that "one nation, and only one, meets the specifications of this prophecy; it points unmistakably to the United States of America. . . . The lamb-like horns indicate youth, innocence, and gentleness, fitly representing the character of the United States."[2]

In 1942, Herbert W. Armstrong, founder of a cult known as the Worldwide Church of God and a magazine called *The Plain Truth*, published a 196-page book titled *The United States and Britain in Prophecy*. "The all-important master key has been found!" Armstrong wrote. "That key is knowledge of the astonishing identity of the American and British peoples—as well as the German—in biblical prophecies. . . . This book will open, to open minds, this hitherto closed vital third of all the Bible. No story in fiction ever was so strange, so fascinating, so absorbing, so packed with interest and suspense, as this gripping story of our [American and British] identity—and our ancestry."[3]

In 1968, S. Franklin Logsdon published a 98-page book titled *Is the U.S.A. in Prophecy?* "Is the U.S.A. mentioned by name in prophecy?" Logsdon asked. "The answer, of course, is 'No.' But, if you ask, Is the U.S.A. in the framework of prophecy? The answer is an unqualified 'Yes' . . . It is unthinkable that the God who knows the end from the beginning would pinpoint such small nations as Libya, Egypt, Ethiopia, and Syria in the prophetic declaration and completely overlook the wealthiest and most powerful nation on the earth."[4]

In 1998, Thomas Ice and Timothy Demy published a 48-page booklet titled *The Truth about America in the Last Days*. They wrote, "Most would agree that neither America, North America, nor the

United States is mentioned explicitly in the Bible, either historically or prophetically, in the way that Scripture speaks repeatedly of Israel, Babylon, Syria, or Egypt. . . . The Western Hemisphere is not specifically mentioned in Scripture."[5]

In 2003, David R. Reagan published a 210-page book titled *America the Beautiful? The United States in Bible Prophecy*. "So, where is the United States in Bible prophecy?" Reagan asked. "A partial answer is that we are not mentioned directly and specifically. We are covered by general prophecies that relate to all nations, but beyond that, our end time destiny is not specifically mentioned. General prophecies that apply to the United States include those that say all nations will be judged (Isaiah 34:2-3). . . . But how could God overlook the world's most important and powerful nation? I don't think He has. I believe America can be found in Bible prophecy, not specifically, but in prophetic type. . . . I believe the biblical prophetic type of the United States is the nation of Judah."[6]

In 2004, Michael D. Evans published a 310-page book titled *The American Prophecies: Ancient Scriptures Reveal Our Nation's Future*. "Is America in prophecy?" Evans wrote. "Yes, it is. . . . After thousands of hours of research, I am totally convinced that America *is* found in prophecy."[7]

In 2009, Terry James published a 292-page book titled *The American Apocalypse: Is the United States in Bible Prophecy?* "Is America in prophecy?" James asked. "The answer, to this writer at least, is a resounding yes! By name, no, but by presence and influence, absolutely!"[8]

Also in 2009, Mark Hitchcock also published a well-researched, well-reasoned 191-page book titled *The Late Great United States: What Bible Prophecy Reveals about America's Last Days*. In it, Hitchcock helpfully cites many more books on the subject, including an 1859 book by Frances Rolleston titled *Notes on the Apocalypse, as Explained by the Hebrew Scriptures: The Place in Prophecy of America and Australia Being Pointed Out*; an 1884 book by Uriah Smith titled *The United States in the Light of Prophecy*; a 1914 book by L. A. Smith titled *The United States in Prophecy*; a 1976 book by Douglas B. MacCorkle titled *America in History and Bible Prophecy*; and a 1977 book by Henry Hoyt titled *Is the United States in Prophecy?*[9]

Clearly, there has been no shortage of discussion on the topic. What, then, is the answer? Is the U.S. clearly and specifically identified in the Bible as part of End Times prophecy or not?

Allusions to America in the Bible

At the minimum, one can certainly and reasonably argue that America is alluded to repeatedly in the Bible. After all, the terms "all nations" and "all the nations" appear a combined total of eighty-nine times in the New American Standard translation of the Bible. The Lord has very specific things to say about what he has done for "all the nations" in the past and what will happen in—or to—"all nations" in the future. This certainly includes the United States.

In Haggai chapter 2, for example, the Lord foretold through the Hebrew prophet that he would shake all the nations of the world in the last days. "For thus says the LORD of hosts, 'Once more in a little while, I am going to shake the heavens and the earth, the sea also and the dry land. I will shake all the nations. . . . I am going to shake the heavens and the earth. I will overthrow the thrones of kingdoms and destroy the power of the kingdoms of the nations'" (vv. 6-7, 21-22). This is certainly coming true in the United States. We are being shaken physically, financially, socially, spiritually, politically, and in numerous other ways, and we can expect this to accelerate and intensify in the years ahead.

In Matthew 24:14, the Lord Jesus says that in the last days, "this gospel of the kingdom shall be preached in the whole world as a testimony to all the nations, and then the end will come." There is no question that the Lord has used the United States for more than two centuries to help train, equip, and deploy pastors, teachers, preachers, and missionaries who have taken the gospel all over the earth. Americans have set up Bible schools, Bible colleges, and seminaries here at home and in many other countries. Americans have translated the Bible into hundreds of languages, printed those Bibles, and distributed millions upon millions of copies around the world. Americans have produced evangelistic films and television and radio programs and Internet materials in hundreds of different languages to reach people all over the globe with the salvation message of Jesus Christ. What's more, the U.S. has long been the "ATM" for the world missions movement, helping to finance much of the missions work that was done in the nineteenth and twentieth centuries, though other countries are increasingly sharing that blessed burden.

Yet according to the Scriptures, the era of the U.S. being the epicenter of Christendom will come to an end. The Lord Jesus said in Matthew 24:9 that at some point during the last days, opponents of Christianity "will deliver you to tribulation, and will kill you, and you will be hated by all nations because of My name." That's painful to hear, but it is true. "All nations" will eventually turn against faithful followers of Jesus Christ, including here in the United States. We are certainly not seeing Christians in America being imprisoned or even killed for their faith by the government as we see in China or in radical Islamic countries—yet—but we have in recent decades begun to witness the climate of American culture shifting significantly and steadily away from its Judeo-Christian roots to one that is increasingly hostile toward faith in Christ. This will go from bad to worse, according to Jesus.

Ultimately, the Bible says that judgment will come upon the United States, as it will upon all the nations. The Lord Jesus warned in Matthew 25:31-33 that "when the Son of Man comes in His glory, and all the angels with Him, then He will sit on His glorious throne.

All the nations will be gathered before Him; and He will separate them from one another, as the shepherd separates the sheep from the goats; and He will put the sheep on His right, and the goats on the left." In his righteousness and holiness, the Lord will judge the individuals from all nations. To some, he will say, "Come, you who are blessed of My Father, inherit the kingdom prepared for you from the foundation of the world" (v. 34). To others, however, he will say, "Depart from Me, accursed ones, into the eternal fire which has been prepared for the devil and his angels" (v. 41). All individuals from all nations will hear one or the other, based on whether or not they received Jesus Christ as Savior and Lord and were born again as described in John 3—and thus lived lives of faith and obedience to the Lord, loving him and loving others.

But aside from such general references, is America ever specifically mentioned in the Bible?

Is America "Babylon"?

Numerous authors and teachers over the years have insisted that the United States—and/or New York City—is the Babylon mentioned in the book of Revelation.

David Wilkerson, for example, the late founder and pastor of Times Square Church in Manhattan, once wrote a book titled *America's Last Call*. "Revelation 18 predicts a graphic scene of a prosperous society falling under judgment in a single hour," Wilkerson explained. "This society is called Babylon—and many theologians have tried to predict who it will be. Some say it will be a revived Rome. Others say it will be a rebuilt version of the literal Babylon in Iraq. Scripture doesn't make clear who this Babylon will be. To me, it sounds much like New York City, with its Wall Street and the United Nations."[10]

A. P. Watchman recently published a book titled *Reaping the*

Whirlwind: The Imminent Judgment of Babylon America. "Truly, the United States is the 'great harlot who sits on many waters with whom the kings of the Earth have committed fornication and the inhabitants of the Earth have been made drunk with the wine of her fornication,'" Watchman argued, equating America with the Babylon described in Revelation 17 and 18. "If we are honest with ourselves, we know that the Rome, Italy, of our day could never match the description given by Jesus in Revelation 18; nor does any other nation or singular city on the earth in our day, with the possible exception of the city of New York."[11]

In 1998, R. A. Coombes published a book titled *America, the Babylon*. One prophecy expert said it "offers the most extensive, in-depth treatment of the American Babylon view that I've been able to find."[12]

The list could go on and on.

Are there similarities between the U.S. and Babylon? Unfortunately, there are. Is the United States becoming Babylon-esque over time, in the sense of being both enormously powerful and spiritually apostate? Tragically, she is.

But the prophecies in question, together with events happening today, indicate to me that the "Babylon" found in End Times Bible prophecy really refers to the nation of Iraq and the actual ancient city of Babylon, which was once the thriving and powerful capital of the nation of Babylon (also known in history as Babylonia in Mesopotamia). Babylon is not the United States or New York City or Rome or Moscow or any of the many other speculations people have made over the years.

Prophecies found in Isaiah, Jeremiah, Ezekiel, and Revelation indicate that Babylon the country and Babylon the city will, in fact, be resurrected and rebuilt in the last days, much as Israel and Jerusalem have been resurrected and rebuilt in recent decades. Indeed, the Bible indicates that the city of Babylon will not only be fully rebuilt but will actually become the wealthiest and most powerful—and eventually the most corrupt and wicked—city on the face of the planet. That may be difficult for many to picture or accept, but it was also difficult for many to picture the "dry bones" of Israel being rebuilt until it happened in the twentieth century.

What's fascinating to me is that such prophecies are already beginning to come to pass in our lifetime.

In my 2006 book, *Epicenter*, I wrote an entire chapter on Saddam Hussein's efforts in the 1980s to begin rebuilding the ancient city of Babylon and on the new Iraqi government's plans to continue and dramatically expand the work that Saddam set into motion. I quoted a story that appeared on the front page of the *New York Times* on April 18, 2006, saying that "Babylon, the mud-brick city with the million-dollar name, has paid the price of war. It has been ransacked, looted, torn up, paved over, neglected, and roughly occupied. . . . But Iraqi leaders and United Nations officials are not giving up on it. They are working assiduously to restore Babylon, home to one of the Seven Wonders of the World, and turn it into a cultural center and possibly even an Iraqi theme park."[13] I also cited my interview with then–Iraqi finance minister Ali Abdul Ameer Allawi, who told me, "Cultural, religious, archaeological, and biblical tourism is a big opportunity for Iraq. I think rebuilding Babylon is a wonderful idea, as long as it is not done at the expense of the antiquities themselves."[14]

Since *Epicenter* was published, much more has been done to rebuild Iraq and establish peace and security in the once and future Babylon. I have had the opportunity to travel to and minister in Iraq four times since the fall of Saddam Hussein, and each time the country was safer and more prosperous than the time I went before. Just as remarkable is that more steps have been taken to rebuild the actual city of Babylon as well, even with American assistance. On February 14, 2009, I wrote a blog post under the headline "U.S. to Help Rebuild City of Babylon in Iraq."

The government of Iraq is moving forward with plans
to protect the archaeological remains of the ancient city
of Babylon, in preparation for building a modern city of
Babylon. . . . The Obama administration is contributing
$700,000 toward "The Future of Babylon" project through
the State Department's budget. "Officials hope Babylon
can be revived and made ready for a rich future of tourism,
with help from experts at the World Monuments Fund
(WMF) and the U.S. embassy," reports the Reuters news
agency. "'The Future of Babylon' project launched last
month seeks to 'map the current conditions of Babylon
and develop a master plan for its conservation, study, and
tourism,' the WMF says. 'We don't know how long it will
take to reopen to tourists,' said Mariam Omran Musa,
head of a government inspection team based at the site.
'It depends on funds. I hope that Babylon can be reborn
in a better image.'"[15]

Two years later, in January 2011, I pointed readers of my blog to
another *New York Times* story, headlined "A Triage to Save the Ruins
of Babylon." "The Babylon project is Iraq's biggest and most ambi-
tious by far, a reflection of the ancient city's fame and its resonance
in Iraq's modern political and cultural heritage," the article reported,
noting that "in November, the State Department announced a new
$2 million grant to begin work to preserve the site's most impressive
surviving ruins."[16]

The article also reported that "the American reconstruction team
has refurbished a modern museum on the site, as well as a model of
the Ishtar Gate that for decades served as a visitors' entrance. Inside
the museum is one of the site's most valuable relics: a glazed brick
relief of a lion, one of 120 that once lined the processional way into
the city. The museum, with three galleries, is scheduled to open this

month, receiving its first visitors since 2003. And with new security installed, talks are under way to return ancient Babylonian artifacts from the National Museum in Baghdad."[17]

Clearly, Bible prophecies are coming to pass. Babylon is rising again. Unfortunately, too few people are paying attention, which brings us back to the question of America.

So, Is America Ever Mentioned in the Bible?

As we have seen, there have been some very creative—and at times, very bizarre—interpretations of the Scriptures by a wide range of people trying to find America in the Bible. But none of them hold water. The United States is not one of the "ten lost tribes" of Israel, as some have suggested. We are not the "land of whirring wings" mentioned in Isaiah 18 or the "young lions" or "merchants of Tarshish" mentioned in Ezekiel 38, as others have suggested. America is not the "great eagle" mentioned in Revelation 12. These and similar arguments are simply not credible.[18]

Are there lessons America can learn from the histories of other nations in the Bible? Yes. Are there commandments in the Bible that all nations, including the United States, must obey? Yes. Are there promises of blessing made to all nations, including the United States, if they follow the Lord? Yes. Are there punishments promised to all nations, including the United States, that turn away from the Lord and his Word? Yes. All these points are important. But those who try to extract more out of Scripture—who try to force the Bible to say more than it does—are standing on shaky theological ground.

The truth is, the United States of America simply is nowhere to be found in the Bible. This may be painful for many to hear. This may be difficult for many to accept. Nevertheless, the fact remains: The U.S. is never directly mentioned or specifically referenced in Bible history or in Bible prophecy. It just isn't.

If Not, Why Not?

When I tell Americans that the United States is not mentioned in Bible prophecy at all, much less as a key player in God's plan and purpose for the last days, some have a hard time accepting it at first. Here's how such conversations often go:

"Joel, you believe we are living in the last days, right?"

Right.

"And you're saying the signs in the Bible that are evidence of the last days are coming to pass, right?"

Right.

"And you believe that the rebirth of Israel is the super sign, the one that proves beyond all doubt that we're moving deeper into the last days, right?"

Right.

"And all kinds of countries are mentioned in the Bible— Egypt, Iran, Iraq, even India and Russia, right?"

Right.

"Then how is it possible that America—the wealthiest, most powerful country on the face of the earth in the history of mankind—is not even mentioned in Bible prophecy at all, much less as a key player in the End Times?"

That's a good question, and the answer is: I don't know. The Bible doesn't say. If the Bible spoke directly, clearly, and precisely to our future as a nation, then I would say so, but it doesn't. So the next question we have to ask, then, is this: "If not, why not?" If America isn't mentioned in the Bible, then why isn't it? What happens to us?

I draw two possible conclusions from the absence of a clearly defined biblical role for the U.S. in the last days:

- First, something happens to the United States in the last days that strips us of our status as the wealthiest, most powerful country on the face of the earth in the history of mankind.
- Second, other countries emerge wealthier, more powerful, and more dynamic than we are, replacing us as the global leader.

We know clearly from Scripture that Israel will emerge as the epicenter of global attention in the last days. Other key nations that will rise and fall include a revived Roman Empire, Russia, Iran, and Iraq, to name just a few. We know, therefore, that nations other than the U.S. will be emerging in the years ahead as more powerful players than ever before. That I have no problem with. However, as an American citizen who loves this country very much and is deeply grateful for the freedom and opportunities my family and I have received and experienced here, it is terribly painful to come to the conclusion that my country will wither, fade, or outright implode.

No American wants to believe such things. I certainly don't. But these are the conclusions I have come to after studying and praying about these questions for many years.

Often when I answer these questions at a conference or in a church or during an interview, the next questions are variations of the following: What do you think could happen to the U.S. to strip us of our status as the world's economic and military superpower? What could cause America to wither or fade or utterly collapse?

Without clear scriptural guidance, it is very difficult to say, of course. So long as you realize that I am speculating at this point, not teaching specific Bible prophecies, here are four scenarios I believe are possible that could make America unable—or unwilling—to play a key role in the unfolding prophetic events of the last days:

- **Economic Implosion**—The United States implodes financially and economically.

- **War or Terrorism**—The United States is devastated by a surprise military or terrorist attack or series of attacks.
- **Natural Disasters**—The United States is devastated by an unprecedented series of natural disasters.
- **The Rapture**—The United States suddenly loses millions, or tens of millions, of people when the Rapture happens, leaving the rest of the American people devastated and triggering any number of cataclysmic events.

Of course, these are not the only things that could lead America to implode. Political paralysis is a real and present danger as well—we could become frozen in partisan political gridlock or be sidelined by widespread political apathy or a new wave of isolationism. But I believe these four scenarios pose the biggest and most dangerous threat to the American way of life as we have known it. In the next four chapters, we will take a closer look at these scenarios and attempt to assess the degree of danger each one poses.

Bottom Line

In the Old Testament book of Job, there is a very important verse about God's sovereignty over men and nations: "He makes the nations great, then destroys them; He enlarges the nations, then leads them away" (Job 12:23).

Some might say the Lord made America great because our founders built this nation upon the teachings of the Scriptures and because the American people responded to the First Great Awakening and the Second Great Awakening and other periods of moral and spiritual renewal. Others would say the Lord allowed America to become great for a time, despite our many mistakes, errors, and sins. Either way, we have now come to a point where people are actively discussing whether the Lord will proactively judge and destroy us or remove his hand of grace and blessing and let us implode, or whether he might give us a second chance—at least for a season—with a Third Great Awakening.

One thing seems clear, however, to nearly all Americans: we are in grave danger both economically and spiritually.

CHAPTER NINE

THE FINANCIAL IMPLOSION SCENARIO

IT'S A SCARY FEELING to wake up each morning without a job. Or to fear you're about to lose the job you have, especially when you don't know how you would get another one that could adequately provide for your family. It's scary to be so deep in personal credit-card debt that you wake up in the middle of the night seized with anxiety and with no idea how you'll ever climb your way out of the hole you're in. It's a scary thing not knowing whether you can still afford to pay the mortgage on your house, to fear the bank will foreclose, to see the value of your house collapse to the point where you literally can't afford to sell it because you'd still owe the bank money when the transaction was all finished. It's scarier still to already be past that point and to have seen the bank take away your home, to feel the shame of failure and try to explain to your spouse and your children that somehow—though honestly you don't know how—it's all going to be okay.

Far too many Americans have experienced such fears firsthand in recent years. They know all too well that the U.S. economy is in serious trouble. They want to believe that with the right leadership in Washington and on Main Street and on Wall Street, we can turn this thing around. But they have also seen the politicians and the bankers and the CEOs blow it time and time again. And they sense intuitively that the situation could get much, much worse. They fear that even if leaders do emerge who demonstrate good ideas, solid experience, strong personal courage, and resolve to make bold changes, perhaps America has passed the point of no return. They worry that the problems we face might be so enormous that no matter how diligent we are as a nation in making critical changes, it might be too little too late. Americans don't want to believe we are on the financial *Titanic*, but many fear we might be and that, even as we see the icebergs dead ahead, we may not have time to change course before we crash. Ocean liners don't turn on a dime. Neither do nations.

These are not minor fears held by a small percentage of Americans. As we noted earlier in this book, nearly eight in ten Americans in the spring of 2010 feared the U.S. economy could collapse entirely,[1] and in the summer of 2011, nearly half of all Americans feared the U.S. was heading for another Great Depression.[2] At the end of 2011, nearly eight in ten Americans believed the country was on the wrong track.[3] Even should these numbers recede somewhat in the short run, Americans will continue to worry about our nation's long-term prospects.

Yet honestly, most Americans don't know the half of it. At best, they are aware of only the proverbial tip of the iceberg. If every person in the U.S. truly understood the magnitude of the icebergs we are racing toward at full steam, I suspect the number of Americans fearing our economy could collapse into a Great Depression would skyrocket.

"Economic Disaster on an Epic Scale"

It is difficult to overstate just how much trouble the American economy is in. According to a growing number of experts, if we don't drastically reduce government spending, balance the federal budget, and make sweeping, fundamental reforms to save and protect Social Security, Medicare, and Medicaid—just to name a few of our biggest fiscal challenges—then the federal debt will continue to explode, and the American economy will soon implode. Consider just a few such experts' statements:

- "These deficits are like a cancer [and] they will truly destroy this country from within if we don't take care of them," warned Erskine Bowles, the Democrat cochair of President Obama's National Commission on Fiscal Responsibility and Reform in 2010.[4]
- "We are accumulating debt burdens that will rival a third-world nation within ten years," warned David Walker in 2010. Walker was appointed by President Bill Clinton to serve as the comptroller general of the United States—essentially the nation's chief financial auditor—and served in that role from 1998 to 2008. "Once you end up losing the confidence of the markets, things happen very suddenly and very dramatically. We've seen that in Greece, we've seen it in Ireland, and we must not see it happen in the United States."[5]
- "We are steadily becoming more vulnerable to economic disaster on an epic scale," said Simon Johnson, a highly respected economist at Massachusetts Institute of Technology's Sloan School of Management and an advisor to the Congressional Budget Office, in testimony before the Senate Budget Committee in 2010.[6]

- America is on an "unsustainable fiscal course" after going through the "worst economic crisis since the Great Depression," wrote the Turkish-born American economist Nouriel Roubini, professor of economics and international business at New York University's Stern School of Business, in an October 2010 op-ed in the *Financial Times*. Roubini, who accurately predicted the collapse of the housing markets and the financial disaster on Wall Street in 2008, believes the U.S. is heading toward a "fiscal train wreck" and that "the risk . . . is that something on the fiscal side will snap."[7]

- "The United States cannot go on borrowing at projected rates," warned Alice Rivlin, a Democrat on the president's Debt Commission and the founding director of the Congressional Budget Office, in testimony before the Senate Budget Committee in 2011. "Without major policy changes, we risk a debt crisis that could severely damage our economy and weaken our influence in the world. . . . We face the prospect of debt crisis and economic disaster if we do not act."[8]

- "It is only a matter of time until our financial house collapses," wrote Stuart Butler of the Heritage Foundation in his 2011 report, "Saving the American Dream: The Heritage Plan to Fix the Debt, Cut Spending, and Restore Prosperity." "We are living on borrowed time and risk an economic catastrophe unless somebody in government exercises real leadership to reduce spending and borrowing."[9]

- "We know we're going to have an economic collapse if we stay on the path we are on," Wisconsin's Republican congressman Paul Ryan, chairman of the House Budget Committee, warned in a 2011 interview with Christiane Amanpour of ABC's *This Week*. "And so to me it's unconscionable as an elected representative of people to know that that's coming and not try to do something to prevent it from happening."[10]

- "This debt is a mortal threat to our country," warned Ohio's Republican congressman John Boehner, Speaker of the House of Representatives, in a 2011 interview. "It is also a moral threat. It is immoral to bind our children to as leeching and destructive a force as debt. It is immoral to rob our children's future and make them beholden to China. No society is worthy that treats its children so shabbily."[11]

How Bad Is America's Economy Today?

In a moment, we will look at the specific numbers and fiscal projections that are causing so many experts to warn of the very real possibility of a coming financial implosion. First, however, let's look at a snapshot of just how much Americans are hurting economically.

- In 2011, nearly 14 million Americans were unemployed, and an additional 8.5 million Americans were underemployed, meaning they were working part-time because they couldn't find a full-time job.[12]
- Since 2006, more than 3 million American families have suffered foreclosures—that is, they have seen their houses repossessed by banks because they could not keep up with their mortgage payments.[13]
  - In 2008 alone, foreclosures shot up 81 percent— a single-year record—resulting in 861,664 families losing their homes.[14]
  - In 2009, another 918,000 American families lost their homes to foreclosure.[15]
  - In 2010, another 1.05 million American families lost their homes to foreclosure, shattering all previous records.[16]
  - In 2011, another 804,423 American families lost their homes to foreclosure, and nearly 1.9 million American

homeowners received notices from their banks that they were in danger of foreclosure.[17]

- An estimated 7 to 8 million homes in the U.S. now stand vacant or in the foreclosure process.[18]
- Even those Americans who still own their homes have suffered significant losses, as average home values across the country in 2011 plunged back to 2004 levels, a loss of some 33 percent from peak values.[19]
- Americans' household net worth has plunged precipitously in recent years, driven down by the implosion of home values and by huge losses in the stock markets. According to Federal Reserve data, between 2007 and 2009, household wealth plunged 23 percent.[20]
- Approximately 7 million Americans filed for personal bankruptcy between 2006 and 2011, and the rate shot up by more than 150 percent during that time.[21]
- Since 2001, some 42,400 American factories have closed their doors.[22]
- A record 45.8 million Americans used government-funded food stamps in 2011 to help put food on their families' tables.[23]

Tragically, Washington has been deeply divided as to how to turn the economy around and get the private sector growing again. Democrats have by and large insisted that trillions of dollars in new federal spending would jump-start the stalled economy and create millions of new jobs—even if that money had to be borrowed from foreign lenders. Republicans have argued that such massive spending has not significantly lowered the unemployment rate or triggered sustained economic growth and that extensive new federal regulation—including President Obama's aggressive environmental regulations and restructuring of the American health care industry

("ObamaCare")—has severely harmed American companies, especially small businesses and entrepreneurs. As the political debates have gotten hotter and the rhetoric has grown more intense, many Americans have become concerned that Washington may not know how to restore the conditions for private-sector growth and job creation, exacerbating fears not only about how America can fully recover, but whether we can. Compounding these fears even further is the issue of our staggering national debt.

How Bad Is America's Debt Crisis?

For the first two hundred years or so of our history, Americans hated the notion of Washington overspending and borrowing, except in extreme national emergencies. Now, we are addicted to both, and the debt crisis has become its own national emergency.

America's Debt History

Let's make sure we begin by putting current events in context. In the first sixty years of our national existence—between 1789 and 1849—the U.S. government accrued a budget *surplus* of some $70 million, according to a report from the White House's Office of Management and Budget. Over the next half century—between 1850 and 1900—a series of emergencies such as the Spanish-American War and the Civil War required Washington to spend more than it took in, and we accumulated a federal deficit of nearly $1 billion. Yet once the emergencies were over, Washington wisely moved to get its fiscal house back in balance.[24]

"Between 1901 and 1916, the budget hovered very close to balance every year," the report noted. "World War I brought large deficits that totaled $23 billion over the 1917–1919 period. The budget was then in surplus throughout the 1920s. However, the combination of the Great Depression followed by World War II resulted in a long, unbroken string of deficits that were historically unprecedented in magnitude. As a result, federal debt held by the public mushroomed from less than $3 billion in 1917 to $16 billion in 1930 and then to $242 billion by 1946. In relation to the size of the economy, debt held by the public grew from 16 percent of GDP [gross domestic product] in 1930 to 109 percent in 1946."[25]

The good news is that once Nazi Germany and Imperial Japan were defeated and World War II ended victoriously for the U.S. and our allies, the Greatest Generation returned home to start growing families and businesses. As a result, the American economy boomed. Tax revenues to Washington surged. Budget deficits were minimal—there were often surpluses—and the federal debt as a percentage of our economy dropped dramatically. But then came the Korean War, the Vietnam War, the Cold War, and the first Gulf War. As a result of these wars, but also of the compounding effects of the New Deal and Great Society policies in Washington, federal spending grew enormously, as did the federal deficit and national debt.

By the early 1990s, Americans were deeply frustrated by the overspending. In the 1994 fall elections, the Democratic Party lost control of the U.S. House of Representatives and the Senate, though President Bill Clinton, also a Democrat, was reelected in 1996. The battle between congressional Republicans and a Democrat in the White House created a dramatic freeze on spending, with both sides resisting each other's spending priorities but also pledging to balance the budget. By 1998, bipartisan efforts in Washington succeeded, and the federal government posted its first surplus ($69 billion) in decades. For four straight years, the federal government continued to post budget surpluses, hitting a high of $236 billion in the year 2000.[26]

All told, between 1789 and 2000—a period of 211 years—the U.S. federal government racked up a national debt of $3.4 trillion.[27] That's an awful lot of money, to be sure. But to put it in context, because our national economy had grown so far and so fast during that time, our federal debt was just 34 percent of our gross domestic product in 2000.[28]

That was barely a decade ago. How quickly things changed.

The Debt Crisis Worsens

President George W. Bush faced numerous extraordinary challenges during his eight years in office, including the terrorist attacks on September 11, 2001, subsequent wars in Afghanistan and Iraq, and a severe recession at the end of his second term. Unfortunately, he also massively overspent and refused to veto big spending bills coming from Congress, even when Congress was controlled by his own political party. By the time he left the White House after the 2008 elections, the federal debt had risen 71 percent to $5.8 trillion.[29] This was a terrible failure of President Bush, for whom I otherwise have great respect. But again, let's keep it in context. Because the U.S. economy had grown so rapidly for most of the Bush presidency (until the end), the federal debt was still only 40.2 percent of GDP.[30] That was a significant increase from when Bush came into office, to be sure, but it was still manageable in historical terms.

To win the presidency, then-Senator Barack Obama, the Illinois Democrat, sharply and consistently (and rightly) criticized President Bush for creating such large budget deficits, driving up the national debt, and having to repeatedly borrow so much money. In 2006, for example, Senator Obama refused to vote in favor of raising the debt ceiling to permit the federal government to borrow more money. "The fact that we are here today to debate raising America's debt limit is a sign of leadership failure," Obama said. "It is a sign that the U.S. government can't pay its own bills. It is a sign that we now depend on ongoing financial assistance from foreign countries to finance our government's reckless fiscal policies. . . . Increasing America's debt weakens us domestically and internationally. Leadership means that 'the buck stops here.' Instead, Washington is shifting the burden of bad choices today onto the backs of our children and grandchildren. America has a debt problem and a failure of leadership. Americans deserve better."[31]

Upon taking the oath of office, however, President Obama abandoned all pretense of opposing massive deficits, debt, and borrowing. In a series of moves that stunned and rattled the nation, President Obama nearly tripled the national debt in just his first three years in office.

- The federal debt stood at $5.8 trillion at the end of 2008.[32]
- The federal debt hit a record $15.11 trillion on December 1, 2011.[33]
- In 2011, our debt-to-GDP ratio was a staggering 100 percent— that is, in 2011 the United States owed as much money as our entire national economic output was in 2010.[34]
- The national debt grew about $3 million a minute in 2011.[35]

How Much Is a Trillion?

The concept of going more than $15 trillion—that's *trillion*, with a *t*—into debt with no end in sight is hard for most Americans to grasp. It is certainly hard for me to get my mind around.

Maybe this will help. According to an interesting website called DefeatTheDebt.com:

- If we were to pay one dollar every second of every hour of every day of every month to pay down our national debt, it would take us almost 32,000 years just to pay off $1 trillion; to pay off $14 trillion would take more than 443,000 years.[36]
- If we were to spend $10 million a day to pay down our national debt, it would take us about 273 years to get to $1 trillion—so it would take us about 3,822 years to pay off $14 trillion.[37]

- One trillion is more than the number of stars in the Milky Way.[38]
- It would take more than ten thousand 18-wheelers to transport one trillion $1 bills. Our national debt today would fill up 30 of the largest container ships ever constructed, each holding more than 4,100 containers full of cash.[39]
- Fifteen trillion $1 bills, laid end to end and side to side, would pave every interstate, highway, and country road in America—twice—with a good amount left over.[40]

America's Debt Crisis: Going from Bad to Worse

President Obama, his senior advisors, and his allies in Congress argued that all their spending and borrowing would stimulate the economy, create new jobs, and drive down the unemployment rate. Obama increased discretionary federal spending—that is, nonessential government spending, not including Social Security, Medicare, Medicaid, or defense spending—by 84 percent with just his first two budgets and his "stimulus" spending bill. The Environmental Protection Agency budget, for example, rose 131 percent in the first two years of the Obama administration. The Department of Energy budget rose 170 percent. The Department of Commerce budget rose 219 percent. The Transportation Department budget rose a stunning 547 percent.[41]

Unfortunately, despite good intentions to get the private economy growing again and to create millions of new private-sector jobs, the Obama administration's efforts accomplished neither of these goals. Rather, unemployment stayed painfully high. Bankruptcies continued at record rates, as did foreclosures. Economic growth sputtered. The markets around the world were rattled by Washington's runaway spending and borrowing train. Then, in August 2011, Standard & Poor's credit rating agency announced that it was downgrading the U.S. credit rating from a triple-A score to a double-A score for the first time since America was given the highest possible credit ranking in 1917.[42] The *Washington Post* reported that the move dealt "a symbolic blow to the world's economic superpower in what was a sharply worded critique of the American political system."[43]

The Moody's credit rating agency did not choose to downgrade the U.S. credit rating at the time. However, the agency sent a strong signal that the federal government would have to drive the debt-to-GDP ratio down to 73 percent by 2015 in order to maintain America's triple-A credit rating.[44]

It is going to be very difficult, however, to bring the debt-to-GDP ratio down without dramatic changes to the way Washington does business. If we stay on the current spending and borrowing path, the Congressional Budget Office projects the total U.S. national debt will explode to nearly $25 trillion by 2020.[45]

Twenty-five trillion dollars of debt is beyond most people's comprehension. Yet as horrifying as that number is, it may actually be too conservative an estimate of the catastrophic level of debt that is coming our way.

Why? Two words: *Unfunded liabilities.*

The Threat Ahead

Over the years, politicians in Washington have made promises to pay the American people certain benefits when they retire or become too sick or disabled to work. Other politicians have then come along and promised to be even more generous than those who made the original promises. It all might have seemed like a good idea decades ago when America's economy was booming and there were more than enough able-bodied workers paying small amounts of taxes to cover the promises the government made to their parents and grandparents.

Now the bills are rapidly coming due, and the fact is we don't have nearly enough money to keep the lavish promises made by politicians who have long since retired or passed away. The term *unfunded liability* refers to financial promises made by politicians who never actually set aside any money to pay those bills.

Congressman Paul Ryan has described just how enormous these unfunded liabilities really are. "Medicare faces the daunting demographic challenge of supporting the baby boomers as they retire. But its much larger problem is that of medical costs, which are rising at roughly double the rate of growth in the economy," Ryan warned. "Today Medicare has an unfunded liability of $38 trillion over the next seventy-five years. This means that the federal government would have to set aside $38 trillion today to cover future benefits for the three generations of Americans: retirees, workers, and children. This translates to a burden of about $335,350 per U.S. household. Moreover, the problem worsens rapidly. . . . By 2014, Medicare's unfunded liability is projected to grow to $52 trillion—or about $458,900 per household."[46]

Take a moment to consider the magnitude of those facts:

- At the moment, Medicare has made promises to the American people that cost $38 *trillion*—more than politicians have set aside to pay for those promises.
- But because some 80 million baby boomers will soon begin to retire, in less than five years Medicare will cost American taxpayers $52 *trillion.*
- To put it another way, each and every American household would have to pay the federal government more than $450,000 to cover our Medicare promises.

If you're thinking, *"That's impossible!"* you're right.

Unfortunately, it gets worse. These, after all, are "only" the coming costs of Medicare. We haven't even talked about Social Security yet. "When Social Security and Medicare are taken together," Congressman Ryan warned, "the total unfunded liability . . . will grow to $57 trillion, or $500,414 per household."[47]

Social Security was originally created in the 1930s with the idea that many workers would help pay for relatively few retirees, but that is no longer the case. In 1945, an average of 41.9 workers paid taxes to cover the benefits of every retiree. By 1980, there was an average of only 3.2 workers paying taxes to cover the benefits of every retiree. By 2020, only 2.4 workers will be paying payroll taxes to cover the benefits of each retiree.[48]

How did this happen? The architects of Social Security did not foresee two critical developments. First, as Americans became wealthier, they generally stopped having as many children as they did in the early- to mid-1900s. This meant that there were now fewer children growing up, becoming educated, and becoming productive workers who were able to pay taxes to adequately cover the benefits of their parents and grandparents. Second, Americans have aborted more than 53 million children since 1973.[49] As morally unconscionable as abortion is in its own right—something we will discuss in an upcoming chapter precisely because it is a terrible national failure— the abortion issue is also coming back to haunt the economy in ways its proponents likely did not anticipate. Those 53 million murdered American citizens are not working. They are not paying taxes. They are not helping to care for their parents and grandparents in their retirement years, and the day of reckoning—fiscally speaking, at least—is quickly approaching.

For years Washington has been collecting a bit more Social Security payroll tax revenues than it needed to pay out in benefits. But rather than putting those surpluses in an interest-bearing account from which funds could be withdrawn when those estimated 80 million baby boomers began to retire, Washington has been spending (some would say wasting) those surpluses, throwing the equivalent of IOUs into the proverbial piggy bank. Now time has run out. The baby boomers are starting to retire. In 2010, Social Security began paying out more in benefits than it collected in taxes, and this will accelerate as these unfunded liabilities come due.[50]

A Cruel Choice: Raising Taxes or Slashing Benefits

The truth is painful, but here it is: there is absolutely no way Washington can keep these promises without raising taxes beyond what we could bear.

Let's be specific. The Heritage Foundation, one of the leading public-policy think tanks in Washington, published a study in 2010 analyzing how these government promises would have to be kept if the politicians decided to raise taxes. The results were chilling. To pay for all of Social Security and Medicare's unfunded liabilities alone (not to mention covering the cost of Medicaid, national defense, and the rest of the government), the federal corporate tax rate would have to be raised from 35 percent today to 88 percent. Considering that many American businesses are already gasping for economic oxygen, such a massive tax increase would amount to financial suicide. Top marginal federal tax rates on the wealthiest Americans would also have to be raised from 35 percent to 88 percent. Nor would middle-income Americans escape a massive tax increase. Rather, they would see their federal tax rates skyrocket from 25 percent to 63 percent.[51]

America could never remain the world's economic leader with federal tax rates this high. Our economy is already struggling with the current level of taxes, spending, and debt. To double or triple tax rates would cause an already-sputtering economy to stall and then implode.

Of course, rather than raise taxes sky-high, Washington could slash benefits. Yet a Heritage Foundation study found that by 2037, presumably even with some modest tax increases, Social Security benefits would have to be gutted by some 22 percent in order for

Washington to be able to cover its costs.[52] Given that Social Security payments are difficult to live on to begin with, these would be extremely painful cuts and unlikely to pass a future Congress.

What other options would Washington have besides raising taxes or slashing benefits? Politicians could print or borrow the money. These, too, would have disastrous results, however. Printing more money would devalue each dollar currently in circulation. This would create inflation. Prices for food, housing, energy, and other staples of American society would skyrocket, further harming American families and suffocating the American economy. Borrowing trillions of dollars would deeply exacerbate the debt crisis and put America's standard of living and our national security in increasing jeopardy, as Washington would no longer be able to afford the size and sophistication of a military capable of defending our interests at home or our values overseas. One also has to consider whether other nations would actually lend us so many trillions, or whether they would conclude that America is no longer a good credit risk and allow us to implode.

As Congressman Ryan noted in his report, "The effect on personal standards of living will be devastating, and it will be felt as those born today are completing college and beginning their careers. By 2050, workers and families will begin seeing the growth in their wages and incomes erode. Standards of living will begin to stagnate and then decline in real terms. By 2058, the economy enters a free fall, beyond which the catastrophe cannot be measured: CBO cannot model the impact because debt rises to levels the economy cannot support."[53]

The Road to Reform . . . ?

Some experts and think tanks believe there is still time to turn things around. At least two have laid out detailed reform plans worth considering.

Congressman Paul Ryan has developed his "Roadmap for America's Future." This detailed legislative proposal cuts tax rates and simplifies the tax code to reignite economic growth. It cuts and restrains federal spending. It reforms Social Security and Medicare in ways that protect the existing system for current retirees and those close to retirement while also improving the system for younger workers. For example, Ryan proposes the retirement age be gradually and incrementally increased from sixty-five years old to seventy years old, since people are living and working longer. He also proposes that younger workers can invest some of their current payroll taxes into tax-free personal retirement accounts that permit low-risk investments in mutual funds and annuities. The Ryan plan also includes specific details to balance the budget and reduce federal debt—all, presumably, before an implosion of the American economy occurs.[54]

The Heritage Foundation has also released a very detailed reform plan. It's called "Saving the American Dream: The Heritage Plan to Fix the Debt, Cut Spending, and Restore Prosperity." While the principles are similar to Congressman Ryan's plan, some of the specifics are different. Both plans call for fully repealing "ObamaCare," and both create personal retirement accounts within the Social Security system for younger workers. However, while the Ryan plan calls for simplifying the federal tax code from its current six marginal tax brackets down to just two (a 10 percent rate and a 25 percent rate), the Heritage plan calls for a single flat tax rate (not yet determined). Whereas the Ryan plan would hold spending at 19 percent of GDP, the Heritage plan would restrain spending to 18.5 percent of GDP.

The Heritage plan was designed to balance the federal budget by 2021 and reduce the national debt to 30 percent of GDP by 2035. By contrast, because the Ryan plan phases in some of the reforms more gradually than the Heritage plan does, the "Roadmap" does not bring the federal budget into balance until after 2055. That may seem like a long time—and it is—but the Ryan plan should be compared not only with the Heritage plan but more importantly with the fact that President Obama has not laid out a reform plan of his own. Under the current trajectory, the Congressional Budget Office projects deficits as far as the eye can see through the twenty-first century. Without significant changes, the budget will never be balanced in our lifetimes. Worse, the CBO indicates that the national debt will hit a horrifying 185 percent of GDP by 2035.[55]

Overall, the Heritage plan is much bolder than the Ryan plan, but there are various policy and political challenges to both. What remains to be seen is whether the American people have the stomach for either plan or a variation of one of them. The point is not that one plan is necessarily better than the other. The point I want to make here is that there are at least two serious, credible plans on the table right now that show us in specific ways how we can boost economic growth, create more jobs, reform our entitlement systems, and get ourselves back on the road to fiscal sanity *before* we implode. Perhaps others will develop bold, creative, and compassionate plans that will improve upon what Congressman Ryan and the Heritage Foundation have offered. I hope so. The more serious ideas in the mix, the better. There is still a way out of this mess, and that is good news, but the window to get started on such reforms is rapidly closing.

. . . Or the Road to Ruin?

If we don't make desperately needed reforms, then we are most certainly on the path to ruin. Indeed, we could be on the road to Greece.

"America is on the road to re-creating Greece's recent debt crisis," noted business magazine *Barron's* in a 2011 issue. "If a country as small and removed as Greece could generate the tremors that it did in the past year, how much worse would a national debt crisis be in the world's largest economy?"[56]

The article notes that "Greece, the world's 27th-largest economy, is a minor player, even in the European Union. Yet a budget deficit of 13.6 percent of gross domestic product spiked its overall debt to 115 percent of GDP. Its debt fell to junk status, and it stood on the edge of bankruptcy. Only the massive May 2010 bailout by the European Union and the International Monetary Fund pulled it back from the brink."[57]

Citing sobering data from the Congressional Budget Office, *Barron's* warned, "If you think debt problems like Greece's can't happen here, think again. . . . [Soon], U.S. debt will hit 132 percent of GDP—well above Greece's 115 percent. Government spending will consume almost one-third of everything America produces—a level only reached at the height of World War II. Even raising taxes to their greatest ratio to the economy in America's history wouldn't offset the automatic spending machine. . . . Washington is on the road to Greece."[58]

Bottom Line

America in 2012 owes more than $15 *trillion* to a range of creditors, many in foreign countries, including Communist China.

That's bad enough, but it gets worse.

Most Americans don't even realize that we owe another $57 *trillion* to cover a range of "unfunded liabilities," including Social Security, Medicare, and Medicaid benefits. America's most respected financial experts—both Republicans and Democrats—are warning us that such staggering levels of current and coming debt could trigger an economic implosion unless we rapidly and courageously make fundamental and sweeping reforms. The good news is that at least two detailed and compelling reforms have been proposed.

Two key questions emerge. First, does Washington have the courage to follow those plans or variations on them? And second, will

Americans reward or punish political leaders in Washington for pursuing such reforms?

As important as those questions are, however, there is another even more important question: Will the Lord give us the time we need to make these changes—however difficult and painful they would be—or will he simply choose in his sovereignty to let America implode financially?

CHAPTER TEN

THE WAR AND TERRORISM SCENARIOS

AMERICA'S ENEMIES SMELL BLOOD IN THE WATER.

Though I have been writing and speaking about this for years, I remain stunned by how few Americans realize that the leaders of al Qaeda and Iran have explicitly been pursuing a policy of economic jihad against the United States. Yet consider the following quotes:

> "If their economy is destroyed, they will be busy with their own affairs rather than enslaving the weak peoples. It is very important to concentrate on hitting the U.S. economy through all possible means."
> —OSAMA BIN LADEN, DECEMBER 2001[1]

> "We will also aim to continue, by the permission of Allah, the destruction of the American economy."
> —DR. AYMAN AL-ZAWAHIRI, TOP DEPUTY TO OSAMA BIN LADEN, SEPTEMBER 2002[2]

"Alongside the mujahadeen in Afghanistan, we bled
Russia for ten years until it went bankrupt and was
forced to withdraw in defeat. . . . We are continuing this
policy to bleed America to the point of bankruptcy. . . .
Al Qaeda spent $500,000 on [the 9/11 attacks], while
the incident and its aftermath have cost America more
than half a trillion dollars. This meant that, by the
grace of God, every dollar al Qaeda spent cost America
a million dollars and a huge number of jobs. . . . This
demonstrates the success of the bleed-until-bankruptcy
plan."
—OSAMA BIN LADEN, OCTOBER 2004[3]

"No politician can be found in the United States who
is capable of saving the U.S. economy from this move
toward the valley of downfall."
—MAHMOUD AHMADINEJAD, APRIL 2008[4]

"These days, [although] no incident has as yet occurred,
oil prices have risen from $12 to $120 a barrel. Now
try to calculate how high [the price] of this essential
commodity will rise if the enemy acts in a foolhardy
manner."
—MOHAMMAD JA'FAR ASSADI, COMMANDER OF
THE IRANIAN REVOLUTIONARY GUARD CORPS,
AUGUST 2008[5]

The weaker the United States has grown economically, the more
emboldened those who wish us harm have become—both to exacerbate our economic woes in the hopes of triggering our implosion
and to steadily build their own strategic, conventional, and unconventional forces to prepare for the day when they believe they can
overtake us or even destroy us.

The Threat of War

The good news: the United States remains the world's only super-power. At the moment, America has the world's most fearsome nuclear weapons force and the world's most powerful and effective Army, Navy, Air Force, Marine Corps, and Coast Guard. It is critical that we maintain strong national defenses, maintain and enhance our ability to project force wherever we need to around the world, and keep a clear eye on our vital national interests.

What are these interests? I believe there are five:

1. We must always safeguard U.S. national security, including carefully protecting our homeland, our coastlines, and our borders.
2. We must prevent major threats by other powers to dominate or control Europe, East Asia, or the Middle East and the Persian Gulf.
3. We must maintain access to foreign trade.
4. We must protect Americans at home and around the globe against threats to their lives and well-being.
5. We must maintain unfettered access to resources, particularly energy resources, while specifically developing and defending our own energy resources.[6]

The bad news: other nations, ideologies, and religious movements are hell-bent on subverting, severely damaging, or outright incapacitating us. They are determined to remove from us the title of "world superpower" and claim it for themselves. Long ago they recognized this would not be easy to accomplish, but they have been patient and persistent, and they increasingly believe the U.S. will soon implode just as the Soviet Union and the Warsaw Pact nations imploded in the late 1980s and early 1990s.

Real and serious threats to our vital national interests are emerging (and in some cases, reemerging) from countries like Russia, China, North Korea, and Pakistan. Each has conventional forces that could threaten our interests. Each has developed chemical and biological weapons. Each has developed nuclear weapons. Each has also developed ballistic missiles capable of delivering these weapons against our homeland or against our allies. What's more, these nations are forming strategic regional alliances against us, and they are selling weapons and technologies to each other and to other enemies of the United States.

While some of these countries could attack us directly, they could also choose to attack our access to oil in the Middle East or our trade routes in Asia, across the Atlantic, through the Panama Canal, or through the Suez Canal in hopes of bringing us to our knees financially. They could seek to unleash terrible biological attacks that would shut down international travel and trade. They could release computer viruses that would attack our banking and financial institutions and our communications systems. Now is no time to lower our guard. An open society like the United States is vulnerable to attack—especially at a time of economic weakness.

The Russian Threat

Russia, for example, is becoming increasingly hostile to the United States and is seeking to intimidate and bully our allies while threatening our interests.

Vladimir Putin, the highly provocative and controversial Russian leader, threatened in 2008 to aim nuclear-armed Russian missiles at American allies in Eastern Europe if the U.S. placed missile-defense systems there.[7] During the brutally cold winters of 2006 and 2009, Russia cut off oil and gas supplies to Ukraine, a democratic ally of ours, to undermine the government there, force Ukrainians to pay drastically higher energy prices, and warn the rest of Europe, which relies on Russian gas supplies, not to cross the Kremlin. In 2008 Russia actually invaded the nation of Georgia, another of our democratic allies in Eastern Europe. More recently, Putin denounced America as a "parasite." He told students in Russia that the U.S. "is living beyond its means and shifting part of the weight of its problems onto the world economy, acting to some extent as a parasite on the global economy and its dollar monopoly position."[8]

Russia, meanwhile, is selling advanced weaponry and even nuclear technology to Iran and other countries opposed to the U.S. The Kremlin has both strategic and conventional forces that could move southward to threaten Israel and attempt to gain control of the oil-rich Middle East. Indeed, as I wrote about in detail in my book *Epicenter*, Bible prophecies found in Ezekiel chapters 38 and 39 indicate that Russia will form an alliance with Iran, Turkey, Libya, Sudan, and other countries in the Middle East and North Africa to come against Israel in the last days. Trends over the last two decades—and notably in the past few years—suggest we are getting increasingly close to the fulfillment of the "war of Gog and Magog" prophecies.[9]

We must, therefore, be increasingly vigilant about this red storm rising. When Russia was the core of the Soviet Union, her leaders in the Kremlin actually threatened to "bury" the United States, and today, in light of certain leaders' words and actions, we cannot assume they have all abandoned this objective.[10]

The Chinese Threat

China is also a serious concern for the United States.

Beijing has a huge and growing conventional military along with its significant nuclear force. Together with an increasingly well-equipped air force, navy, and ground forces—including the launch in 2011 of its first aircraft carrier and the intensive development of a ballistic missile capable of destroying American aircraft carriers—Beijing has the ability to cut off our trade routes in the Pacific Rim, deny us passage through the Panama Canal (which they now effectively own), or seize the democracy of Taiwan, one of our key allies in East Asia.[11]

Yes, China is heavily engaged in commercial trade with the U.S., which binds our countries together. And no, China is not currently posing a direct military threat against us. But Beijing's national strategy is known as *taoguangyanghui*, which can be translated as, "Hide our capabilities; bide our time."[12] That is exactly what the Chinese are doing: carefully—at times stealthily—building their military forces while biding their time and waiting for the best moment to move. A careful study of the writings and sayings of the Communist leaders in Beijing clearly indicates they want to dominate the Pacific Rim and become a world superpower, if not *the* world superpower.

There should be no question that some Chinese leaders are prepared to use lethal force—even nuclear weapons—against the United States when and if they feel the time is right or if the U.S. gets in the way of one of their most cherished objectives. In late 1995, a top Chinese general told a Clinton administration official that the U.S. would not defend Taiwan if China were to attack and seize the technology-rich island democracy. Why? Because Americans "care more about Los Angeles than they do about Taiwan," the general said in a statement widely perceived as a Chinese threat to rain nuclear weapons down on the California city if the U.S. were to get in China's way.[13]

Then came this headline in the *New York Times* in 2005: "Chinese General Threatens Use of A-Bombs If U.S. Intrudes." "China should use nuclear weapons against the United States if the American military intervenes in any conflict over Taiwan, a senior Chinese military official said Thursday," the *Times* reported. "'If the Americans draw their missiles and position-guided ammunition onto the target zone on China's territory, I think we will have to respond with nuclear weapons,' the official, Maj. Gen. Zhu Chenghu, said at an official briefing."[14]

China, along with other countries around the world, is also

developing additional strategies to threaten us, including increasingly advanced cyberwarfare capacities to infiltrate, corrupt, and take down the computer systems that run our national defenses and national economy; antisatellite weapons to disrupt our military and civilian communications systems; and electromagnetic pulse (EMP) capabilities that could suddenly and catastrophically render our electrical and electronic networks, including our communications and banking systems, ineffective. As with the Russians, we dare not let down our guard with the Chinese.

The Iranian Threat

The Islamic Republic of Iran is of particular concern because its senior leaders believe that the Islamic Revolution that began in 1979 is now reaching its climax. They have stated publicly that the end of the world is increasingly close at hand. They have taught that the way to hasten the arrival or appearance on earth of the so-called Islamic messiah known as the "Twelfth Imam" or the "Mahdi" is to destroy Israel, which they call the "Little Satan," and the United States, which they call the "Great Satan."

What's more, they have explicitly vowed to annihilate the United States and Israel and have urged Muslims to envision a world without America and Zionism. They believe Allah has chosen them to create chaos and carnage on the planet. The key leaders in Iran seem determined to accomplish their apocalyptic, genocidal mission. They are steadily enriching uranium and developing nuclear weapons. Tehran is building alliances with Russia, China, and North Korea and has cooperated with those countries on the development of offensive and defensive weapons systems. For example, they are building and buying increasingly longer-range ballistic missiles capable of delivering nuclear warheads. These missiles are capable of hitting Israel and our allies in the Middle East and Europe. Before long, Iranian long-range missiles will be able to reach the continental United States. Already,

Iran (along with several other countries) has the ability to attack the U.S. homeland or our allies around the world by firing short- and medium-range missiles from commercial container ships.[15]

Iranian leaders also continue to aggressively export their Islamic Revolution to countries throughout the Middle East and around the world. They are harboring scores of al Qaeda terrorists and leaders inside Iranian cities and allowing terrorists to crisscross their territory. They are making a concerted effort to enlarge the reach of terrorist operations by building strategic alliances with other jihadist organizations, regardless of their theological differences. They claim to be building a network of between forty thousand and seventy thousand suicide bombers ready to strike Israeli, American, and British targets.[16] What's more, over the past decade they have sent suicide bombers, other insurgents, money, and weapons into Iraq and Afghanistan to attack American and coalition forces.

Also troubling are the alliances Iran is making with countries like Venezuela, an increasingly hostile Turkey, and an Egypt troubled by growing chaos, all of which are demonstrating growing anti–U.S. sentiments. Some dismiss Iran as a nuisance and not a threat, but the mullahs and ayatollahs who rule Tehran and believe in the coming of the Twelfth Imam are truly evil and must not be overlooked or underestimated, for to misunderstand the nature and threat of evil is to risk being blindsided by it.

The Threat of Al Qaeda and Other Terror Groups

The events of September 11, 2001, taught us the hard way that terrorism—especially from radical Islamic jihadists such as al Qaeda and the Taliban, but also from the Muslim Brotherhood, Hezbollah, Hamas, and other non-state actors—represents a clear and present danger to the United States. Unfortunately, even after a decade of hot war with the jihadists, this is still true.

In *Inside the Revolution*, I posed the question "How many Radicals are there worldwide?" To find the answer, I looked to authors John Esposito and Dalia Mogahed, who in 2007 published *Who Speaks for Islam? What a Billion Muslims Really Think*. Esposito is a professor of Islamic studies at Georgetown University and founding director of the school's Prince Alwaleed Bin Talal Center for Muslim-Christian Understanding. Mogahed, herself a devout Muslim, is executive director of the Gallup Center for Muslim Studies. The book these two experts wrote presents the findings of "a mammoth, multiyear Gallup research study . . . the largest, most comprehensive study of contemporary Muslims ever done."[17]

The good news from their research was that approximately 93 percent of Muslims worldwide fit Esposito and Mogahed's definition of a "moderate"—peaceable, nonviolent, and traditionally religious but unlikely to pose a threat to Western security interests. The deeply disturbing news, however, was that about 7 percent would be classified as Radicals. That is, they are supportive of anti-American and anti-Western terrorism, believe it is fully justified, and thus are sympathetic of and potentially helpful to violent Islamic extremists. Unlike the moderates, these people pose a serious threat to American national security and to our allies and interests worldwide.

While 7 percent may at first seem like a relatively small number, the implications of such results are daunting. Seven percent of 1.3 billion Muslims equals 91 million people. It may comfort some Americans to know that the vast majority of the world's Muslims are peaceful people. But it is far from comforting to know that 91 million Muslims are politically radicalized. After all, were these 91 million people to form their own country—the Islamic Republic of Radicalstan, for example—they would represent the twelfth-largest country on the planet, having about twice the population of Spain, nearly three times the population of Canada, almost ten times the population of Sweden, and more than twelve times the population of Israel. What's more, some researchers say Gallup's 7 percent figure significantly *underestimates* the number of Radicals out there, meaning there may be many more.[18]

What does this mean for the U.S. in terms of national security? For one thing, if the U.S. and our NATO allies completely withdraw from Afghanistan before the country is secure and the government in Kabul is truly stable and capable of using its military and police forces to keep terrorists out of the country, Afghanistan could once again become a safe haven for our enemies. We must not take our eye off the ball. We must make sure the Afghan threat is neutralized.

The same is true of Iraq. In my view, President Obama made a serious mistake by pulling all U.S. forces out of Iraq by the end of 2011. He seriously failed in his negotiations with Baghdad to maintain an American presence. We certainly made progress toward establishing a peaceful, stable Iraq, but by withdrawing precipitously, I am concerned the Obama administration may have unwittingly created a political and military vacuum that the Radicals of Iran, al Qaeda, and elsewhere could exploit, leading to new threats in Iraq to us, our allies, and our national interests.

We should all be deeply grateful to our brave and heroic military and intelligence forces for killing Osama bin Laden and capturing numerous top operatives since 9/11. At the same time, we must remember that the al Qaeda terrorist network and similar radical Islamic groups remain a major threat to the national security and economic vitality of the United States, the State of Israel, and our Western allies. While al Qaeda in particular has certainly been badly damaged by U.S. and coalition forces in recent years, they are by no means defeated. Rather, they are doing everything they can to reconstitute themselves in Somalia, Yemen, Pakistan, North Africa, sub-Saharan Africa, and elsewhere around the world. They are building new alliances, recruiting new jihadists, raising more money, acquiring more weapons, and plotting new attacks. We must remain vigilant.

The jihadists, after all, no longer want to merely frighten us; they want to annihilate us. They are no longer interested in merely inflicting minor damage on planes, trains, buses, restaurants, malls, and other "soft targets." Rather, they are plotting to inflict catastrophic damage on the U.S. and our allies. To accomplish their objectives, they are actively seeking to acquire weapons of mass destruction—chemical, biological, and nuclear—along with ballistic missiles capable of reaching all of Europe and the United States. They are recruiting followers who are religiously and ideologically committed to helping them carry out their plans and ready to infiltrate the American homeland and set off catastrophic attacks from the inside.

In 1998, Osama bin Laden was asked whether al Qaeda had nuclear or chemical weapons. Bin Laden's response was that "acquiring weapons for the defense of Muslims is a religious duty. If I have indeed acquired these weapons, then I thank God for enabling me to do so."[19] What was particularly troubling was that bin Laden made the statement the same year Pakistan tested nuclear weapons.

In the summer of 2002, Suleiman Abu Ghaith, a Kuwaiti-born spokesman for al Qaeda, posted the following statement on the Internet: "Al-Qa'ida has the right to kill 4 million Americans, including one million children, displace double that figure, and injure and cripple hundreds of thousands."[20]

In May 2003, al Qaeda unveiled a fatwa from a leading Saudi cleric that sanctioned the use of nuclear weapons against the U.S. and permitted the killing of up to 10 million Americans.[21]

During his tenure as director of the Central Intelligence Agency, George Tenet became convinced that al Qaeda's top priority is to acquire nuclear weapons and detonate them inside the United States. In his 2007 memoir, *At the Center of the Storm: My Years at the CIA*, Tenet wrote concerning his discoveries about al Qaeda's intentions:

What we discovered stunned us all. The threats were real. Our intelligence confirmed that the most senior leaders of al-Qa'ida are still singularly focused on acquiring WMD. . . . Moreover, we established beyond any reasonable doubt that al-Qa'ida had clear intent to acquire chemical, biological, and radiological/nuclear (CBRN) weapons, to possess not as a deterrent but to cause mass casualties in the United States.[22]

Terrorists' acquiring weapons of mass destruction is a nightmare scenario that we must avoid at all costs. To prevent the worst from happening, the U.S. and other Western governments must constantly remain vigilant. After all, what these fanatics need most in order to accomplish their goals are Western ignorance, apathy, and lack of moral clarity. If the West can be lulled to sleep, the Radicals will have a much better chance of pulling off a series of attacks that make 9/11 pale by comparison.

The Pakistani Threat

When I was writing *Inside the Revolution*, I interviewed Porter Goss, the former director of the Central Intelligence Agency. For Goss, Pakistan stood near the top of the list of serious threats facing the United States. Pakistan, a country of questionable political stability, has more than one hundred nuclear warheads and many ballistic missiles and is a center for extreme Sunni fundamentalism. Should Radicals suddenly seize control of the country, or should the country disintegrate into chaos or civil war, Pakistan could in a matter of hours or days become the most dangerous country on the face of the planet.

I feel this is now the new Doomsday Scenario, if one of these nuclear weapons or this capability falls in the hands of irresponsible people who have declared that they want to wipe out our Western form of civilization because it is apostate. The all-too-possible nightmare of assassination, chaos, and anarchy in Pakistan could lead to the country's nuclear capability falling into wrong hands. . . . It would be a disaster if the Pak military lost control of the serious weaponry in Pakistan—including WMD.[23]

I couldn't agree more. One can only imagine the horrible implications to American and international security if Pakistani nuclear weapons should end up in the hands of al Qaeda or the Taliban—or the Iranians. America—known to many Pakistanis as the "Great Satan"—would suddenly be in grave danger.

For the foreseeable future, therefore, Pakistan is a country we must watch closely.

Do Americans Have the Resolve to Remain Engaged?

What I have briefly described are just a few of the emerging threats facing the U.S. There are many more. On numerous fronts—but particularly in the Middle East—we face what Winston Churchill once called a "gathering storm." Evil is rising, and we must confront it decisively, or we risk being blindsided as we were at Pearl Harbor in 1941 or on September 11, 2001.

Will American leaders—and the American people—have the resolve to stay focused on national-security issues and remain engaged in a hostile world when economic and social problems are so pressing here at home? Will we invest the time, technology, and national resources it takes to defend ourselves from cataclysmic, paralyzing, even decapitating attacks by enemy states and terrorist organizations, even when budget cuts are needed elsewhere?

I hope so, but to be honest, these are open questions at the moment.

Admiral Mike Mullen, then chairman of the Joint Chiefs of Staff, made headlines in August 2010 when he publicly stated that "the most significant threat to our national security is our debt."

Mullen warned that if America's debt continues eating up more and more of the federal budget, the Pentagon may not be able to fully and adequately defend the vital interests of the country. "The reason I say that is because the ability for our country to resource our military—and I have a pretty good feeling and understanding about what our national security requirements are—is going to be directly proportional . . . to help our economy," Mullen said. "That's why it's so important that the economy move in the right direction, because the strength and the support and the resources that our military uses are directly related to the health of our economy over time."[24]

The following month, Secretary of State Hillary Clinton publicly agreed with Chairman Mullen. In a speech to the Council on Foreign Relations, Secretary Clinton said, "Our rising debt levels (pose) a national security threat."[25]

Mullen and Clinton were right, of course. But that doesn't mean the politicians will refrain from gutting the defense budget and calling it a "peace dividend." I saw it happen when I first came to Washington in 1990 as the Cold War came to an end. I am concerned it will happen again.

What's more, the winds of isolationism are moving across Washington and the nation. A growing number of Republican leaders have been calling for the U.S. to withdraw our forces as rapidly as possible from Afghanistan, echoing widespread sentiments among Congressional Democrats.[26]

Interest in taking decisive action to stop Iran from getting or using nuclear weapons has been hard to find in Washington in recent years. I was particularly surprised to see Senator John McCain signal that the U.S. would not fight another war in the Middle East and imply that he would not support such a war. In a live television interview during the ceremonies honoring the tenth anniversary of 9/11, Senator McCain—a war hero, leading hawk, and ranking member of the Senate Armed Services Committee—told Fox News Sunday, "I think we did the right thing there [in Iraq and Afghanistan]. But I also think we have learned a lot of lessons. And frankly, I don't think you are going to see the United States of America in another war in that part of the world."[27]

Does that mean Senator McCain is ruling out any and all American preemptive military action to stop Iran from obtaining or using nuclear weapons? Does that mean the U.S. would not come to the defense of Israel if she were attacked by Iran or Russia or any other enemy? Does that mean the U.S. would not come to the defense of the democratic government of Iraq, were she invaded? Or defend our access to oil in Saudi Arabia and the Gulf states? These are just a few of the scenarios that could warrant another war in the Middle East. No American wants another war in the region, but it was noteworthy to hear Senator McCain rule one out. If he wouldn't support U.S. military action in the epicenter, how many in the U.S. Senate would?

Bottom Line

The Bible clearly indicates that there will be terrible wars and acts of terrorism and lawlessness in the last days. Could we see catastrophic wars or crippling terrorist attacks foisted upon the United States in the months and years ahead? Yes, this is very possible. Could such attacks cause or hasten the implosion of the U.S. as a world power? Yes, I'm afraid this, too, is possible. Indeed, even the constant threat of war and terrorism could, over time, lead to America becoming emotionally and spiritually exhausted, increasingly isolationist, or politically gridlocked. This, in turn, could cause us to become neutralized in terms of our involvement on the world stage, effectively leading to the end of the U.S. as the world's only superpower. I shudder to think of the implications, but given our current trajectory, this possibility cannot be ruled out.

CHAPTER ELEVEN

THE NATURAL DISASTER SCENARIOS

WHILE AMERICA COULD BE SUDDENLY and unexpectedly neutralized as a key world player due to financial implosion, an incapacitating war, or an unprecedented terrorist strike or series of strikes, these are not the only threats we face. In his sovereignty, God could choose to send natural disasters—be they hurricanes, tornadoes, earthquakes, fires, droughts, floods, volcanoes, pandemic diseases, or any number of other disasters—that would essentially neutralize us or render us unable or unwilling to engage in other global events.

Natural disasters continue unfolding one after another here at home and around the world as they always have. But have you stopped to notice that so many recently are described as "historic" and "unprecedented"?

- Eight of the ten most expensive hurricanes in American history have happened since 9/11. The worst was Hurricane

Katrina, which nearly wiped out an American city and ended up costing more than $100 billion.[1]

- Hurricane Irene made 2011 the worst year in American history for natural disasters, with ten separate catastrophes costing $1 billion or more.[2]

- In 2011, America experienced the worst outbreak of tornadoes in nearly half a century.[3]

- In 2011, Texas suffered the worst fires in the history of the state, amid the worst drought in Texas history.[4]

- In 2011, Virginia—and much of the East Coast—experienced its biggest earthquake since 1875.[5]

The fact that these events were "historic" or "unprecedented" in nature doesn't necessarily mean they were all devastating in terms of lives lost. But that was the grace of God. What if he had decided to allow the United States to suffer disasters of the magnitude that Haiti or Japan or Indonesia or Chile or Pakistan suffered in recent years? What if he allows such disasters to happen in the near future?

Let's take a moment and briefly look at a few worst-case scenarios.

The Threat of Earthquakes

As we have seen, Bible prophecy warns that earthquakes will occur in the last days. In Matthew 24:7, we read that "in various places there will be famines and earthquakes." In Luke 21:11 we read that in the End Times "there will be great earthquakes . . . and there will be terrors and great signs from heaven." In the books of Ezekiel and Revelation, we also read of cataclysmic earthquakes that will shake everyone on the face of the earth and do damage beyond our worst nightmares.

The question is: Why does God send earthquakes? Let's consider two reasons.

First, the Bible teaches that God often uses earthquakes to wake people up and get them to focus on him and on his only begotten Son, the Lord Jesus Christ. After the crucifixion of Christ, for example, God sent an earthquake to Israel:

> Now from the sixth hour darkness fell upon all the land until the ninth hour. About the ninth hour Jesus cried out with a loud voice, saying, *"Eli, Eli, lama sabachthani?"* that is, "My God, My God, why have you forsaken Me?" . . . And Jesus cried out again with a loud voice, and yielded up His spirit. And behold, the veil of the temple was torn in two from top to bottom; and the earth shook and the rocks were split. The tombs were opened, and many bodies of the saints who had fallen asleep were raised; and coming out of the tombs after His resurrection they entered the holy city and appeared to many. Now the centurion, and those who were with him keeping guard over Jesus, when they saw the earthquake and the things that were happening, became very frightened and said, "Truly this was the Son of God!"
>
> MATTHEW 27:45-54

Likewise, God sent an earthquake during the resurrection of Christ:

> Now after the Sabbath, as it began to dawn toward the first day of the week, Mary Magdalene and the other Mary came to look at the grave. And behold, a severe earthquake had occurred, for an angel of the Lord descended from heaven and came and rolled away the stone and sat upon it. And

his appearance was like lightning, and his clothing as white as snow. The guards shook for fear of him and became like dead men. The angel said to the women, "Do not be afraid; for I know that you are looking for Jesus who has been crucified. He is not here, for He has risen, just as He said. Come, see the place where He was lying. Go quickly and tell His disciples that He has risen from the dead; and behold, He is going ahead of you into Galilee, there you will see Him; behold, I have told you." And they left the tomb quickly with fear and great joy and ran to report it to His disciples.

MATTHEW 28:1-8

God also sent an earthquake to wake up Roman government officials who were persecuting the believers and to draw one of them to Christ.

But about midnight Paul and Silas were praying and singing hymns of praise to God, and the prisoners were listening to them; and suddenly there came a great earthquake, so that the foundations of the prison house were shaken; and immediately all the doors were opened and everyone's chains were unfastened. When the jailer awoke and saw the prison doors opened, he drew his sword and was about to kill himself, supposing that the prisoners had escaped. But Paul cried out with a loud voice, saying, "Do not harm yourself, for we are all here!" And he called for lights and rushed in, and trembling with fear he fell down before Paul and Silas, and after he brought them out, he said, "Sirs, what must I do to be saved?" They said, "Believe in the Lord Jesus, and you will be saved, you and your household." And they spoke the word of the Lord to

him together with all who were in his house. And he took
them that very hour of the night and washed their wounds,
and immediately he was baptized, he and all his household.
And he brought them into his house and set food before
them, and rejoiced greatly, having believed in God with his
whole household.

ACTS 16:25-34

Second, God uses earthquakes to judge those who reject him.
John Wesley preached a sermon in the mid-1700s titled "The Cause
and Cure of Earthquakes." In it he argued that "of all the judgments
which the righteous God inflicts on sinners here, the most dreadful
and destructive is an earthquake. . . . Earthquakes are set forth by
the inspired writers as God's proper judicial act, or the punishment
of sin: sin is the cause, earthquakes the effect, of his anger. . . . Now,
that God is himself the Author, and sin the moral cause, of earthquakes . . . cannot be denied by any who believe the Scriptures."
Wesley argued that "God waits to see what effect his warnings will
have upon you."[6]

Wesley drew his case from the Bible. Consider these passages:

- "Thus I will punish the world for its evil and the wicked
  for their iniquity. . . . Therefore I will make the heavens
  tremble, and the earth will be shaken from its place at the
  fury of the LORD of hosts in the day of His burning anger"
  (Isaiah 13:11-13).
- "From the LORD of hosts you will be punished with thunder
  and earthquake and loud noise, with whirlwind and tempest
  and the flame of a consuming fire" (Isaiah 29:6).
- "And in that hour there was a great earthquake, and a tenth
  of the city fell; seven thousand people were killed in the
  earthquake, and the rest were terrified and gave glory to the
  God of heaven" (Revelation 11:13).

Experiencing an Earthquake

Might God decide to humble America through a series of devastating earthquakes? It is a very real possibility.

Having lived on the East Coast of the United States all my life—upstate and central New York and the Washington, DC, area—I have never had any anxiety or fear about earthquakes like some folks on the West Coast have. Indeed, the first earthquake I ever experienced was the 5.8-magnitude quake that occurred in August 2011, while I was writing this book.

At first I thought our four sons were wrestling so hard that they were shaking the house. In fact, I was just in the process of shouting upstairs to them, "Hey, what in the world are you guys doing that's making the house shake so much?" when food started falling out of the pantry and pictures tumbled off the walls and my young nieces who were visiting began screaming. Suddenly, we realized what was happening and gathered in the center of our home, away from any windows or things that could fall on us, and prayed. After about a minute, it was all over, and we thanked the Lord that it really wasn't so bad after all.

The earthquake—whose epicenter was in rural southern Virginia—shook DC and New York City and was felt in twenty-two states. It briefly interrupted cell phone coverage in spots along the eastern seaboard, triggered evacuations of the White House, the Capitol Building, and the Pentagon, and closed many schools. The quake caused several cracks in the Washington Monument and other minor damage but—again by God's grace—no serious injuries or fatalities. News reports called the quake "rare"[7] and "significant."[8] It certainly was. *National Geographic* reported that "before this latest quake . . . the largest earthquake on record in central Virginia was a magnitude-4.8 [quake] that occurred in 1875, according to the U.S. Geological Survey."[9]

Curiously, on the same day, the *New York Times* ran this headline: "Rare Strong Earthquake Hits Colorado." "The largest natural earthquake in Colorado in more than a century struck Monday night in the state's southeast corner," the *Times* reported. "The last known natural event of comparable size was an earthquake in 1882 in what is now Rocky Mountain National Park."[10]

I was grateful the effects of both were so mild, but I couldn't help but wonder what would have happened if either of these earthquakes had had its epicenter not in a rural area but under a major American city.

Fearing the "Big One"

Americans living on the West Coast, in particular, fear the "Big One"—an enormous, even apocalyptic, earthquake that would devastate life and property on a scale previously unimagined.

In January 2010, CBS *Evening News* ran a story headlined "Haiti Revives Fears of 'Big One' in Calif." The story noted that "the fault under Haiti is the same type as the San Andreas fault—the 800-mile-long scar slicing through California. Pressure has been building in the southern end near Los Angeles for more than 300 years. Scientists say the so-called 'Big One' here is not a matter of if, but when."[11]

In March 2010, *USA Today* ran this headline: "Chilean Earthquake Hints at Dangers of 'Big One' for USA." "One of the really 'Big Ones' to shake the United States was a magnitude-9.0 earthquake along the Pacific Northwest coast more than 300 years ago, before the arrival of huge numbers of people and development, that sent a catastrophic tsunami to Japan," the article reported. "Were something like that 1700 quake to occur today—and it certainly could, seismologists say—enormous destruction and loss of life would result in a region that is home now to big cities and millions of people. The magnitude-8.8 earthquake that rocked Chile and sent tsunami fears across the Pacific on Saturday—nearly seven weeks after the enormously deadly quake that destroyed parts of Haiti—serves as a vivid reminder of the perils posed to the United States by countless fault lines and shifting plates. 'It's not a matter of if, only of when an event like this strikes the people of the United States,' says Marcia McNutt, director of the U.S. Geological Survey. 'Shame on us if we don't prepare.'"[12]

Such fears are grounded in historic reality. In 1906, a powerful earthquake rocked San Francisco, California, and triggered a horrendous fire. The quake—which some scientists say was magnitude 7.7; others say it hit 8.3 on the Richter scale—was felt from Oregon to Nevada. The damage was extensive. An estimated three thousand people were killed, some 28,000 buildings were destroyed, and nearly a quarter of a million people were made homeless. The cost of rebuilding topped $400 million, an enormous sum at the time.[13]

What if the same quake occurred in San Francisco this year or next? "The 'Great 1906 San Francisco Earthquake' is one of the strongest ever recorded on the North American continent," noted a group of earthquake experts at the California Institute of Technology. "If a similar earthquake occurred in northern California today, after many decades of rapid urban growth, thousands of people would likely be killed and economic losses might be in the hundreds of billions of dollars. Such an event would easily be the worst natural disaster in the nation's history."[14]

What Is the Probability of a Catastrophic Earthquake?

Just how likely is it that such a devastating quake will happen in northern California again? "Because of extensive urban development in northern California since 1906, the strong earthquakes expected in the coming decades may be very destructive," the CIT scientists wrote. "For example, a magnitude-7 earthquake occurring today on the Hayward Fault (a part of the San Andreas Fault system, along the densely populated eastern side of San Francisco Bay) would likely cause hundreds of deaths and almost $100 billion of damage. In 1999, the USGS reported that there is a 70 percent chance that one or more quakes of about magnitude 6.7 or larger will occur in the San Francisco Bay area before the year 2030."[15]

Residents of Southern California also fear the "Big One." They experience small and moderate quakes rather frequently, but in 1994, a 6.7-magnitude quake rocked the Northridge area of Los Angeles, killing fifty-seven people, injuring thousands, and doing between $20 billion and $40 billion worth of damage.[16]

Could something worse be coming? Unfortunately, the experts say yes. A well-respected 2007 study known as the Uniform California Earthquake Rupture Forecast offered dismal news—it found that "powerful quakes . . . are inevitable in California's future." According to the U.S. Geological Survey, the federal government's main earthquake research and tracking agency, "In a new comprehensive study, scientists have determined that the chance of having one or more magnitude-6.7 or larger earthquakes in the California area over the next 30 years is greater than 99 percent." That, in scientific terms, is essential certainty. "Such quakes can be deadly, as shown by the 1989 magnitude-6.9 Loma Prieta and the 1994 magnitude-6.7 Northridge earthquakes. The likelihood of at least one even more powerful quake of magnitude 7.5 or greater in the next 30 years is 46 percent—such a quake is most likely to occur in the southern half of the state. Building codes, earthquake insurance, and emergency planning will be affected by these new results, which highlight the urgency to prepare now for the powerful quakes that are inevitable in California's future."[17]

Killer Quakes Threaten Supercities

A 2003 article in *National Geographic* warned that urbanization is making the world more vulnerable to catastrophic earthquakes. As more people move to cities and more buildings are erected closer together, the probability of great destruction increases. The article noted that some of the world's largest "supercities" of 2 million or more people—including major American cities—are becoming extremely vulnerable to extinction-level events.

"Unless protective measures are taken, once every century or so when the earth trembles in a violent release of pent-up tension, buildings will tumble, streets will buckle, and pipelines will snap, leaving upwards of a million people crushed beneath the debris," noted reporter John Roach, referencing the research of Roger Bilham, a geological scientist at the University of Colorado at Boulder.[18]

Other scientists around the world share this view. "As population grows, and it is growing in earthquake-prone regions, we are susceptible to large earthquakes causing huge numbers of fatalities," said Andy Michael, a geologist with the U.S. Geological Survey's Western Earthquakes Hazard Team in Menlo Park, California, in an interview with *National Geographic*.[19]

"People do not like to think in terms of an earthquake disaster of one million fatalities. Nevertheless, I am convinced this is possible," Max Wyss, director of the World Agency of Planetary Monitoring and Earthquake Risk Reduction in Geneva, Switzerland, was quoted in the article as saying.[20]

Perhaps the big question, however, is not whether merely one such catastrophic quake could hit one major American city but whether the U.S. could be hit with multiple "killer quakes."

The Threat of Tsunamis

Recent devastating tsunamis in Asia and India left untold destruction and stunned and saddened people all over the world. Could such events ever happen here in the U.S.? Bible prophecy certainly warns us to be watching for such disasters in the last days. In fact, the Lord Jesus himself said in Luke 21:25 that prior to his return, there will be "dismay among nations, in perplexity at the roaring of the sea and the waves."

Consider, then, this disturbing headline from a 2005 article in *National Geographic*: "Tsunamis More Likely to Hit U.S. than Asia."[21] Scientists believe that tsunamis resulting from major earthquakes in the Pacific Ocean are actually more likely to reach the United States than the Asian continent, and Americans living along that coast would have precious little time to get to safety if a cataclysmic event occurred.

"If a magnitude-9 earthquake were to strike in the Pacific Northwest and generate a tsunami, we'd have less than 15 minutes' warning [before it hit the shore]," said Robert Yeats, a professor emeritus of geosciences at Oregon State University in Corvallis.[22]

Obviously, major tsunamis are rare along the Pacific Coast of the United States, but they have happened. "A 1946 Aleutian quake, which generated a tsunami that struck Hawaii, and the 1964 Alaska event led the United States to establish a federal tsunami-monitoring system, managed by the National Oceanic and Atmospheric Administration," *National Geographic* reported. "Today six deep-ocean monitors, located from Alaska's Aleutian Islands to the middle of the Pacific Ocean, watch for patterns that could hint at an earthquake or landslide capable of generating a tsunami. A recorder's readings are beamed up to a buoy and relayed to NOAA's network of weather satellites. The satellite data is analyzed at NOAA's tsunami warning centers in Hawaii and Alaska, which issue alerts to emergency officials and the U.S. military in the event of a tsunami."[23]

Is it possible, then, that a series of massive, unprecedented earthquakes or tsunamis could level American cities, kill hundreds of thousands or even millions of people, and cause such extensive damage that the U.S. would be hard-pressed to recover emotionally or economically? Given that Bible prophecy tells us massive earthquakes are coming, one cannot rule out the possibility of the U.S. being neutralized by them.

The Threat of Hurricanes

Hurricanes along the East Coast and Gulf Coast also pose grave dangers for us.

While I was writing this book, Hurricane Irene swept the East Coast of the United States in August 2011, causing the largest evacuation in American history as millions of Americans fled the storm's path.[24] When Irene hit, some 5 million Americans were left without power.[25] Thousands of homes and businesses were damaged or destroyed, and dozens of people lost their lives. Irene became one of the top ten costliest hurricanes in American history.[26] Yet it could have been much worse. At its peak, Hurricane Irene was about six hundred miles wide, or about the size of the state of Texas.[27] Had it remained a category 3 storm—or even increased in intensity—it could have created the greatest natural disaster catastrophe in the history of the United States.

Fortunately, that's not what happened. The storm lost speed and power as it approached land, and by the time it reached New York City, most of its "teeth" had been removed. As the cleanup began, critics said the storm was hyped up and overblown by government officials and weather forecasters. But did the experts really badly misjudge Irene, or did God hear people's prayers and have mercy on us by weakening the storm faster than the experts had predicted? I think both are true. I am grateful to the Lord for his grace and mercy on us.

But what if God had not been so gracious? What if rather than shaking us and waking us up to what he could do, he actually let us experience what other nations around the world have experienced?

What if a Hurricane Hit New York City?

As Hurricane Irene was approaching, the *New York Times* noted that "tropical cyclones in and around New York City and the northeastern United States are fairly rare but not unprecedented" and that since 1900, at least twenty such serious storms "have made landfall north of the Mason-Dixon line with tropical-storm-force winds (at least 39 miles per hour) or higher, twelve of which made direct hits on either Long Island or New Jersey."[28]

The *Times* then offered a sobering analysis by hurricane experts of some worst-case scenarios. Reporter Nick Silver wrote that a hurricane that hit Manhattan at its full category 2 storm strength would likely flood New York's subway system, flood homes and businesses in neighborhoods throughout the city, and cause $35 billion in damage, which the story noted is "equivalent to roughly half of New York City's annual budget."[29]

"It is theoretically possible that an even stronger storm might hit the city at some point in the future," Silver added. "A category 3 hurricane, one with wind speeds of 111 miles per hour or higher, could plausibly produce an economic impact in excess of $100 billion if its eye were to pass directly over Manhattan." A stronger category 3 storm, Silver reported, "could rival or exceed the roughly $235 billion in economic damage estimated to have been caused by the Japanese earthquake and tsunami. What happens beyond that gets into highly speculative territory: in recorded history, no storm has made landfall in the northeastern United States while stronger than a category 3."[30]

Silver reported that "meteorologists debate whether a category 4 storm hitting New York is literally physically impossible, so unlikely as to be practically impossible, or a plausible occurrence but one that will happen less than once in a generation." But he wrote that "if such a storm were to occur, it would be exceptionally devastating to New York City, and its economic effects would plausibly run into the trillions of dollars, tantamount to the estimates that some scholars have provided of a Tohoku-strength earthquake striking directly under Tokyo (something that almost certainly is physically possible)."[31]

Specifically, a category 4 direct hit on Manhattan could do $2 trillion to $6 trillion dollars in damage. What's more, since New York's annual gross domestic product is roughly 10 percent of the nation's

GDP, "if much of the city were to become dysfunctional for months or more, the damage to the global and domestic economies would be almost incalculable."[32]

Are Other Parts of the U.S. at Risk?

Is it really possible that American cities could be wiped out—or nearly wiped out—by direct hits from major hurricanes? Before Hurricane Katrina, few could have even imagined such a horrific scenario. Now anything seems possible.

Seven of the deadliest hurricanes in American history have occurred in the past twenty-five years, according to the National Hurricane Center (NHC), run by the federal government's National Oceanic and Atmospheric Administration (NOAA). Two-thirds of the costliest hurricanes occurred during the same period.[33]

An August 2011 report by the agency warned that the NHC has "repeatedly emphasized the great danger of a catastrophic loss of life in a future hurricane if proper preparedness plans for vulnerable areas are not formulated, maintained, and executed." The study showed that "85 percent of U.S. coastal residents from Texas to Maine had never experienced a direct hit by a major hurricane," and that now "an estimated 50 million residents have moved to coastal sections during the past twenty-five years" and are in jeopardy of the next major storms.[34]

None of us can know precisely what the future holds. But the experts are warning that some of history's worst hurricanes have happened quite recently, raising the possibility that even worse is still ahead. During the course of my research, for example, one piece of data really caught my attention and, I have to admit, unnerved me. "The biggest hurricane ever recorded was Typhoon Tip," reported a website called Live Science, noting that hurricanes in the western Pacific Ocean are called typhoons. "The 1979 storm, which made landfall in southern Japan, was nearly 1,400 miles wide at one point. That's almost half the size of the continental United States."[35]

Could that ever happen here? I wondered. Is it possible that a hurricane half the size of the U.S. could hit the continent—and do so at a category 3, 4, or 5 intensity? Could we recover from such a disaster? Such an apocalyptic event might neutralize America for years to come.

"Weather historians who have studied the cycles of Atlantic hurricanes said such a massive storm so far north was long overdue," noted a story in the *Wall Street Journal* as Hurricane Irene made landfall. "As a fading hurricane, it was the first major storm to cross Long Island since 1991. If the historical pattern holds true, the northeastern U.S. can expect even stronger hurricanes soon."[36]

Hurricane scholar Richard Schwartz in Alexandria, Virginia, author of *Hurricanes and the Middle Atlantic States*, told the *Journal*, "Irene wasn't a fluke, and we are due for worse." Schwartz, who has analyzed hurricanes dating back to the 1600s, added that "we have been in an active hurricane cycle that began in 1995. It is amazing that there has not been a hurricane like Irene or worse coming into the New York area in all that time."[37]

The Threat of Volcanoes

The first time I ever recall hearing of a volcano erupting in the United States was in 1980, when I was thirteen years old and Mount St. Helens in Washington State erupted. Back then, I didn't really look closely at what happened. After all, I was growing up in upstate New York, on the other side of the country, and this was before the days of cable news and Google. When I eventually looked into that eruption, however, I was stunned by the destructive impact of that fateful day.

An article on a U.S. government website offers the following description:

Shaken by an earthquake measuring 5.1 on the Richter scale, the north face of this tall, symmetrical mountain collapsed in a massive rock debris avalanche. In a few moments this slab of rock and ice slammed into Spirit Lake, crossed a ridge 1,300 feet high, and roared fourteen miles down the Toutle River. The avalanche rapidly released pressurized gases within the volcano. A tremendous lateral explosion ripped through the avalanche and developed into a turbulent, stone-filled wind that swept over ridges and toppled trees. Nearly 150 square miles of forest was blown over or left dead and standing. At the same time a mushroom-shaped column of ash rose thousands of feet skyward and drifted downwind, turning day into night as dark, gray ash fell over eastern Washington and beyond. Wet, cement-like slurries of rock and mud scoured all sides of the volcano. Searing flows of pumice poured from the crater. The eruption lasted nine hours, but Mount St. Helens and the surrounding landscape were dramatically changed within moments.[38]

Though most people in the area had been evacuated, fifty-seven people lost their lives. Prior to Mount St. Helens, only two people in American history had died from volcanic eruptions. According to the U.S. Geological Survey, more than two hundred houses and cabins were destroyed, as were 185 miles of roads and fifteen miles of railways. "Many tens of thousands of acres of prime forest, as well as recreational sites, bridges, roads, and trails, were destroyed or heavily damaged."[39]

Could volcanoes in the future pose even more serious threats to life as we know it in the United States? Apparently, they could.

Consider this MSNBC headline from the summer of 2011: "Keeping an Eye on Yellowstone's Supervolcano: When Next 'Big One' Will Be Is Anyone's Guess—But You Don't Want to Be Here." The story begins:

It's no mere doomsday pseudoscience: The Yellowstone supervolcano really could be the end of us all. When the Yellowstone Caldera—the name of the national park's geographic structure, which roughly translates as *cauldron*—blows its lid, much of the continental United States will get covered in a blanket of ash. That ash will clog the atmosphere enough to block out the sun, disrupting the global climate enough to cause mass extinctions.[40]

Consider, too, this headline from the London *Daily Mail* in the winter of 2011: "Could Yellowstone National Park's Caldera Super-Volcano Be Close to Eruption?" The article paints a bleak picture:

Scientists are predicting that the world's largest supervolcano in one of America's most popular national parks could erupt in the near future. Yellowstone National Park's caldera has erupted three times in the last 2.1 million years, and researchers monitoring it say we could be in for another eruption. They said that the supervolcano underneath the Wyoming park has been rising at a record rate since 2004—its floor has gone up three inches per year for the last three years alone, the fastest rate since records began in 1923. It would explode with a force a thousand times more powerful than the Mount St. Helens eruption in 1980. Spewing lava far into the sky, a cloud of plant-killing ash would fan out and dump a layer ten feet deep up to 1,000 miles away. Two-thirds of the U.S. could become uninhabitable as toxic air sweeps through it, grounding thousands of flights and forcing millions to leave their homes. But hampered by a lack of data, they have stopped short of an all-out warning, and they are unable to put a date on when the next disaster might take place. When the eruption finally happens, it will dwarf the effect of Iceland's Eyjafjallajökull volcano, which erupted in April last year, causing travel chaos around the world.[41]

Is this all just media hyperbole? It certainly sounds like it at first. However, such reports are actually backed up by scientists working for the federal government. According to the U.S. Geological Survey, "the term *supervolcano* implies an eruption of magnitude 8 on the Volcano Explosivity Index, meaning that more than 1,000 cubic kilometers (240 cubic miles) of magma (partially molten rock) are erupted." Such a giant eruption, these government scientists say, "would have regional effects such as falling ash and short-term (years to decades) changes to global climate. The surrounding states of Montana, Idaho, and Wyoming would be affected, as well as other places in the United States and the world."[42]

In fact, federal scientists and geologists say that "if another large caldera-forming eruption were to occur at Yellowstone, its effects would be worldwide. Thick ash deposits would bury vast areas of the United States, and injection of huge volumes of volcanic gases into the atmosphere could drastically affect global climate," dramatically altering life in this country as we have known it.[43]

Bottom Line

While the Bible doesn't specifically tell us which natural disasters will hit which countries in the last days, Scripture clearly warns us that a wide range of game-changing, life-altering disasters will occur with growing frequency and intensity as we get closer to the return of Jesus Christ. We can currently see "historic," "rare," and "unprecedented" disasters happening with growing frequency around the world and here in the United States. Furthermore, scientists say we are due for even more powerful and cataclysmic disasters.

Can we say with certainty that America will be neutralized by such natural disasters and thus unable or unwilling to play a key role in events prophesied in the Bible? No, we cannot go that far; the Bible doesn't give us that level of specificity. However, based on the general direction of Bible prophecies, we unfortunately cannot rule out such a possibility.

CHAPTER TWELVE

THE RAPTURE SCENARIO

UP TO NOW, we have been examining bleak scenarios by which the United States could implode or become neutralized and thus unable or unwilling to be a powerful and influential nation in the last days as key Bible prophecies come to pass. In this chapter, we will change perspectives and look at a radically different possibility.

This is the Rapture scenario. The Bible describes a remarkable event that will take place during the last days. This biblical event is the sudden "catching away" of the followers of Jesus Christ, something Bible scholars call the Rapture. It is this amazing event that captured the imagination of millions around the world when Tim LaHaye and Jerry B. Jenkins wrote their biblically based Left Behind series of novels, selling more than 65 million copies in the process. The novels tried to depict what it would feel like if those in the world who follow Jesus suddenly disappeared "in the twinkling of an eye." But Christians' understanding of the Rapture predates the writings of

LaHaye and Jenkins by nearly two thousand years. This is, therefore, a scenario worthy of closer consideration.

While the Bible does not indicate precisely when the Rapture will happen, it does teach that all true followers of Jesus Christ will be removed from the earth prior to the beginning of the Tribulation. Because God has not chosen believers to suffer the wrath of the Tribulation, people who have received Christ as their Savior and Lord prior to the Rapture will thus be rescued from the worst of the persecution, wars, natural disasters, and judgments that the book of Revelation, the book of Daniel, and other Scriptures explain will occur during the seven years leading up to the Day of the Lord. People who are not born-again believers in Christ at the moment of the Rapture will remain on the earth. If a person honestly and genuinely repents of his or her sins and receives Christ as his or her personal Savior and Lord at any point during the Tribulation, that person will without a doubt be forgiven of all sin, be regenerated by the Holy Spirit of God, and be saved from ultimate judgment. This is God's grace and mercy, and it will be available even after the Rapture, though the Bible indicates that such new believers will still have to endure the terrors that will occur on the earth during that time. Many will face martyrdom. Only those who are believers before the Rapture will be saved both spiritually *and* physically from the wrath to come.

While we cannot preclude the possibility that the U.S. could implode before the Rapture happens, the Bible tells believers to comfort one another with the certain knowledge that as bad as events get on earth, people who trust Christ before the Rapture will be spared from the worst that the prophecies tell us is coming. In this chapter, we will look specifically at the implications for America if the Rapture were to happen in the near future.

First, however, we need to define our terms.

What Does the Word Rapture *Mean?*

The most famous passage describing what theologians refer to as the Rapture is found in 1 Thessalonians 4:13-18. The apostle Paul writes:

> But we do not want you to be uninformed, brethren, about those who are asleep, so that you will not grieve as do the rest who have no hope. For if we believe that Jesus died and rose again, even so God will bring with Him those who have fallen asleep in Jesus. For this we say to you by the word of the Lord, that we who are alive and remain until the coming of the Lord, will not precede those who have fallen asleep. For the Lord Himself will descend from heaven with a shout, with the voice of the archangel and with the trumpet of God, and the dead in Christ will rise first. Then we who are alive and remain will be caught up together with them in the clouds to meet the Lord in the air, and so we shall always be with the Lord. Therefore comfort one another with these words.

While the word *rapture* does not appear in modern English translations of the Bible, the concept is rooted in Scripture. The word itself comes from the Vulgate, the Latin translation of the Bible. In 1 Thessalonians 4:17 in the Vulgate, the Greek word *harpazō* is translated *rapturo* or *raeptius*, which means "to seize, carry off by force; to seize on, claim for one's self eagerly; or to snatch out or away."[1] Most English translations of the Bible—including the King James Version, the New King James Version, the New American Standard Bible, and the New International Version—have, therefore, translated the word *harpazō* as "caught up." But English-speaking Bible scholars who studied the Latin Vulgate decided the word *rapture* was a useful and suitable term to express the scriptural concept of believers being suddenly removed from the world.

If "you happened to pick up a copy of the Latin Vulgate at a garage sale, produced by Jerome in the early 400s, you would indeed find the word *rapture*," Bible scholars Mark Hitchcock and Thomas Ice have noted. "The Vulgate was the main Bible of the medieval Western church until the Reformation. It continues to this day as the primary Latin translation of the Roman Catholic church. . . . It should not be surprising to anyone that an English word in regular use today was developed from the Latin. That word, of course, is *rapture*."[2]

How Does the Bible Describe the Rapture?

In 1 Thessalonians 4:13-18 we find significant and important clues about the Rapture. Among them:

- God does not want believers to be ignorant or "uninformed" about the last days or the Rapture like people who "have no hope" (v. 13).
- Rather, the Lord wants believers to be aware, ready, and expectant for "those who have fallen asleep in Jesus" (born-again believers who have physically died) to be resurrected in the last days—indeed, "the dead in Christ will rise first" (vv. 14, 16).
- The Lord also wants believers who are still alive in the last days to be aware, ready, and expectant for the fact that we will be united with the Lord Jesus Christ and with resurrected believers during the Rapture (vv. 15-16).
- During the Rapture, the Lord Jesus Christ will descend from heaven with a shout, with the archangel of God and the sound of the trumpet of God (v. 16).
- During the Rapture, as the Lord descends from heaven, believers will be caught up or snatched up from earth to meet the Lord in the air (v. 17).

- Unlike the Second Coming, Christ does not come all the way down to earth during the Rapture. He only comes down partway to meet us and take us to heaven, where we will remain with him until we join him at the Second Coming. The key, the Scriptures tell us, is that "we shall always be with the Lord." Christ will never leave nor forsake us. To the contrary, we will always be at his side and worshiping him for who he is and what he has done for us (v. 17).
- The Rapture should be a comfort to believers because it will be a supreme act of God's grace (unmerited favor) and his love and mercy as he rescues them out of the traumas of the age from the even-more-horrific traumas to come during the Tribulation (v. 18).

We learn more important details about the Rapture in the apostle Paul's next chapter to the church in Thessalonica. Consider these verses from 1 Thessalonians 5:1-11:

Now as to the times and the epochs, brethren, you have no need of anything to be written to you. For you yourselves know full well that the day of the Lord will come just like a thief in the night. While they are saying, "Peace and safety!" then destruction will come upon them suddenly like labor pains upon a woman with child, and they will not escape. But you, brethren, are not in darkness, that the day would overtake you like a thief; for you are all sons of light and sons of day. We are not of night nor of darkness; so then let us not sleep as others do, but let us be alert and sober. For those who sleep do their sleeping at night, and those who get drunk get drunk at night. But since we are of the day, let us be sober, having put on the breastplate of faith and love, and as a helmet, the hope of salvation. For God has not destined

us for wrath, but for obtaining salvation through our
Lord Jesus Christ, who died for us, so that whether we are
awake or asleep, we will live together with Him. Therefore
encourage one another and build up one another, just as
you also are doing.

Notably, in this passage we learn that:

- The Lord isn't going to tell us the specific time when the
  Rapture will occur (v. 1). The day of the Lord's coming for us
  (different in this context from the final Day of the Lord, his
  judgment after seven years of wars and traumas) will be "just
  like a thief in the night"—that is, it will come at a time when
  unbelievers will be surprised because they are not paying
  attention (v. 2).
- When unbelievers are saying, "Peace and safety!" then the
  Rapture will occur, and destruction will follow—and all this
  will come upon the world "suddenly like labor pains upon a
  woman with child, and they will not escape" (v. 3).
- In describing these "labor pains," the apostle Paul echoes the
  words of the Lord Jesus when he explained in Matthew 24
  and Luke 21 that the world will be experiencing "birth pangs"
  in the last days (v. 3).
- Thus, while we don't know exactly when or how the Rapture
  will occur, it seems to come not specifically during a time of
  intense "contraction" (major wars, terrorist attacks, etc.), but
  during a time of "release," a time when things seem to the
  non-Christian world to be relatively more peaceful and safe
  than they had previously been (v. 3).
- This means the Rapture cannot take place during the
  Tribulation, because no one in their right mind could possibly
  describe any moment during that seven-year period of

apocalyptic wars and natural disasters and persecution and divine judgment as a time of "peace and safety" (v. 3).

- Believers are not supposed to be caught off guard by the Rapture but are to remain "alert and sober" (vv. 4-8).
- The truth of the Rapture is meant to encourage believers. The apostle Paul, after all, tells us that because we know the Rapture will occur and the true church will be rescued and removed from the world before the Tribulation begins and the Antichrist emerges and conquers the world, we are to "encourage one another and build up one another" (v. 11).

Do Other Scriptures Shed Light on the Rapture?

Do other New Testament passages shed more light on the Rapture? Yes, they do. The apostle John gives us additional details in his Gospel account, and the apostle Paul provides more information in his first letter to the church in Corinth as well as in the first chapter of 1 Thessalonians. We also see evidence of the Rapture in the book of Revelation.

In John 14:1-6, the Lord Jesus, in a conversation with his disciples, said:

"Do not let your heart be troubled; believe in God, believe also in Me. In My Father's house are many dwelling places; if it were not so, I would have told you; for I go to prepare a place for you. If I go and prepare a place for you, I will come again and receive you to Myself, that where I am, there you may be also. And you know the way where I am going."

Thomas said to Him, "Lord, we do not know where You are going, how do we know the way?"

Jesus said to him, "I am the way, and the truth, and the life; no one comes to the Father but through Me."

Here, Christ promised to leave earth to prepare heaven for our arrival. Then he promised to come back from heaven to get us and take us to heaven. Therefore, we are not to worry or let our hearts be troubled, because he will eventually come and rescue his church from the troubles of this world.

In 1 Corinthians 15:51-52, the apostle Paul writes, "Behold, I tell you a mystery; we will not all sleep, but we will all be changed, in a moment, in the twinkling of an eye, at the last trumpet; for the trumpet will sound, and the dead will be raised imperishable, and we will be changed."

When Paul says "we will not all sleep," he means not all believers will physically die. We will "all be changed"—that is, all believers will be spiritually transformed. Some will die physically but will be resurrected from the dead and given new, immortal bodies. Others will not die physically but will be "changed" during the Rapture and given new, immortal bodies.

In 1 Thessalonians 1:9-10, the apostle Paul explains that believers will be rescued from the coming wrath of the Tribulation, explaining that we serve "a living and true God" and that we currently "wait for His Son from heaven, whom He raised from the dead, that is Jesus, who rescues us from the wrath to come."

The book of Revelation gives us interesting clues about the Rapture as well. In Revelation 3:10, the Lord Jesus reinforces his promise to remove those who are faithful to him from the wrath of the Tribulation when he says, "Because you have kept the word of My perseverance, I also will keep you from the hour of testing, that hour which is about to come upon the whole world, to test those who dwell on the earth."

Notably, the word *church* or *churches* is mentioned eighteen times in the first three chapters of Revelation. The apostle John is being told by the Lord to give his messages to a range of different types of church congregations, some who are walking very faithfully with the

Lord, but most of whom (five out of seven) are being told to repent or face judgment. Then a striking turning point occurs.

Suddenly, as chapter 4 begins, the apostle John is no longer focused on the churches. Rather, he is caught up to heaven and sees events unfolding from the perspective of heaven. "After these things I looked, and behold, a door standing open in heaven, and the first voice which I had heard, like the sound of a trumpet speaking with me, said, 'Come up here, and I will show you what must take place after these things.' Immediately I was in the Spirit; and behold, a throne was standing in heaven, and One sitting on the throne" (4:1-2).

The word *wrath* is mentioned eleven times in the book of Revelation to describe the events during the Tribulation. One of the main reasons for the Rapture, the apostle Paul tells us, is to remove the church from the wrath to come during the Tribulation. "For God has not destined us for wrath, but for obtaining salvation through our Lord Jesus Christ" (1 Thessalonians 5:9).

Remarkably, beginning in Revelation chapter 4, neither the word *church* nor *churches* is used during any of the descriptions of Tribulation events in the next eighteen chapters. Only in the final chapter of the book of Revelation, when all the events of the End Times have been described, does the Lord turn his attention back to the existing churches on earth and say, "I, Jesus, have sent My angel to testify to you these things for the churches" (Revelation 22:16). The fact that churches are referred to so frequently at the beginning of the book and then not again until the last chapter is because the church—the institution as we have known her for the past twenty centuries—is not a factor during the events of the Tribulation. People are still coming to faith in Christ, but they are not operating as the church during that time. Rather, the church has been removed, snatched away, caught up, or raptured prior to the Tribulation.

Examples in the Bible of People Who Were Raptured

One of the things that has intrigued me in the study of the Bible and prophecy—specifically the concept of the Rapture—is that the Lord has given us two examples of people who were raptured in the Old Testament. In a sense, they are examples or "prophetic pictures" of what is coming for all believers at a certain moment in the not-too-distant future.

In the book of Genesis, we learn about a righteous servant of the Lord named Enoch. The Bible tells us that "Enoch walked with God; and he was not, for God took him" (Genesis 5:24). In other words, Enoch obeyed the word of the Lord while living his physical life on earth, and then the Lord decided that rather than requiring Enoch to die physically before going to heaven, he would simply snatch Enoch away while he was still physically alive. The book of Hebrews confirms this interpretation. "By faith Enoch was taken up so that he would not see death; and he was not found because God took him up; for he obtained the witness that before his being taken up he was pleasing to God" (Hebrews 11:5). Think about that for a moment. The Lord was so pleased with Enoch that he made him the first example of a person raptured from the earth. Enoch, however, was not the last.

In the book of 2 Kings, we read about the Hebrew prophet Elijah. The Lord was so pleased with Elijah that he sent a chariot of fire to whisk the prophet away to heaven while he was still alive and walking alongside his young protégé, Elisha. "As they were going along and talking, behold, there appeared a chariot of fire and horses of fire which separated the two of them, and Elijah went up by a whirlwind to heaven. Elisha saw it and cried out, 'My father, my father, the chariots of Israel and its horsemen!' And he saw Elijah no more. Then he took hold of his own clothes and tore them in two pieces. He also took up the mantle of Elijah that fell from him and returned and stood by the bank of the Jordan" (2 Kings 2:11-13). The text goes on to tell us that fifty Israelites then proceeded to search for the living Elijah—or at least his dead body—for three full days, but they were unable to find him. Why? Because Elijah had not simply been moved to another location by the Lord. Elijah had not physically died. He had become the second person in the Bible to be raptured.

The Lord Jesus himself gives us the picture of another type of rapture. While the circumstances are not precisely the same as what the apostle Paul describes in 1 Thessalonians, they do shed some light on what the Rapture will be like. Christ, of course, was crucified, killed, and buried. Then he was raised from the dead on the third day, according to the Scriptures. After that, he spent time with the believers on earth. During that time, he had a real body, but it was a body that had been dramatically changed. For example, the Lord Jesus spoke, walked, ate, cooked, and traveled with those he loved. He had real flesh and blood, as he demonstrated to Doubting Thomas in John chapter 20. But he also appeared, disappeared, and walked through walls.

In Acts 1, Christ beautifully and amazingly demonstrated this type of rapture:

> And after He had said these things, He was lifted up while
> they were looking on, and a cloud received Him out of their
> sight. And as they were gazing intently into the sky while
> He was going, behold, two men in white clothing stood
> beside them. They also said, "Men of Galilee, why do you
> stand looking into the sky? This Jesus, who has been taken
> up from you into heaven, will come in just the same way
> as you have watched Him go into heaven."
> ACTS 1:9-11

Can you imagine that? One moment Jesus was talking to his disciples on the Mount of Olives. The next moment he was floating up to heaven through the clouds. Someday soon, believers will experience something very similar.

Not every Christian has studied these Scriptures about the Rapture, or understands them, or believes them. Nevertheless, the Bible teaches that every single person who has received the free gift of forgiveness and salvation through faith in Jesus Christ—and who is physically alive when the Lord decides the moment has come—will be caught up from the earth to meet Jesus in the air. What a glorious thing that will be. I hope it happens in my lifetime. I am really looking forward to it, as are my wife and children. We are eager to see the Lord Jesus face-to-face. We are excited about his return and amazed by these promises he has made us.

If the Lord had called the church to go through the Tribulation, then we would endure it willingly and for his glory. We would do so knowing that the Holy Spirit would give each of us the strength, the courage, the boldness, and the words to witness for Jesus Christ in the darkest hours of human history. After all, the Lord Jesus tells us what he told the apostle Paul: "My grace is sufficient for you, for power is perfected in weakness" (2 Corinthians 12:9). At the end of Matthew 28, Christ said, "All authority has been given to Me in heaven and on earth." Then He commanded us, "Go therefore and make disciples of all the nations, baptizing them in the name of the Father and the Son and the Holy Spirit, teaching them to observe all that I commanded you." And he promised, "I am with you always, even to the end of the age" (vv. 18-20). So we may be assured of his grace, mercy, love, and presence through all circumstances.

But the Lord didn't call believers to endure the Tribulation. Instead, he promised to remove the church before the wrath comes. For this we are grateful, and we want more believers to know and understand and be encouraged by these powerful promises.

The Rapture will be a great blessing for believers in the last days.

But there will be serious implications for all countries, including the United States.

What Will Happen to America after the Rapture?

As we have seen, when the Rapture occurs, every single American who is a born-again believer in Jesus Christ will suddenly disappear. This will cause enormous disorientation and disruption for all the unbelievers who are left behind as their lives suddenly change and they are forced to handle the aftermath and adapt to the new and rapidly shifting conditions.

Think of how dramatically life in the United States changed after we lost some three thousand Americans on September 11, 2001. First and foremost, the emotional impact was devastating. Then the way we travel changed. The way we conduct foreign policy changed. Our economy changed. Our government institutions changed. So many areas of life changed that it is difficult to adequately categorize them, much less catalog them.

Now try to imagine the U.S. losing a million people in the blink of an eye. Or 5 million people. Or 25 million people. Or more.

If you're riding in a car driven by a believer who suddenly disappears, that car very well could crash. If you're on a plane flown by believers who suddenly disappear, that plane also could crash. Highly valuable and experienced military commanders and business leaders and medical professionals will disappear, perhaps in the middle of critical projects or medical procedures. The impact will be catastrophic.

Consider, too, the emotional devastation for people who suddenly and irretrievably lose a spouse, children, parents, friends, colleagues, neighbors, and other loved ones. There will be no long illnesses during which one can get prepared, no dead bodies to identify, no human way to find closure. Consider the horror that will be experienced by millions of people who long described themselves as Christians but suddenly realize that they were not included in the Rapture, people who realize that they never actually received for themselves the free gift of forgiveness and salvation offered by Jesus Christ. Consider how sickened they will feel when they realize that despite having gone to church and perhaps having occasionally read the Bible and done good works and been "religious" in some way, they never really understood or accepted God's simple plan of salvation.

Consider, too, the terror felt by atheists and agnostics and people of other religions when they see their country and their world imploding and realize that their family members and friends who had been followers of Jesus Christ were right, and thus are gone, but that they themselves were left to face the wrath to come. Can such people fall on their knees the minute after the Rapture and receive Christ's free gift of salvation for themselves? Absolutely, and they should. If they do, the Bible teaches that their sins will be instantly forgiven and their souls saved forever. They can know without the shadow of a doubt that they are going to heaven when they die and will spend eternity with Christ Jesus, not in the lake of fire with no way of escape. But as wonderful and real and true as all that redemption will be, such people who receive Christ as their Savior and Lord after the Rapture will also be struck by the daunting realization that they and their remaining family members and friends and neighbors will have to endure previously unimaginable suffering in a country that will neither be nor seem like anything they have ever known, a country that has neither the strength nor the will to oppose the Antichrist or the persecution that is coming.

Imagine, too, the economic implications of the Rapture. If you think U.S. banks have a foreclosure problem now as millions of Americans cannot afford to pay their mortgages, imagine what will happen when millions of American homeowners suddenly disappear, never to make another mortgage payment again. What will happen when millions of business owners are suddenly no longer around to pay their bills? Or pay their employees? Or continue delivering vital goods and services? What will happen to the federal government when millions of taxpayers are no longer providing Washington much-needed revenues? What will happen to state governments? What will happen when nonprofit agencies and medical clinics and hospitals that care for the poor and needy here in the United States and are run by and funded by believers suddenly stop operating? What will happen when humanitarian relief organizations and adoption agencies and other charitable organizations that are run by and funded by believers in Jesus Christ stand empty? Those who sneer at Christianity and mock the do-gooders and the missionaries will suddenly realize how much of a blessing believers actually have been in the U.S. and around the world.

All of this traumatic change in the United States will be compounded by the fact that hundreds of millions of believers around the world—possibly a billion people or more—will have suddenly disappeared at the exact same moment. They will stop returning phone calls and e-mails. They will stop paying their bills and compensating their employees. They will stop being a force for good and hope in the world. They will simply be gone.

The foreign-policy implications for the U.S. must also be considered. With such an immediate, enormous, and unprecedented shock to American society and economy from the loss of millions of people, it is difficult to imagine how the U.S. could remain a superpower. How could we quickly replace all our Christian intelligence and foreign-policy officials who would suddenly be gone? How could we quickly replace all the officers and NCOs throughout the ranks of our military who are born-again believers? With all the resulting chaos and dislocation caused by the Rapture, how could the U.S. move rapidly and effectively to defend a threatened or invaded ally or defend our vital interests around the world? How could we defend our own homeland?

Are You Ready?

The question is not whether the Rapture will occur. The question is whether you will be spiritually ready to meet Jesus Christ face-to-face when it happens and be caught up in the air with him and all believers, or whether you will not be ready and have to remain on earth to face the wrath of the Tribulation.

If you're not 100 percent certain at this point in your life that your sins are forgiven, that your soul is saved, and that you will go to heaven whether you face natural death or the Rapture, then may I encourage you to read the following verses and receive Jesus Christ right now as your personal Savior and Lord?

- In John 3:3, the Lord Jesus told a religious leader who came to him seeking spiritual guidance, "Truly, truly, I say to you, unless one is born again he cannot see the kingdom of God." One's physical birth into a religious family, Jesus was saying, is not enough. Nor is being a very religious person. Nor even a religious leader. Something else has to happen on the inside. Thus, as you read the New Testament, it becomes clear that *born again* is a biblical term referring to a person who 1) is fully convinced that faith in Jesus Christ's death on the cross and resurrection from the dead is the only way to be forgiven of his sins and adopted into God's family; and 2) has consciously, willfully, and purposefully asked God through prayer to wash his sins away and save him through the death and resurrection of Jesus Christ.
- In John 1:12, we learn that "as many as received Him [Jesus Christ], to them He gave the right to become children of God."
- Jesus said in John 3:16 that "God so loved the world, that He gave His only begotten Son, that whoever believes in Him shall not perish, but have eternal life."

- In Romans 10:9-10, the apostle Paul explains how to be born again: "If you confess with your mouth Jesus as Lord, and believe in your heart that God raised Him from the dead, you will be saved; for with the heart a person believes, resulting in righteousness, and with the mouth he confesses, resulting in salvation."
- Then, in 2 Corinthians 5:17-18, Paul tells us the result of being born again: "If anyone is in Christ, he is a new creature; the old things passed away; behold, new things have come. Now all these things are from God, who reconciled us to Himself through Christ and gave us the ministry of reconciliation."
- In Revelation 3:20, Christ encourages you to make this decision immediately and not to refuse him or shut him out of your life any longer. "Behold, I [Jesus] stand at the door and knock; if anyone hears My voice and opens the door, I will come in to him and will dine with him, and he with Me."

Would you like to make that decision? You can receive Jesus Christ as your Savior and Lord right now. Here is a suggested prayer that has been helpful to many people all over the world—including my father and me—in becoming followers of Christ and in sharing the gospel with others. The key is not so much the precise words as the attitude of your heart.

Lord Jesus, thank you for loving me. Thank you for having a wonderful plan and purpose for my life. I need you today— I need you to forgive me for all of my sins. Thank you for dying on the cross to pay the penalty for my sins. Thank you for rising again from the dead and proving that you are the Way, the Truth, and the Life and the only way to get to heaven. I open the door of my heart and my life right now. I receive you as my Savior and Lord. Thank you for forgiving my sins and giving me eternal life. Please change my life. Please fill me with your Holy Spirit. Please take control of my life and make me the kind of person you want me to be so I can serve you and please you forever. Thank you so much. I love you, and I want to follow you. Amen.

If you just prayed with sincere faith in Christ's death and resurrection, then congratulations! You've just been adopted into God's family. Welcome! Let me give you a quick snapshot of seven wonderful things that have just happened.

1. **You have a new spiritual life.** The apostle Paul put it this way in 2 Corinthians 5:17: "Therefore if anyone is in Christ, he is a new creature; the old things passed away; behold, new things have come."

2. **You have made everyone in heaven happy.** According to the words of Jesus in Luke 15:10, there is great rejoicing in heaven because you have become a follower of the living God. "I tell you," Jesus said, "there is joy in the presence of the angels of God over one sinner who repents."

3. **You are going to heaven when you die or when the Rapture happens.** According to the words of Jesus in John 3:16, you now have eternal life. You will *not* go to hell and perish eternally when you die physically. Rather, you will go to heaven and live forever with God and with all those who have been adopted into his family through faith in Jesus Christ. In fact, the New Testament was written precisely to show people how to find eternal life through faith in Jesus Christ. As we read in 1 John 5:13, "These things I have written to you who believe in the name of the Son of God, so that you may know that you have eternal life."

God wants you to know beyond the shadow of a doubt that you are now forever safe in his family. Take confidence in his promises.

4. **You have the Holy Spirit living within you.** According to the words of the apostle Paul in Ephesians 1:13-14, your salvation has been sealed and secured forever by God's Holy Spirit, who now lives within you. "In Him [Jesus Christ], you also, after listening to the message of truth, the gospel of your salvation—having also believed, you were sealed in Him with the Holy Spirit of promise, who is given as a pledge of our inheritance, with a view to the redemption of God's own possession, to the praise of His glory."

5. **You have access to a supernatural source of peace.** According to Philippians 4:7, you now have access to a supernatural peace with God and internal peace of mind, regardless of whatever external circumstances come your way. "The peace of God, which surpasses all comprehension, will guard your hearts and your minds in Christ Jesus."

6. **You have access to a supernatural source of hope.** According to the words of Hebrews 6:18-19, all followers of Jesus Christ are encouraged to "take hold of the hope set before us" and to view "this hope we have as an anchor of the soul, a hope both sure and steadfast."

7. **You have access to God's supernatural wisdom.** According to James 1:5, "If any of you lacks wisdom, let him ask of God, who gives to all generously and without reproach, and it will be given to him."

Now, I strongly encourage you to find some people who also love Jesus and are his faithful followers and tell them what you have just done. Allow them to rejoice with you, and ask them to help you find a good, solid, Bible-believing and Bible-teaching church congregation where you can begin attending. Start asking the Lord for an older, wiser follower of Christ to begin discipling you—that is, to begin teaching you the Scriptures, answering your questions, praying with you, and encouraging you to actually put into practice in your life all that the Lord teaches us in the Bible.

I would also encourage you to choose three people who are not born again and tell them what you've just discovered about God's love and forgiveness and why you chose to receive Christ into your life and become his follower. Answer their questions as best you can. Perhaps give them a copy of this book to help them understand why you've made this decision. Better yet, find out if they have a Bible, and if they don't, offer to go to a bookstore and help them pick one out to begin studying and reading on their own. Now is not the time to keep the miracle that has just happened in your life to yourself—go tell people! And don't stop at three. Tell as many as will listen. Tell them lovingly and gently. Don't force it down their throats, of course. But don't be shy, either. They need to know these truths and make a choice one way or the other, just like you did.

Bottom Line

Not all Christians understand it or believe it, but the Bible teaches us that the Rapture is coming in the last days. And so it will.

The effect of the Rapture on the United States and other countries around the world will be far more devastating than the worst war or natural disaster in all of human history to date. With most of those wars came some degree of warning. Not so with the Rapture. The people who do not disappear will be stunned and horrified by the disappearance of so many others. What's more, if the United States economy and society have not imploded prior to this cataclysmic event, the Rapture itself will likely trigger the implosion.

America will be forever altered in the blink of an eye and from that moment forward will have no chance of recovering her former glory of freedom, peace, and prosperity.

The good news is that you don't have to go through the Tribulation. That's why it's essential that you pray to receive Jesus Christ as your Savior and Lord immediately, without delay, lest the Rapture come and you miss it.

Moreover, you don't want your family or friends or neighbors or colleagues to go through the Tribulation either. That's why it's essential that you begin sharing the gospel with them, answering their questions, and encouraging them to receive Christ right away.

Neither you nor I can stop the Rapture or the Tribulation or the traumas that are coming for America and the world. But we can be spiritually ready, and we can help others to be spiritually ready as well. What hope will we have if we do nothing while time is running out?

CHAPTER THIRTEEN

THE LAST BEST HOPE

★ ★ ★ ★ ★ ★ ★ ★ ★ ★ ★ ★ ★ ★ ★ ★ ★ ★ ★ ★

WE DON'T KNOW WHICH of the various scenarios we have explored will come to pass. Nor do we know *when* these events may occur. Perhaps a combination of scenarios will cause the United States to be unable or unwilling to engage in the major world events at the end of human history as described in the Bible. Only time will tell, but any of the possibilities we've discussed are plausible.

In the meantime, what should we do? How should we live? And how should we respond to the anxious cries of frightened people all around us?

As we have seen, the outlook in regard to our economic stability is bleak. Our national security is at risk. We have noted the ever more frequent and intense natural disasters in recent years. Are all these things the beginnings of the end? Or are they simply warnings? Is it possible that there may be another stretch of peace and strength for America? I certainly hope so.

I don't want to see America implode. To the contrary, I want to see this country revived and transformed by Christ's love and power and used by the Lord to bless other nations for many more years. I'm sure this is true of you as well. A country cannot recover or be revived, however, if her people are sleeping. And a nation is in even worse danger if the church is largely sleeping too. After all, the church is the institution ordained by God to be a light to the nations. While America isn't mentioned as a key player in the last days, the church certainly is. While some have called America the "last best hope" of a turbulent world, the truth is that the church is the "last best hope" of America. It is the church who is supposed to be Christ's instrument to bring hope and supernatural power and change to lost people and their nations. It is the church through whom Christ chooses to reveal that he alone has the ultimate answer for the ills that plague any nation. A weak church—one whose members give lip service to Jesus but are really spiritually asleep or intoxicated by the things of the world rather than walking in the light of God's Word and the power of the Holy Spirit—can provide little help to a weak nation in danger of imploding.

Yet this, I'm afraid, is where the U.S. is now. Alarm bells are going off all around us. Lights on the dashboard are flashing, *Warning! Warning!* Yet America is sleeping through the alarms, blind to the warning lights. And tragically, for the most part, the church—God's chosen instrument to bless individuals, families, communities, and nations—is asleep as well. I shudder to imagine where we are heading if we don't wake up soon, plead for the Lord's forgiveness, and ask him to use us to love our neighbors and revitalize our country.

The Wake-Up Call on 9/11

As I was working on this book, we as a nation marked the tenth anniversary of the horrific terror attacks on September 11, 2001. Clearly,

9/11 was a day that changed our country forever. I believe the Lord allowed evil to win a battle that day. Why? To shake us out of a stupor and open our eyes to realities we have long avoided.

Thousands of years ago, God told the prophet Haggai to write down these words: "For thus says the LORD of hosts, 'Once more in a little while, I am going to shake the heavens and the earth, the sea also and the dry land. I will shake all the nations. . . . I am going to shake the heavens and the earth. I will overthrow the thrones of kingdoms and destroy the power of the kingdoms of the nations'" (Haggai 2:6-7, 21-22).

This is Bible prophecy. This is an intercept from the mind of the all-knowing, all-seeing God of the universe. It is a weather report from the future, if you will, a storm warning. It was given to us so that we would be awake and ready and faithful and walking close to Jesus when the tempests come. God told us well in advance that he was going to "shake *all* the nations." That certainly includes the United States.

Do you remember where you were on September 11, 2001? Do you remember how you felt when you saw the Pentagon burning, the smoldering wreckage in Pennsylvania, the Twin Towers imploding? I'm sure you do. Not since Pearl Harbor had so many Americans been killed in a single attack. None of us will ever forget that day— nor should we.

God didn't cause the terrible events of 9/11 to happen. Radical Islamic jihadists caused the death and destruction of that day. Fanatics devoted to false teachings were responsible for what happened on 9/11. But the true and living God—the God of the Bible—let it happen to shake America, to get our attention. The tragedy of 9/11 was a wake-up call for America and particularly for the church.

On September 11, 2011—the tenth anniversary of the 9/11 attacks—I was invited to participate in a broadcast and webcast called *A Wake-Up Call* that was seen in all fifty states and in two hundred countries around the world and was heard live on more than five hundred radio stations throughout the U.S. The organizer was Anne Graham Lotz, the internationally renowned Bible teacher and daughter of the world-famous evangelist Billy Graham. Specifically, Anne asked me to shed some light on all the traumas that were going on in our country and around the world and to explain what they meant in the light of Bible prophecy. Given my wife's and my own deep concerns about the future of our country and the church, we were honored to accept Anne's invitation. You see, while the economic, political, and security failings of our country are deeply troubling, there is a much more insidious danger facing our country. It is a danger that threatens to make restoration and revival impossible. I am speaking of the spiritual blindness in America. This blindness is the cause of deep moral brokenness. And unfortunately, the church too often acts as though she either is blind herself or is unwilling to be the source of the only true light available to mankind.

I began my portion of the evening by asking some questions. "On this anniversary of 9/11, are you morally and spiritually better off than you were ten years ago? Is your family? Is your church? Now is an appropriate time to take a spiritual audit, to assess how you're doing morally and spiritually, how your family is doing, how your congregation is doing. Ten years ago, God shook us. The question is: Were we listening?"

These questions are as relevant today as they were then. I would encourage you to take some time right now and really think about your answers to these questions.

- Are you morally and spiritually better off than you were on 9/11?
- Is your family morally and spiritually better off?
- Is your church morally and spiritually better off?

The writer of the book of Hebrews implored his readers, "See to it that you do not refuse Him [Christ] who is speaking. For if those did not escape when they refused him who warned them on earth, much less will we escape who turn away from Him who warns from heaven. And His voice shook the earth then, but now He has promised, saying, 'Yet once more I will shake not only the earth, but also the heaven'" (Hebrews 12:25-26).

Our Lord Jesus Christ, while sitting with his disciples on the Mount of Olives in Jerusalem, also warned in Matthew 24 that we would be shaken in the last days leading up to his return. "The sun will be darkened, and the moon will not give its light, and the stars will fall from the sky, and the power of the heavens will be shaken," Jesus said. And then he added that when people least expect it, "the sign of the Son of Man will appear in the sky, and then all the tribes of the earth will mourn, and they will see the Son of Man coming on the clouds of the sky with power and great glory" (Matthew 24:29-30).

When God tells us to wake up, it isn't wise to hit the snooze button, much less to do so repeatedly. Yet isn't it fair to say that overall that's what America has done since 9/11?

The State of Our Culture

We need to take a long, hard look in the mirror. God is shaking us physically, with earthquakes and hurricanes and tornadoes and fires and droughts and floods. Our own mistakes and failures are causing us to be shaken financially, with the severe current economic downturn, our skyrocketing debt, and the even more severe debt crisis that looms just around the corner. Yet as serious as this all is, there is more.

Consider the state of our culture.

In 2012, America became a country of more than 312 million people, of whom more than 234 million are 18 years of age or older.[1]

What do we believe as a nation? What are our values? How are we living? Where are we heading? Sadly, it is not a pretty picture.

"Since 1960, our population has increased by 48 percent," William Bennett wrote in his book *The Index of Leading Cultural Indicators: American Society at the End of the Twentieth Century.* "But since 1960, even *taking into account* recent improvements, we have seen a 467 percent increase in violent crime; a 463 percent increase in the number of state and federal prisoners; a 461 percent increase in out-of-wedlock births; more than a 200 percent increase in the percentage of children living in single-parent homes; more than a doubling in the teen suicide rate; a more than 150 percent increase in the number of Americans receiving welfare payments; an almost tenfold increase in the number of cohabiting couples; a doubling of the divorce rate; and a drop of almost 60 points on SAT scores."[2]

Unfortunately, it gets worse. Consider abortion, for example. Only six in ten Americans (59 percent) believe that abortion ends a human life.[3] What's more, only half of all Americans (between 51 percent and 55 percent, depending on the poll) believe abortion is "morally wrong."[4] As a result, Americans have had more than 53 million abortions since 1973.[5] That means Americans have murdered more than 53 million of their own children in the past four decades, yet there is little remorse and no end of this holocaust in sight. True, many Americans are praying for the Lord to end this horrific practice. And many have been working tirelessly since abortion became legal in 1973 to change public opinion in favor of life, persuade pregnant women to bring their children to term and consider raising the children themselves or putting them up for adoption, create legal restrictions against abortion, and eventually support a constitutional amendment banning abortion. As a result, some progress has been made. Some important legislation has been passed. The number of annual abortions has declined somewhat. And this is good.

But it is not nearly enough. Abortion is a terrible stain on our nation. The Scriptures teach us that human life is precious, even before birth. King David once prayed to the Lord, "For you created my inmost being; you knit me together in my mother's womb. I praise you because I am fearfully and wonderfully made" (Psalm 139:13-14, NIV). How long will the creator and sustainer of life bless the United States rather than judge and punish us when we take the lives of well over one million innocent children every year? Indeed, for this reason alone one has to wonder why God has not allowed the U.S. to implode already.

Consider, too, the pandemic of pornography in our country. Only two out of three American adults (66 percent) say they believe pornography is "morally wrong," while fully 30 percent say it is morally acceptable.[6] In a country the size of ours, that means some 70 million Americans not only believe but will admit to pollsters that pornography is morally acceptable. How many more believe it is not acceptable yet indulge in it anyway? Today, pornography revenues in the United States from movies, videos, pay-per-view, magazines, the Internet, and other forms of media exceed the revenues of ABC, CBS, and NBC—*combined*.[7] Indeed, the revenue of the pornography industry—which is largely, though not exclusively, based in the United States—is larger than the revenues of Microsoft, Google, Amazon, eBay, Yahoo!, Apple, Netflix, and EarthLink—combined.[8]

If this weren't bad enough, based on current trends, pornography sales will likely surge higher still in the decades to come as even more Americans become ensnared, addicted, and degraded. Why? Because polls show that younger Americans view pornography as far more acceptable than older Americans do. Nineteen percent of Americans age 55 and older say pornography is morally acceptable. But 29 percent of Americans 35 to 54 years old say pornography is acceptable. Worse, a stunning 42 percent of Americans 18 to 34 years old say it's acceptable.[9] Unless hearts and minds are radically changed soon, as these young people get older and earn more disposable income, their ability to purchase pornography will increase—particularly as technology makes it easier to purchase in one's home through fiber-optic television and broadband Internet connections.

Concurrent with this explosion in the availability, sales, and viewing of pornography has come a dramatic increase in sexual crimes, the number of sexual predators, sexual abuse of children, divorce, and related social pathologies. In 1960, approximately 17,000 forcible rapes occurred in the U.S., according to FBI statistics. Forty years later, the number of forcible rapes had more than quadrupled to some 90,000 in the year 2000 alone.[10] In 2011, there were more than 730,000 sexual predators registered online with the National Center for Missing & Exploited Children.[11]* The number of sexual offense cases involving juvenile perpetrators has shot up 40 percent over the past two decades, climbing from 24,100 cases in 1985 to 33,800 in 2004.[12] A 2001 report by the U.S. Department of Justice found that 42 percent of juvenile sexual offenders had been "exposed to hardcore pornography."[13]

Thirty-five times in the Bible, the Lord warns against the sin of lust. Dozens more times, the Scriptures warn us against sexual immorality. Jesus said in Matthew 5:27-29, "You have heard that it was said, 'You shall not commit adultery'; but I say to you that everyone who looks at a woman with lust for her has already committed adultery with her in his heart. If your right eye makes you stumble, tear it out and throw it from you; for it is better for you to lose one of the parts of your body, than for your whole body to be thrown into hell." The apostle Paul writes in 1 Thessalonians 4:2-3 (just before writing about the Rapture), "For you know what commandments we gave you by the authority of the Lord Jesus. For this is the will of God, your sanctification; that is, that you abstain from

---

*Some have expressed that caution should be used in assessing the true number of sexual offenders and predators, as there are cases of people who might not truly qualify but end up on the list anyway. Experts and government officials should be extremely careful to make sure no one is put on such a national registry for reasons other than convictions of sexual crimes. Still, few question that we have seen an epidemic of sexual crimes over the past few decades.

sexual immorality." How much longer, then, can we expect the Lord to show America grace and mercy when we are so flagrantly violating his commands to be holy?

Consider, too, the surge in support of homosexuality in the United States. The number of people declaring themselves to be homosexual is growing. The open discussion of homosexuality is expanding on television, in the movies, and throughout popular culture. Open support and approval for homosexual marriage is dramatically expanding as well. In 1996, only 27 percent of Americans supported the legalization of homosexual marriages, while 68 percent were opposed. By 2011, a majority of Americans supported same-sex marriages; support had climbed to 53 percent, while opposition had fallen to 45 percent.[14]

And it's not just attitudes; now it's legislation. In 2011, New York became the seventh state to formally legalize homosexual marriages (after Massachusetts, Connecticut, California, Iowa, Vermont, and New Hampshire; though not a state, the District of Columbia has also legalized same-sex marriages).[15]

In both the Old Testament and the New Testament, the Bible is clear that homosexuality is not just a sin in God's eyes but an "abomination." In Leviticus 18:22, the Lord instructed, "You shall not lie with a male as one lies with a female; it is an abomination." In 1 Corinthians 6:9-10, the apostle Paul writes, "Do you not know that the unrighteous will not inherit the kingdom of God? Do not be deceived; neither fornicators, nor idolaters, nor adulterers, nor effeminate, nor homosexuals, nor thieves, nor the covetous, nor drunkards, nor revilers, nor swindlers, will inherit the kingdom of God."

It is becoming politically incorrect to accept the Bible's teachings on these and other moral issues or to talk about them publicly. Nevertheless, the Kingdom of Heaven is not a democracy. The Lord is not running for political office. He's not trying to cobble together a majority. He is the King of kings and the Lord of lords. What he says goes. How blessed is the man or woman who follows the Word of God, not his or her own desires.* And how blessed is the nation that follows the Word of God as well. As we read in Psalm 33:12, "Blessed is the nation whose God is the LORD." That said, the Bible also teaches that a nation that loses its vision of the Lord and willfully and systematically disobeys the Word of God will not be blessed but will eventually perish.

- "Where there is no vision, the people perish: but he that keepeth the law, happy is he" (Proverbs 29:18, KJV).
- "When there is moral rot within a nation, its government topples easily. But wise and knowledgeable leaders bring stability" (Proverbs 28:2, NLT).
- "If the foundations [of a nation] are destroyed, what can the righteous do?" (Psalm 11:3).

Once again, therefore, we need to ask the question: How much longer will the Lord keep America from imploding if our society keeps moving in direct opposition to the expressed will of God?

The State of the Church

As deeply grieved as I am by the spiritual blindness and the shocking moral brokenness of our nation, I am even more deeply grieved by the state of the church in America. Where are the Christians? Where is the church? What difference are we making? The answer is painful to hear, but we must say it anyway. Too many people who say they are Christians are asleep or distracted or intoxicated by the world. Like the old country song says, too many people who say they are Christians are "looking for love in all the wrong places." They have

---

*For examples, see Psalm 1:1, Psalm 34:8, Psalm 40:4, Psalm 112:1.

been seeking love and meaning and purpose outside of Christ and his love. As a result, the church is as weak as—or even weaker than—the culture itself.

In 2011, George Barna, the Christian pollster and researcher, released a fascinating but sobering book titled *Futurecast*, which I commend to your attention. In it he devoted considerable time to analyzing the state of Christianity in America today. What he found was revealing.

- 85 percent of Americans identify themselves as Christians.[16]
- 84 percent of Americans consider the Bible a holy or sacred book.[17]
- The typical American household owns four Bibles.[18]

Think about that for a moment. More than eight in ten Americans say they are Christians and consider the Bible a holy book. Yet over the last few decades, our country has experienced a moral and spiritual breakdown of unprecedented proportions. We have faced war and depression and even insurrection in our country's history. But never have we seen such a wholesale abandonment of God and his commandments. How is this possible in a country where 85 percent of the people claim to be Christians?

Clearly, there is a serious disconnect between who Americans say they are, what they say they believe, and how they are living.

For example, there is no statistical difference between the percentage of married non-Christians who have been divorced (33 percent) and the percentage of married "born-again Christians" who have been divorced (32 percent).[19] Lynn and I have seen this happen among our own friends and acquaintances. People we know who once said they loved Jesus and were committed to helping build his church then betrayed the Lord and their spouses and let their marriages and families implode. Knowing that Christ warned in Matthew 24 that in the last days betrayal and apostasy would accelerate and people's love for one another would grow cold hasn't lessened the resulting pain and heartbreak.

At the same time, sexual sin is metastasizing through the church like cancer. In the year 2000, Focus on the Family reported that 63 percent of men—two-thirds of whom were in church leadership—who attended "Men, Romance & Integrity" seminars had admitted to struggling with using pornography in the previous year.[20] Focus on the Family also reported in 2000 that one in seven calls to the organization's pastoral care line were regarding struggles with Internet pornography.[21] All over the U.S., pastors continue to resign from their pulpits because they are having adulterous affairs. According to *Christianity Today's Leadership Journal*, "Four in ten pastors online have visited a pornographic website. And more than one-third have done so in the past year." After assessing the increasing prevalence of such problems among pastors, the editors of the magazine warned, "If you think you can't fall into sexual sin, then you're godlier than David, stronger than Samson, and wiser than Solomon."[22]

The apostle Paul called the church to be different from the world and thus a witness to the world of Christ's redeeming power. "Therefore I urge you, brethren, by the mercies of God, to present your bodies a living and holy sacrifice, acceptable to God, which is your spiritual service of worship," Paul writes. "And do not be conformed to this world, but be transformed by the renewing of your mind, so that you may prove what the will of God is, that which is good and acceptable and perfect. . . . Do not be overcome by evil, but overcome evil with good" (Romans 12:1-2, 21).

The statistics from recent research on America's social and spiritual crises are sobering, and there is ample evidence of the disconnect between what Christians say they believe and the way they are living. Allow me to share two more troubling examples.

First, only half of all born-again American Christians say they

try to share the gospel with even one unsaved person one time—
one time—per year.[23]

Second, only 15 percent of American Christians are being men-
tored or discipled, and only 2 percent of all American Christians say
that discipling others, teaching them about Jesus, and helping them
grow spiritually is a goal of theirs and would make them spiritually
successful.[24]

How is this possible? How can the church be salt and light to
the lost world if it is no different from that lost world? How can we
possibly hope for a spiritual revival or a Third Great Awakening in
this land if Christians are barely sharing their faith in Jesus Christ
with one person a year and not following Christ's great commission
to preach the gospel and make disciples of all nations?

Jesus said in Luke 6:46, "Why do you call Me, 'Lord, Lord,' and
do not do what I say?" This is an important question for all of us at
this hour.

Four Reasons God Is Shaking Us

The Bible teaches us that in the last days, God "will shake all the
nations" (Haggai 2:7). This shaking is not to punish people, though
judgment will eventually come during the Tribulation and on the
Day of the Lord. As we pray and hope for revival and healing in our
country and around the world, we should thank the Lord for the
time we have left, however much that is. We should also thank the
Lord for shaking us in all kinds of ways. These shakings are sometimes physical and sometimes metaphorical, and I believe they have
four key purposes.

Because He Loves Us and Wants Us to Wake Up and Turn to Christ

In John 3:16, the Lord Jesus was crystal clear about God's attitude
toward the world. He said, "God so loved the world, that He gave

His only begotten Son, that whoever believes in Him shall not perish, but have eternal life." God sent his Son to offer forgiveness and eternal salvation to anyone who would repent. In other words, God doesn't want us as individuals, families, or nations to implode or perish. Rather, he wants us to put our faith in Jesus Christ and follow him. Sometimes, therefore, he shakes people to get their attention and help them realize their need for him.

In his letter to the Romans, the apostle Paul pleads with the church to wake up. "This is all the more urgent, for you know how late it is; time is running out. Wake up, for our salvation is nearer now than when we first believed. The night is almost gone; the day of salvation will soon be here. So remove your dark deeds like dirty clothes, and put on the shining armor of right living" (Romans 13:11-12, NLT).

The proper response to this kind of divine shaking, the Bible indicates, is to repent. But what is repentance?

Lynn and I have tried to teach our four sons what repentance means in a very simple way. Our youngest is Noah. Sometimes I'll bring Noah over to my side and say, "Noah, start running away from me, out of the family room, through the kitchen, and to the dining room. Ready? Go!" So Noah starts running. Then suddenly I say, "Stop, Noah!" And he stops. And I say, "Repent, Noah." And he turns around. And I say, "Come back to Daddy!" And he comes running to me and jumps into my arms, and I hug him and kiss him. That's repentance. God is telling us to stop because we're running in the wrong direction, away from him. He tells us to repent—to turn around—and to come running back to him so he can forgive us and show us his love and restore us. And that's why he shakes us. He is trying to get us to let go of anything and everything we are holding—every form of ideology, philosophy, religious beliefs, political beliefs, or material possessions—whatever we're holding on to that we think will give us hope and peace and security other than Jesus Christ.

Because He Wants Us to Realize There Is No One Else Who Can Give Us True Peace and Security

God doesn't simply want us to stop going in the wrong direction. He wants us to move in the right direction, toward him, because he is the only answer to all of our personal and national problems.

In the Old Testament—in Jeremiah 17:13-14—we read, "Those who turn away on earth will be written down, because they have forsaken the fountain of living water, even the LORD." So the prophet prays, "Heal me, O LORD, and I will be healed; save me and I will be saved, for You are my praise."

In the New Testament, the Lord Jesus said, "If anyone is thirsty, let him come to Me and drink. He who believes in Me, as the Scripture said, 'From his innermost being will flow rivers of living water.'" Jesus "spoke of the [Holy] Spirit, whom those who believed in Him were to receive" upon salvation (John 7:37-39). Nothing else will quench our spiritual and emotional thirst except Christ's "living water." The Lord wants us to discover him and draw near to him and drink the water only Jesus Christ gives us.

Because He Has a Mission for His Church and for Each of His Followers

The apostle Paul writes in Ephesians 2 that born-again believers were "created in Christ Jesus for good works, which God prepared beforehand so that we would walk in them" (v. 10). In that same chapter, Paul makes it clear that we are not saved by doing good works. Rather, we are saved by faith, in part so that we will do good works that the Lord long ago planned for us to accomplish for him. As such, God doesn't want us to miss the blessing of serving him and seeing him bear fruit through our lives of obedience.

One of the most remarkable examples in the Bible of God shaking a man to get him to stop, repent, and get back to the important mission of serving the Lord is found in the Old Testament book of

Jonah. Much of the narrative of that book is focused on a key biblical city in northern Iraq. I've had the opportunity to travel into northern Iraq four times in recent years to preach the gospel, teach the Word of God, assist with humanitarian relief efforts, and strengthen the local believers. In the spring of 2010, I was invited to bring a team of pastors and staff from the Joshua Fund, the nonprofit organization Lynn and I created to bless Israel and her neighbors, to conduct a pastors' conference in northern Iraq, near the province of Nineveh. We have a son named Jonah, and he really wanted to go with me so he could see Nineveh. Lynn and I weren't so sure about that, but we prayed about it and felt God's peace, so Jonah came with me. But as we were flying in, a big storm came up and prevented our flight from landing in northern Iraq. We were diverted back to Amman, Jordan. There, I texted Lynn and told her what had happened and said Jonah and I were disappointed and weren't sure what was going to happen next. She texted back to say, "Don't worry. This would be the first time in history that a Jonah *wanted* to go to Nineveh and God prevented him from going. I think God is going to actually let you and Jonah get to Nineveh after all."

She was right.

In the Bible, the Lord gave the prophet Jonah a mission: to take a warning of judgment and the urgency of repentance to the people of Nineveh (in what was then Assyria and is now northern Iraq), lest they face God's wrath and implode. Jonah, however, refused to obey. Instead, he tried to run away from the Lord by boarding a ship that was heading for Tarshish, in modern-day southern Spain.

What happened? God began to shake Jonah's world. Let's pick up the story in Jonah 1:4-6.

> The LORD hurled a great wind on the sea and there was a
> great storm on the sea so that the ship was about to break
> up. Then the sailors became afraid and every man cried to

his god, and they threw the cargo which was in the ship into the sea to lighten it for them. But Jonah had gone below into the hold of the ship, lain down and fallen sound asleep. So the captain approached him and said, "How is it that you are sleeping? Get up, call on your god. Perhaps your god will be concerned about us so that we will not perish."

You probably know the rest of the story. Jonah was tossed overboard by the ship's crew, was saved from drowning by being swallowed by a huge fish, and three days later was belched up onshore, shaken to his core but essentially unharmed. From there he hightailed it to Nineveh and carried out God's instructions. He could have avoided a lot of pain and hardship if he had just obeyed God to begin with, but eventually he repented and did as God had told him. And because of his words, the people of Nineveh—one of the most notoriously evil cities of the day—repented as well.

The story turns out well, but not without a whole lot of shaking going on. Jonah—a man of God, a prophet of God, a teacher of God's Word—was on the run from God. He was asleep to God's voice and resistant to God's will. How convicting is this: that a pagan ship captain had to shake a teacher of God's Word and wake him up and beg him to pray for his salvation?

What about you? What mission has God given you? Are you obeying, or are you on the run from the Lord and asleep to his voice?

Because Jesus Christ Is Coming Back Soon, and Time Is Running Out

The Old Testament prophet Joel pleaded with the people of God to wake up. "Let all the inhabitants of the land tremble," he said. Why? "For the day of the LORD is coming; surely it is near" (Joel 2:1).

How do we know Christ is coming back? Because the Bible says so repeatedly, and Jesus said so himself numerous times. Here's one example: in Revelation 22:12, Jesus said, "Behold, I am coming quickly, and My reward is with Me, to render to every man according to what he has done." We are seeing the signs that the Bible says will precede Christ's return. We are experiencing the birth pangs that Scripture foretold for the days before Jesus' second coming. We are being shaken, as prophecy warned, because Jesus wants to wake us up. He wants us to be ready.

As we have already seen, we don't know the day or the hour of the Rapture, but Jesus said we would know the season. Thus, we should be living as though his hand is on the doorknob, so to speak, ready to reenter human history at any moment. In Matthew 24:42, Jesus said, "Therefore be on the alert, for you do not know which day your Lord is coming." In the next verses, Jesus said, "For this reason you also must be ready; for the Son of Man is coming at an hour when you do not think He will" (v. 44).

The world is not ready for Christ to return. People are lost. They don't believe in the Resurrection, much less the Rapture. But the church is supposed to be the last best hope of any nation. The church is supposed to be ready and eager for the Lord to come, helping others wake up and get ready too. Yet how can the church be ready and be faithful in reaching the world with the gospel if she is asleep?

God's Call to a Sleeping Church

In the book of Revelation, we read these words the Lord Jesus sent to the church in Sardis, a now-deserted city in modern-day Turkey:

> I know your deeds, that you have a name that you are alive,
> but you are dead. Wake up, and strengthen the things that
> remain, which were about to die; for I have not found your
> deeds completed in the sight of My God. So remember
> what you have received and heard; and keep it, and repent.

Therefore if you do not wake up, I will come like a thief,
and you will not know at what hour I will come to you.

REVELATION 3:1-3

Is it possible that Christ's words describe you? Or your family? Or the church congregation that you attend or serve at or pastor? Perhaps you have "a name"—a reputation—that you are spiritually alive. Yet maybe that's not how Jesus sees you. Maybe he sees you as dead inside. Maybe you're not obeying him. Maybe you're not worshiping him—not really—with your whole heart. Maybe you're not sharing the gospel with your family or friends. Maybe you're not making any disciples, here at home or in any other country. Maybe you've never made a single disciple. Maybe you don't even know what it means to make a disciple, even though Jesus commanded in Matthew 28:19, "Go therefore and make disciples of all the nations."

Now, then, is the time to wake up, for we are steadily running out of time.

Bottom Line

The 9/11 attacks, like other historic shocks in recent years, stunned us. They shook us emotionally and financially and militarily. They drove Americans back to church by the millions. But did it last?

George Barna's research shows that "after the 9/11 attacks, religious activity surged, but within two months, virtually every spiritual indicator available suggested that things were back to pre-attack levels."[25] In other words, the wake-up call came, and startled people jumped out of bed—but before long, they went back to sleep, back to business as usual.

Where are you at this moment? Are you awake or asleep? Are you running *with* Jesus, or are you running *from* him and from the mission he has for your life, like Jonah did?

God is shaking us because he loves us and he wants us to repent, because he wants us to know that Jesus Christ is the only one who can give us peace and security, because he has a mission for us, and because Jesus Christ is coming back sooner than most people think. Americans desperately need to wake up from the moral and spiritual slumber we are in. Most importantly, the church in America needs to wake up, purify herself, abide in Christ more faithfully and passionately than ever before, and once again offer families, communities, our nation, and the world the wonder-working power of Christ Jesus and his Holy Spirit.

For the church truly is America's last best hope. If we don't show the way back to the Lord, who will?

CHAPTER FOURTEEN

A CAUSE FOR OPTIMISM: INSIDE AMERICA'S FIRST GREAT AWAKENING

THE OUTLOOK MAY BE BLEAK, but I don't believe it is hopeless. The U.S. is in dire straits, but we have not yet imploded.

Yes, the American business community is plagued by failure and bankruptcy, but there are glimmers of hope; we do see some true innovators and creative geniuses out there creating new industries and trying to revive old ones, and more are struggling to rise. Yes, the American political community is awash with corruption and ineptitude, but we also see notable exceptions; there actually are some political leaders out there—and more are emerging—who are holding fast to the Constitution and are willing to stand on the principles upon which this great country was founded, rather than selling out and giving up. Yes, the American church has been far too weak and ineffectual for far too long and thus seemingly irrelevant to helping Americans cope with—much less fix—the multiple crises we face. But not all is lost; some Americans are beginning to wake up to their need for a personal relationship with Jesus Christ, and some pastors and congregations are actually becoming more faithful to the Word of God and shining even more brightly, as lighthouses in a dark and troubled land. May their tribes increase.

It is critical that we as a nation seriously consider, understand, accept, and then discuss with our fellow Americans just how precarious our situation really is. We must not put our heads in the sand. Rather, we need to honestly confront the grave challenges before us. We must not allow ourselves to become paralyzed by fear or consumed by the thought that our fate is sealed and there are no steps we can take to turn this ship of state around and get it back on the right course.

The central question we now face is this: Will God in his mercy unleash a dramatic period of sweeping spiritual revival and moral renewal and reform that will fundamentally transform our nation and help us get back on the right track before it's too late?

While it is by no means guaranteed, I believe such a dramatic revival is possible. The prophet Habakkuk once prayed, "O LORD, revive Your work in the midst of the years, in the midst of the years make it known; in wrath remember mercy" (Habakkuk 3:2). If the Hebrew prophet chose to pray for revival, we should too.

The good news is that twice before in American history we have experienced periods of broad, deep national revival. In fact, these movements were so game-changing that both secular and Christian historians were compelled to call them the "Great Awakening" and the "Second Great Awakening." Unfortunately, few Americans know the history of the two spiritual revivals that swept this land in the early- to mid-1700s (pre–Revolutionary War) and in the early- to mid-1800s (pre–Civil War). I certainly don't recall learning much of this history growing up. My parents didn't talk about it, as they hadn't been taught about it, and I don't recall learning any of this at church or in the public schools I attended.

I first began developing an interest in America's Great Awakenings while I was working as an advisor to Steve Forbes. As I set out to write this book, however, I decided to undertake a closer look at how God moved so powerfully to save our country in the past. I was absolutely fascinated and deeply encouraged by what I read. And as a result, I contend that it would be very valuable for all of us to review a bit of that history and then ask whether another such awakening could happen again.

The First Great Awakening (1700–1760s)

Let's begin with some context. Many of the pilgrims who came to this continent in the 1600s and 1700s were strong followers of Jesus Christ, eager to experience religious freedom from the state-run churches of Great Britain and the European continent and to build vibrant faith communities in the New World. But by no means were all those who came faithful believers. Some were businessmen, soldiers, government officials, bureaucrats, and tradesmen who came with little or no religious heritage or faith. These came to work, not to advance the Kingdom of God. Some who arrived here were convicts sent essentially to provide slave labor until others from Africa and the Caribbean were cruelly captured and enslaved and brought to the New World. In time, therefore, the British colonies became a hodgepodge of different religious beliefs.

Unfortunately, while there were some boldly evangelistic ministers and laypeople in the colonies, most believers who were here did little to preach the gospel or make disciples capable of spiritual reproduction—that is, making other disciples who could and would make still more disciples. In other words, the Christians who came to the colonies tended to remain in their churches and in their pews and made little spiritual impact on those around them.

To be sure, they faced enormous challenges. They were battling the exhaustion of building a new society from scratch. They faced disease and the death of many of their family members, friends, and loved ones. They often struggled against harsh weather conditions. They also faced political oppression from the British and skirmishes with the Native Americans (whom they called Indians). However, rather than see these as opportunities to boldly share the life-changing message of the gospel with the rest of the colonists, most believers instead retreated into the safety of their families and tight-knit communities.

Yet this inward and almost-isolationist approach by the believers had unintended consequences. By the late 1600s, various ministers throughout the colonies had begun to despair of the moral and spiritual condition of the people and the rising apathy toward the things of God. So they began preaching of the need for a purification of the church and a revival of interest in hearing and obeying the Word of God. They also began praying more diligently for God to do something that the pastors couldn't do on their own: turn increasingly sluggish and secular hearts and minds toward Christ.

To these ministers' horror, however, events in the colonies took a terrible turn for the worse, not the better. There came a sudden, furious, and devastating war with the Indians, which became known as King Philip's War—referring to Metacomet, the leader of the Native American forces, who was known to the British colonists as King Philip. Not many Americans today know much about it. Indeed, few have ever even heard of it. Yet it was this brutal conflict that helped shake the foundations of colonial American life to its core and set into motion a chain of events that would lead to an astounding outpouring of God's amazing grace.

Historian Jill Lepore, in her award-winning book *The Name of War: King Philip's War and the Origin of American Identity*, described the conflict:

In 1675, Algonquian Indians all over southern New England rose up against the Puritan colonists with whom they had

lived peacefully for several decades. The result was the
bloodiest war in American history, a terrifying conflict
in which the Puritans found themselves fighting with a
cruelty they had thought only the natives were capable
of. . . . In proportion to population, their short, vicious war
inflicted greater casualties than any other war in American
history. . . . By August 1676, when the severed head of
the Wampanoag leader, King Philip, was displayed in
Plymouth, thousands of Indian and English men, women,
and children were dead. More than half of the new towns
in New England had been wiped out, and the settlers'
sense of themselves as civilized people of God had been
deeply shaken.[1]

"The mood in New England following King Philip's War
(1675-76) was bleak and raw," noted historian Thomas S. Kidd in
his intriguing book *The Great Awakening: The Roots of Evangelical
Christianity in Colonial America*. Kidd wrote of two pastors from the
Northeast who thought it increasingly obvious that "we are a people
in extream [sic] danger of perishing, in our own sins and under Gods
Judgements [sic]." Moreover, the pastors feared that "'all ordinary
means' of promoting moral reformation had failed," causing them
to ask themselves whether "our degeneracy and apostasy may not
prove . . . perpetual."[2]

Desperate for the Lord's grace and mercy, a growing number of
Protestant ministers began devoting themselves to prayer and fasting
for a revival in the colonies. A growing number of laypeople began
to pray for widespread revival as well. They asked God to have mercy
on them and their neighbors and countrymen, and they patiently
waited for the Lord to show his powerful hand. Yet what then began
to unfold starting around 1700, building through the 1740s and lasting well into the 1760s, was more than even the most faithful prayer

warriors had hoped for, dreamed of, or imagined. For suddenly there emerged two new dynamics.

- First, there entered into the drama preachers who proclaimed the gospel and taught the Scriptures with great care, passion, and conviction—and with a supernatural power few had seen or heard from their ministers before.
- The leaders of the Great Awakening—preachers like the American-born Jonathan Edwards and British-born missionaries such as George Whitefield, John Wesley, and Charles Wesley—tended to be well-educated men who had attended universities such as Yale and Oxford and were trained theologians. Yet they didn't allow their higher learning to create an intellectualism or an elitism about the Bible that would make it difficult for laypeople to understand them. They carefully studied the Scriptures. They were empowered by the Holy Spirit. They had demonstrable spiritual gifts of teaching, preaching, and evangelism. And they believed that the Word of God— not they personally—had the power to save souls, change lives, and alter nations.
- Second, there emerged in this drama millions of people who *wanted* to hear the gospel preached with great passion and conviction. These people realized that their hearts were full of sin and that they needed to repent and get right with God. A revival cannot take place if there is no one to preach the Word with God's power. But nor can it take place if no one will listen to God's Word and be transformed by it.

By the grace of God, there emerged in America at that time a historic convergence of preachers and hearers, and no one in the New World had ever seen such dramatic results.

The Rise of Jonathan Edwards (1703–1758)

Few men were more instrumental in the First Great Awakening than Jonathan Edwards. Edwards was born in East Windsor, Connecticut, in 1703, into a family of well-educated and well-respected pastors and theologians. Edwards's father was a pastor, and his mother's father was the Reverend Solomon Stoddard, a famous pastor who shepherded the nation's largest and most influential church, in Northampton, Massachusetts, about eighty miles from Boston, and who saw God bring a series of small revivals to his congregation that foreshadowed the revivals to come.[3] Eventually, Edwards married Sarah Pierpont, the daughter of James Pierpont, a pastor and theologian who was the founder of Yale University.

Edwards himself was a brilliant young man. He graduated from high school at the age of thirteen and was immediately accepted to Yale. Four years later, in 1720, he graduated as the valedictorian of his class. After continuing his theological studies at Yale, he became an assistant pastor and understudy to his grandfather Stoddard. But it is unlikely that Edwards understood exactly what the Lord was going to teach him next.

"On Sunday evening, October 29 [1727], a terrible earthquake shook the homes of New Englanders, awakening many both physically and spiritually," one historian noted. "This was followed by a long series of aftershocks, which kept the threat fresh in the minds of penitents. Immediately churches filled with seekers anxious to secure their salvation, lest they be caught unprepared for their own death."[4] Remarked one layperson who survived the earthquake, "God has by the late amazing Earth-quake layd open my neglect before me that I see no way to escape. But by fleeing to Christ for refuge. God in that hour Set all my Sins before me. When I was Shaking over the pit looking every moment when the earth would open her mouth and Swallow me up and then must I have been miserable for ever & for ever."[5] In towns throughout Massachusetts, churches continued to fill as people repented and gave their hearts to Christ.

The Lord used Reverend Stoddard to minister to people powerfully during this time, and his grandson was at his side to assist him. And three years before Stoddard went home to be with the Lord in 1729, the twenty-six-year-old Jonathan Edwards became senior pastor of Stoddard's church.

Though relatively young and inexperienced, Edwards could see God was shaking his town and his community, both literally and spiritually. He could see the hunger people had to find forgiveness and redemption and to grow closer to Christ. Most importantly, he firmly believed the Scriptures spoke clearly of God's ability and desire to save many souls and reverse a nation's drifting from the Lord. He believed God's words from 2 Chronicles 7:14, when the Lord declared, "If my people, who are called by my name, will humble themselves and pray and seek my face and turn from their wicked ways, then I will hear from heaven, and I will forgive their sin and heal their land" (NIV). Edwards understood the similarities between what was going on around him and the spiritual revivals that occurred in the books of Ezra and Nehemiah, when the entire nation of Israel listened to the Word of God and repented of their sins. So Edwards began to pray that God would use him to effect great change, and he began to preach with the faith that the Lord would hear and answer his prayer.

The Impact of Jonathan Edwards

Beginning in 1734, Edwards saw God move even more powerfully in his congregation and community. During a short period of time, several people died in a way that rattled observers to the core. One young man whom Edwards described as being "in the bloom of his youth" was unexpectedly stricken with pleurisy (an inflammation in the chest cavity), experienced intense pain, was delirious for two days, and then was gone.[6] Then a young married woman unexpectedly developed a terrible illness and passed away. "This was followed with the death of an elderly person, which was attended with many unusual circumstances," Edwards recalled. The tragic deaths reminded people of their own mortality and focused them on the prospect of spending eternity either in heaven or in hell. Five or six people suddenly came to the church and converted, Edwards observed. Then a well-known immoral woman came to the church and was saved, and something dramatic began to happen.

Concerning this conversion, Edwards would later write:

> The news of it seemed to be almost like a flash of lightning, upon the hearts of young people, all over the town, and upon many others. Those persons amongst us, who used to be farthest from seriousness, and that I most feared would make an ill improvement of it, seemed to be awakened with it. Many went to talk with her, concerning what she had met with; and what appeared in her seemed to be to the satisfaction of all that did so.
>
> Presently upon this, a great and earnest concern about the great things of religion and the eternal world, became universal in all parts of the town, and among persons of all degrees, and all ages. . . . Other discourse than of the things of religion would scarcely be tolerated in any company. The minds of people were wonderfully taken off from the world, it was treated amongst us as a thing of very little consequence.[7]

A revival in Northampton was under way.

Edwards described the events taking place in his community as nothing short of miraculous. He wrote:

The work of conversion was carried on in a most astonishing manner, and increased more and more; souls did as it were come by flocks to Jesus Christ. . . . The number of true saints multiplied, soon made a glorious alteration in the town: so that in the spring and summer following, anno 1735, the town seemed to be full of the presence of God: it never was so full of love, nor of joy, and yet so full of distress, as it was then. . . . It was a time of joy in families on account of salvation being brought to them; parents rejoicing over their children as new born, and husbands over their wives, and wives over their husbands. The doings of God were then seen in His sanctuary, God's day was a delight, and His tabernacles were amiable. Our public assemblies were then beautiful: the congregation was alive in God's service, every one earnestly intent on the public worship, every hearer eager to drink in the words of the minister as they came from his mouth; the assembly in general were, from time to time, in tears while the word was preached; some weeping with sorrow and distress, others with joy and love, others with pity and concern for the souls of their neighbors.[8]

Edwards called what he was witnessing "a shower of divine blessing."[9] Indeed, to me these accounts of the early days of the revival read like the exciting and supernatural events of Acts 2, when God poured out his Holy Spirit and created the church in Jerusalem on the Day of Pentecost.

In 1738, Edwards published a powerful tract titled *A Faithful Narrative of the Surprising Work of God*. He described what God had just done, why he believed God had done it, and how Edwards and his congregation had responded to this outpouring of the Holy Spirit. He wrote about how people had begun fasting and praying for the lost and how young people had begun to share the gospel with their friends and neighbors and with complete strangers.

In a world without radio, television, or the Internet, the well-written tract caught people's imagination and spread like wildfire. Copies were quickly snapped up, devoured, and shared with others, even as more were being printed. As other ministers and laypeople throughout Massachusetts and the other colonies heard of the revival and read Edwards's pamphlet, many began to beseech the Lord to do in their churches and communities what he had done in Northampton.

And the Lord answered their prayers. The revival soon spread through thirty-two communities near Boston, then throughout New England and the rest of the colonies. Edwards's tract was published in London and spread widely through Great Britain, Scotland, and Wales, where pastors and laypeople were enthralled and began praying and preaching for revivals in their nations as well.

In the years that followed, Edwards went on to plant other church congregations, serve as a missionary to Native Americans, and preach the gospel in congregations throughout New England (including his most famous sermon, "Sinners in the Hands of an Angry God" in 1741).[10]

But arguably his most lasting impact was through his published works. He produced a series of highly influential publications to help others develop sound biblical theology and further the revival. These included *The Distinguishing Marks of a Work of the Spirit of God* (published in 1741), *Some Thoughts Concerning the Present Revival* (published in 1742), and *A Treatise Concerning Religious Affections* (published in 1746). Each of these was used by God to shape Christian thinking in Edwards's day. In 1758, Edwards accepted the position of president at the College of New Jersey (later renamed Princeton University). The school was founded in 1746 by four pastors specifically for the purpose of "educating Ministers of the Gospel" as well as to be "useful in other learned professions—ornaments of the State as well as the Church."[11]

Edwards was increasingly determined to train future pastors, theologians, and Christ-centered laypeople. He felt that by strengthening and revitalizing the college, he could advance the Kingdom of Christ even further. Sadly, he died of complications from a smallpox vaccination only a few months after accepting the post.

Despite his strong faith in Christ and love of the Scriptures, Edwards was by no means a perfect man. Among his flaws was the fact that he could occasionally have an explosive temper. He also, unfortunately, like many men of his day, was a slave owner. In time, however, "he came to oppose the slave trade as an impediment to spreading the gospel in Africa, thereby providing a basis for the abolitionism espoused by his son Jonathan Jr. and disciples such as Samuel Hopkins."[12]

God used Edwards despite his flaws, and fortunately the remarkable positive legacy of Jonathan Edwards did not end with his death. In many ways his impact had only begun to be felt throughout the young and growing country. Edwards and his beloved wife, Sarah, had eleven children together, eight daughters and three sons. Ten of their children lived to adulthood, and the Edwardses invested heavily in them all, making certain they were well educated (including the girls), teaching them the Scriptures, praying with them, playing with them, and preparing them to make a difference for Christ in the world. They succeeded beyond their parents' wildest dreams.

In 1900, a reporter by the name of A. E. Winship conducted a study of what had become of the 1,400 descendants of Jonathan and Sarah Edwards. "He found they included thirteen college presidents, sixty-five professors, one hundred lawyers and a dean of a law school, thirty judges, sixty-six physicians and a dean of a medical school, and eighty holders of public office, including three U.S. senators, mayors of three large cities, governors of three states, a vice president of the United States, and a controller of the United States treasury. They had written over 135 books and edited 18 journals and periodicals.

Many had entered the ministry. Over one hundred were missionaries and others were on missions boards."[13]

The Rise of George Whitefield (1714–1770)

Another incredibly influential figure in the First Great Awakening was George Whitefield,* a passionate preacher of the gospel and missionary to the American colonies.

Born in 1714 in Gloucester, England, Whitefield was one of seven children. When he was only two years old, his father died, leaving his mother a grieving, struggling widow who would not remarry for another eight years. But George grew into a brilliant young man, and he was determined to make something of himself. He studied hard and eventually attended and graduated from Oxford University. It was there that he met two young men whom God would use to change his life, John Wesley (1703–1791) and Charles Wesley (1707–1788), who eventually became world-famous gospel preachers, teachers, and songwriters, went on to found the Methodist church, and were key figures in revivals going on in England and in the American colonies.

At Oxford, however, the young Whitefield was only beginning his spiritual journeys. Though he had been raised in the church, he was only now taking his quest for God more seriously. It was Charles Wesley who invited Whitefield to get involved in a men's Bible study and prayer group that Wesley led with his older brother John. The group was derided by fellow students as the "Holy Club," but the Wesleys liked the name and embraced it; Whitefield embraced it as well. Early on, the group consisted of just eight or nine men. At its peak, about two dozen men participated. But few realized then the spiritual revolution that was going to emerge from their midst.

---

*His name is pronounced "*Whit*-field."

The group resolved to resist what they saw as their fellow students' lives of luxury and waste of time and money. The members of the Holy Club fasted two days a week. They took Communion together. They devoted themselves to caring for the poor. They ministered to prisoners. And all the while they kept rigorous schedules and sought to keep each other accountable to maintaining strict, disciplined, and austere lives. The young men were well meaning, to be sure, but there was a problem: they were trying to earn God's favor through their good works rather than accepting the free gift of God's forgiveness and peace through faith in Jesus Christ alone.

Whitefield would become the first to discover his mistake—that while newly religious, he didn't actually have a personal relationship with Christ—and radically change course.

One day, Whitefield asked Charles Wesley for a list of books to read and began to devour them one by one. His favorite was written in 1677 by a Scottish theologian named Henry Scougal, titled *The Life of God in the Soul of Man*. The work had a profound, life-changing impact on Whitefield. "God showed me that I must be born again, or be damned!" he would later write. "I learned that a man may go to church, say prayers, receive the sacrament, and yet not be a Christian." Whitefield was startled, even offended. "Shall I burn this book? Shall I throw it down? Or shall I search it?" he wondered. "I did search it, and holding the book in my hand I thus addressed the God of heaven and earth: 'Lord, if I am not a Christian, or if not a real one, for Jesus Christ's sake show me what Christianity is, that I may not be damned at last!' God soon showed me, for in reading a few lines further, that 'true Christianity is a union of the soul with God, and Christ formed within us,' a ray of divine light was instantaneously darted into my soul, and from that moment, and not till then, did I know I must become a new creature."[14]

Such radical new thoughts troubled Whitefield at first. He embarked on a course of deep soul-searching as he completely rethought his understanding of Christianity, his involvement in the Holy Club (which he would leave for a time), and his place in the world. Whitefield bought a Greek copy of the New Testament and began studying it, reading it whenever and wherever he could. As he did, God began to open the young scholar's eyes, ears, and heart to the truths in his Word of what it means to be born again. He learned how a man can—and must—be saved and be adopted into God's family not through being religious but through receiving the free gift of salvation by faith in Jesus Christ. And then one day in 1735, it was as though the clouds over the young man parted. The gospel suddenly made sense, and Whitefield—at the age of twenty—got down on his knees and said "Yes!" to Christ. "God was pleased to remove the heavy load, to enable me to lay hold of his dear Son by a living faith, and by giving me the Spirit of adoption, to seal me, even to the day of everlasting redemption," Whitefield later wrote. "O . . . what joy—joy unspeakable—even joy that was full of and big with glory!"[15]

Whitefield began to wake at five each morning for prayer and Bible study in both Greek and English, praying over every word and line. "I began to read the Holy Scriptures upon my knees," he recalled. "This proved meat indeed and drink indeed to my soul. I daily received fresh life, light, and power from above. . . . Oh, what sweet communion had I daily."[16]

Whitefield immediately started sharing his faith in Christ with others and was excited when "God made [him] instrumental to awaken several young people."[17] By the following year, he had completed his schooling, become an ordained Anglican minister, and preached his first sermon. He found it exhilarating. He had found his life's calling, and he continued preaching as opportunities presented themselves. He also served for a while as a missionary in what eventually became the American state of Georgia, where in addition to preaching, he helped start an orphanage.

But it was after Whitefield's return to England that the Lord's favor truly came upon him. The young Christian was soon preaching the life-changing gospel message with more conviction and power than anyone in the U.K. had ever seen before. Churches were packed wherever he spoke, and people were getting saved. The problem was that many of the Anglican clergymen Whitefield encountered were not born again themselves and were cold to his series of messages, which he called "The New Birth," based on John 3. Before long, Whitefield found himself banned from one pulpit after another and under severe criticism from the religious establishment.

Yet it was at precisely this time that God gave Whitefield a radical idea: What if he preached the gospel to the lost in the open air—in fields, factory yards, and town squares? Whitefield had heard of a layman named Howell Harris who was preaching in homes and at outdoor events in Wales. He'd even corresponded with Harris and had been encouraged by Harris's passion for Christ and by the results he was seeing. So on a cold February day, Whitefield simply couldn't wait any longer. He headed to a coal-mining district near the city of Bristol, called several hundred miners and their families together, and began preaching the gospel to them. Today, this might not seem so remarkable. Today, we know the stories of evangelists such as D. L. Moody and Billy Graham preaching outside of church walls. In the 1700s, however, this was considered by the Anglican hierarchy as outright religious fanaticism. But Whitefield didn't care. He kept preaching, and he saw people praying to receive Christ and developing a hunger for God's Word.

"Blessed be God!" he later wrote. "I have broken the ice. I believe I was never more acceptable to my Master than when I was standing to teach those hearers in the open fields. Some may censure me, but if I thus pleased men I should not be the servant of Christ."[18]

Interest in Whitefield and his message began to grow. Soon he was preaching thirty outdoor meetings a week around Bristol, then in towns and cities throughout England. Three months after that first experiment, he was preaching daily to crowds in London ranging from ten thousand to fifteen thousand. Not long after that, he preached to a gathering of some eighty thousand people.

Word about Whitefield was already spreading across the Atlantic. Pastors throughout New England, then the Mid-Atlantic colonies, and then the South wanted Whitefield to come and preach in their pulpits. They had read Jonathan Edwards's pamphlet on revival. Now they were hearing about an evangelist who seemed to have the hand of God upon him. What if God could use Whitefield to bring revival to their communities?

Sensing God's call to revisit the colonies, Whitefield set sail and reached America on October 30, 1739. He immediately went to Philadelphia and preached in churches that were packed to overflowing. He also spoke in New York, Delaware, Virginia, North Carolina, and South Carolina. He was frequently forced to add extra meetings and then outdoor gatherings to accommodate all the people interested in hearing the Word of God taught with more passion and strength than they had ever heard it before.

In November, Whitefield wrote to Jonathan Edwards, asking the well-known reverend if Whitefield could visit the site of the famous revival in Northampton.[19] Edwards seized the opportunity to meet this kindred spirit. He immediately wrote back to welcome Whitefield, offering him the opportunity not just to visit but to preach in his town and also in Boston and the surrounding areas. Edwards also learned that the governor of Massachusetts wanted to hear Whitefield as well.

The impact was stunning. Whitefield spoke to students and faculty at Harvard and saw many pray to receive Christ. He spent four days in Northampton, preaching, teaching, and comparing notes with Edwards about what they were seeing God do to bring revival to the colonies. And the crowds just kept growing.

"When he preached in New England during the fall of 1740, Whitefield addressed crowds of up to 8,000 people nearly every day for over a month," noted one historian, describing that evangelistic tour as "one of the most remarkable episodes in the whole history of American Christianity."[20] In his final message before departing the colonies, Whitefield preached the gospel to a crowd of at least twenty thousand on Boston Common.

The Impact of George Whitefield

We need to be careful about how we evaluate numbers, of course. A man's ministry should be measured primarily by his faithfulness to God's calling on his life, not by how many people show up to listen or by how many respond to an invitation to receive Christ. Indeed, a pastor, missionary, or layperson can be a wonderful and truly faithful minister of the Word of God and the gospel and never see big crowds or much fruit. As Bill Bright, founder of Campus Crusade for Christ, liked to say, we should share Christ in the power of the Holy Spirit and leave the results to God.[21]

Jesus drove this point home best of all. In the parable of the talents in Matthew 25, he told us that God wants us to wisely and effectively invest the spiritual gifts, natural talents, and financial resources he has given us, and he wants us to get a good "return," as it were, on our investments. But in the end, God will not grade us on our external results; he will grade us on our internal faithfulness. To those who are successful in their spiritual investments, he will say, "Well done, good and faithful servant! You have been faithful with a few things; I will put you in charge of many things. Come and share your master's happiness!" (Matthew 25:21, NIV).

That said, if God chooses to bear much fruit through a man and his team, we need not deny it. We should rejoice in it, as long as we are giving praise to Christ and not to the man or his ministry. We are all just servants, after all. The glory belongs to Jesus.

In that context, then, the more I learn about the things God did through George Whitefield, the more I rejoice. The man wasn't perfect, of course. But he was used mightily.

"For decades [in the early 1700s] preachers had lamented the absence of grace and the apparent indifference of their congregations," wrote one historian of the Great Awakening. "In sermon after sermon ministers unsuccessfully urged sleepy sinners to awake to their danger. An individual now and again detected signs of the Spirit operating in him, and in the 1720s and 1730s a number of congregations reported seasons of spiritual refreshment. But not until the 1740s did men in large numbers lay claim to the divine power which their theology offered them. Then they suddenly awoke to God's glory and experienced a moral transformation as promised. In the Awakening the clergy's pleas of half a century came to fulfillment."[22]

The powerful preaching of George Whitefield was one of the catalysts of this movement sweeping across the colonies. College presidents invited Whitefield to address their student bodies. Local government leaders wanted to meet and discuss faith with him. The governor of Massachusetts came to see Whitefield preach in Boston. Even the esteemed Benjamin Franklin, not known to be a man interested in the Bible or the things of Christ, could not resist striking up a friendship with Whitefield and engaging him in many conversations, starting with Whitefield's first visit to Philadelphia.

Franklin actually soon became an admirer of both the crowds Whitefield was drawing and the cultural impact he was having. For Franklin could see that people were not just hearing Whitefield preach; they were responding to his message with weeping, with genuine repentance, and with changed lives and conduct. "In 1739 there arrived among us the Rev. Mr. Whitefield [and] the multitude of all sects and denominations that attended his sermons was enormous,"

Franklin would later write, noting that he had attended one particular open-air sermon that he personally calculated was heard "by more than thirty thousand."[23]

Franklin observed, "It was wonderful to see the change soon made in the manners of our inhabitants. From being thoughtless or indifferent about religion, it seemed as if all the world were growing religious" after hearing Whitefield's sermons, "so that one could not walk thro' the town in an evening without hearing psalms sung in different families in every street."[24]

Franklin would go on to publish Whitefield's sermons and even financially invest in Whitefield's ministry, though there is no evidence that this founding father ever personally prayed to receive Christ as Savior.

Others, too, were struck by the impact of Whitefield's preaching.

Said one observer of the Great Awakening in Boston in November of 1741, "The apostolical times seem to have returned upon us; such a display has there been of the power and grace of the divine Spirit in the assemblies of his people, and such testimonies has he given to the word of the Gospel."[25]

Declared a pastor in Connecticut who was amazed by what God was doing through men like Whitefield, Edwards, and the Wesleys, "I believe the people [in my congregation] advanced more in their acquaintance with the Scriptures, and a true doctrinal understanding of the operations of the Holy Spirit in conviction, regeneration, and sanctification, in six months' time than they had done in the whole of my ministry before, which was nine years."[26]

Over the course of his thirty-three-year ministry, Whitefield preached an estimated fifteen thousand sermons.[27] The pace and intensity of his ministry eventually exhausted him, and he actually died during a preaching tour. When Whitefield passed from this life and went to heaven on September 30, 1770, his dear friend John Wesley preached his eulogy. He said, "Have we read or heard of any person, who called so many thousands, so many myriads of sinners to repentance?"[28]

George Whitefield was without question one of the preeminent leaders of the Great Awakening in America in the eighteenth century, and he was used powerfully by God throughout England as well. As one religious historian has usefully noted, Whitefield "initiated almost all of [the eighteenth century's] enterprises—the open-air preaching, the use of lay preachers, the publishing of a magazine, the organizing of an association, and the holding of a conference. And by his thirteen crossings of the ocean, he provided the international scope of the movement. Among his accomplishments there must be recognized the host of men and women he led to Jesus Christ and the large part he played in this great work of revival on both sides of the Atlantic."[29]

Confirmed another historian of the eighteenth century, "The very magnitude of the revivals, which won for the Awakening the appellation 'Great,' is one indication of their importance. From Whitefield's 1740 tour until 1743, the period when the revival was at its peak, thousands were converted. People from all ranks of society, of all ages, and from every section underwent the new birth. In New England virtually every congregation was touched. It was not uncommon for 10 or 20 percent of a town . . . to join the church in a single year."[30]

The Rise of John Wesley (1703–1791) and Charles Wesley (1707–1788)

John Wesley was born on June 17, 1703, in Epworth, England, the fifteenth of nineteen children. His brother Charles was born four years later on December 17, 1707, the eighteenth child of Samuel Wesley, an Anglican minister, and Susanna Wesley, the daughter of a minister. Together, these two remarkable brothers—in concert with George Whitefield—would be used by God to launch a movement of gospel preaching, church planting, pastor recruitment and training, disciple making, and Christian praise and worship that would impact much of the Western world. Yet one of the most fascinating aspects of their early lives is how they set out to convert the lost before they themselves were actually converted.

As I noted earlier, while attending Oxford University, the Wesley brothers led a men's Bible study and prayer group known as the Holy Club. It was Charles who founded the group and later recruited John to help him lead it. But neither of them actually knew Christ personally, and unfortunately when their friend George Whitefield was powerfully converted in early 1735, the Wesley brothers were so busy, or so distracted, that they didn't take the time or effort to grasp precisely what had happened to him. They were excited about his enhanced zeal, but they didn't see how it directly affected them.

The two brilliant and disciplined young men were certainly deeply devoted to serving God, and when they graduated, both were ordained as Anglican ministers like their father. Then they decided to accept an invitation from Georgia governor James Oglethorpe to come to the colony, pastor a church there, and serve as missionaries to the Native Americans. They departed on a ship to the New World on October 14, 1735.

Along the way, the vessel encountered a terrible storm that threatened to sink it. Everyone aboard was terrified—all but a group of Moravian Christians. These Moravian believers didn't seem bothered by the wind or the waves. Rather, they sang songs and remained calm throughout the entire ordeal. The Wesley brothers were intrigued by such depth of faith. They began to get to know the Moravians and spent long hours discussing with them what they believed and how they practiced their faith. It was a relationship that would deeply mark the two men.

The Wesleys reached Savannah, Georgia, on February 8, 1736,

and tried to settle into new routines. Charles became a secretary to Governor Oglethorpe. John began pastoring a congregation and trying to convert a tribe of Native Americans to Christ.

From the beginning, everything seemed to go wrong. Few of the roughneck Georgians seemed interested in the Wesleys' highly intellectualized teaching or style of worship. The Indians didn't seem much interested either. As one religious historian noted of Charles, "this well-bred, well-educated, earnest High Churchman was completely out of his element. His experiences, including one Sunday (March 21, 1736) when his sermon was disrupted by gunshots and an irate matron threatened to blow him up as a religious hypocrite, were mostly discouraging. In late July 1736 he resigned his position and by early August was headed back to England."[31]

John endured for about another year but fared little better. He couldn't find a way to connect with the people. He couldn't seem to convince them by his preaching, and he found himself embroiled in theological arguments at every turn. "More trouble followed when he fell in love with Sophia Hopkey, the niece of Georgia's chief magistrate. When she married another man, Wesley banned her from Holy Communion, damaging her reputation in the community. His successful romantic rival sued him; but Wesley refused to recognize the authority of the court, and the man who would eventually found a major Protestant denomination in America left Georgia in disgrace on December 2, 1737."[32]

Both young Wesley men were discouraged and confused. What had gone wrong? Why hadn't they made the impact for which they had prayed and worked so hard? And why had they failed so spectacularly, when God was so radically blessing the work of their friend George Whitefield?

John began to reflect on a conversation he'd had with one of the Moravian believers. "My brother, I must first ask you one or two questions," the Moravian had said to him. "Have you the witness within yourself? Does the Spirit of God bear witness with your spirit that you are a child of God?"

John had been stunned by the questions and unsure how to answer.

The Moravian had seen this and pressed further. "Do you know Jesus Christ?"

John had replied, "I know he is the Saviour of the world."

"True," the man had said, "but do you know that he has saved you?"

Again John hadn't known what to say. "I hope he has died to save me," was all he could muster, but he feared his words were in vain.[33]

For the next few months, John wrestled with his questions and his fears. Simultaneously, Charles was going through a similar process. Together they sought out some Moravian Christians who were living and ministering in London. They asked a lot of questions but couldn't for the life of them understand what they were doing wrong. By May, the struggle in both men was intensifying. Charles became quite ill but kept praying, pleading with God to show him the way. "I waked [one night] hungry and thirsty after God," he wrote in his journal on May 12, 1738. The next night he wrote, "I waked without Christ; yet still desirous of finding him." On May 14 he wrote, "I longed to find Christ, that I might show him to all mankind; that I might praise, that I might love him."[34]

Another week went by. Charles again sought out the Moravians and studied Paul's epistle to the Galatians with them. And finally, on Sunday, May 21, Charles's eyes were opened. Until then, his religion had been an intellectual affair. It had not yet penetrated his heart. Now he understood what Christ meant when he said a man must be "born again," and he prayed to receive Christ as his personal Savior and Lord. "I found myself at peace with God and rejoiced in hope of loving Christ." And he quickly wrote a hymn, likely "Christ the Friend of Sinners," expressing the joy of his newfound, life-transforming faith.[35]

John, too, was reading his Bible, discussing it with the Moravians, and spending much time wrestling with God in prayer. And that very month, he began to realize that his religion had been a purely intellectual pursuit and that he himself didn't actually have a personal relationship with Jesus Christ. On May 24, 1738—just three days after his younger brother—he, too, was born again. "In the evening, I went very unwillingly to a society in Aldersgate Street, where one was reading Luther's preface to the epistle to the Romans," John wrote in his journal. "About a quarter before nine, while he was describing the change which God works in the heart through faith in Christ, I felt my heart strangely warmed. I felt I did trust in Christ, Christ alone for salvation, and an assurance was given me that he had taken away my sins, even mine, and saved me from the law of sin and death."[36]

In the days that followed, both John and Charles read the Bible with new eyes and new insight. They felt a deep sense of joy and inner peace that they had never previously experienced. They were no longer trying to earn God's love; rather, they found themselves enjoying his favor and thanking him profusely.

At one point, John wrote something quite telling in his journal: "I left my native country in order to teach the Georgian Indians the nature of Christianity. But what have I learned myself in the meantime? Why . . . that I who went to America to convert others was never myself converted to God."[37]

Now he and his younger brother were genuinely converted and eager to serve the Lord with renewed fervor. Almost immediately, they were contacted by Whitefield, who asked them to come help him preach the gospel in the open air, for he was overwhelmed with the enormous response and desperately needed assistance. At first the Wesleys were appalled by the radical concept of preaching the Word of God outside the walls of a church building. But they couldn't deny that the Spirit of God was moving powerfully, and they truly wanted to let Christ lead them rather than trying to follow their own strategies. Their lives were about to change forever.

Charles dove into open-air preaching almost immediately. From June 24 through July 8, 1738—barely a month after his conversion—he preached to crowds of ten thousand people. Later he preached the gospel to a crowd of twenty thousand at Kennington Common. He preached whenever and wherever the Lord told him, regardless of the size of the audience. In fact, from 1739 to 1743, Charles tabulated the number of people to whom he had preached, and the figure came to more than 149,000.[38]

And Charles was not even considered the gifted preacher between the brothers—John was. Charles's real passion—indeed, his genius—was writing hymns and urging people to praise and worship the risen Christ.

John certainly had a passion for preaching and teaching the Word of God as well, but he soon discovered that his real spiritual gifting lay in leadership and administration, and his genius was organization. He didn't simply want to see the gospel preached and the Word taught. He wanted to organize people into small groups to study the Scriptures and pray for one another. He wanted to recruit and train pastors. He wanted to help these young new pastors plant churches. He wanted to organize conferences to better equip pastors and lay leaders. He wanted to make sure churches had excellent hymnals filled with theologically sound psalms, hymns, and spiritual songs—many written by Charles. And he didn't simply want to reach England. He wanted to make disciples of all nations, just as the Lord commanded in Matthew 28:18-20.

John wanted to recruit, train, and send missionaries all over the world—and especially to the American colonies—to preach the gospel and plant more churches. These, John believed, were the methods by which the gospel would be spread and the church strengthened and expanded. And thus was set into motion the beginnings of what would become known in England and America as the Methodist church.

The Impact of the Wesley Brothers

It is difficult to overstate how powerfully God used the Wesley brothers to fan into flame the great spiritual awakenings under way on both sides of the Atlantic, but especially in America. For while the brothers invested most of their time in England, their most lasting impact was in America, as they sent well-trained pastors and missionaries to establish Christ-centered Methodist churches from north to south.

Having perceived themselves as failures with their Holy Club on one side of the pond, and then failures as missionaries in the New World, the Wesleys were clearly determined to make up for lost time. They beseeched the Lord to give them faith, courage, and clarity of purpose and to allow them to truly make a significant difference for Christ at home and abroad. And the Lord certainly heard and answered their prayers.

Charles established a remarkable legacy. In addition to much preaching and teaching of his own, he published some six thousand hymns in his lifetime and wrote nearly four thousand more that weren't published while he was alive. Among his compositions are great classics of the faith such as "Hark! the Herald Angels Sing," "O for a Thousand Tongues to Sing," "And Can It Be?," "Christ the Lord Is Risen Today," "Rejoice, the Lord Is King," and "Christ, Whose Glory Fills the Skies." Truly, Charles helped believers throughout America (as well as England and Europe) learn solid, biblical theology while also learning to praise and worship the Lord in song.

John's impact was no less profound. "In an era when Britain enjoyed virtually no reliable roads," one historian noted, "John Wesley traveled constantly to spread the good news of grace in Christ. After [his conversion] in 1738, his preaching tours took him about a quarter of a million miles (mostly on horseback), and he delivered forty thousand sermons (that is, an average of more than two a day). . . . Only in his seventies did Wesley abandon his horse for a carriage. Only in his mid-eighties did Wesley give up preaching before dawn."[39]

John Wesley wasn't only faithful to the Lord's calling to preach and teach, however. He was also faithful in making disciples and establishing trained and gifted shepherds to continue the work long after he was gone. By the time he died in 1791, he had helped recruit and train 294 preachers in Britain and established the Methodist church in England with 71,668 members. He had also helped recruit and train 198 preachers across the Atlantic and established the American Methodist church with 43,265 members.[40]

Yet this was just the beginning. As we will see in the next chapter, the Methodist church was soon growing exponentially in the young United States as more and more pastors were recruited and trained to preach the gospel and plant theologically solid, Bible-believing congregations. The methods were working because they were rooted in biblical principles and because God was showing tremendous favor to the humble and faithful Methodist shepherds.

Without question, God used the Wesleys to make an enormous impact in the Great Awakening in the eighteenth century, and as we will also see, they helped plant seeds that would bear enormous fruit in the Second Great Awakening in the nineteenth century as well.

Bottom Line

In the early 1700s, the American people were living in darkness. Their political leaders were corrupt and oppressive. The culture was coarsening. The churches were weak. Yet God in his mercy heard the prayers of some faithful pastors and laypeople and sent a series of revivals that dramatically transformed individuals, families, and a continent.

During the Great Awakening, God raised up:

- a brilliant but humble theologian, pastor, and author by the name of Jonathan Edwards to advance the Kingdom of God through the pulpit and the printed word

- a powerful itinerant evangelist by the name of George Whitefield to advance the Kingdom of God through open-air preaching, an new and unconventional form of ministry
- a passionate and tireless shepherd with a genius for organization by the name of John Wesley to advance the Kingdom of God through discipleship, pastor training, and church planting
- a tremendously gifted hymn writer by the name of Charles Wesley to advance the Kingdom of God through praise and worship

What's more, God raised up myriad other faithful pastors and laypeople to teach, pray, give, and serve sacrificially as God poured out his Holy Spirit on the American people far beyond what any of them could have ever imagined.

Was every lost soul in the thirteen colonies saved during the Great Awakening? No. Did every pastor and every person in every congregation on the American continent rededicate his or her life to Jesus Christ at the time? No. Did every believer then (or now) agree with every point of theology that Edwards, Whitefield, the Wesleys, and the others taught? No.* This spiritual revival was not a one-size-fits-all solution to every social problem. It didn't create a perfect society. Indeed, the Bible makes it clear that society will never be perfect until the new heaven and the new earth described in the book of Revelation.

But the goal of the revivalists in the early 1700s wasn't perfection; it was progress. Their Scriptural basis for this was sound. The apostle Paul didn't require perfection in his disciple Timothy or expect him to save the whole city of Ephesus when he directed the young pastor

---

*Whitefield and the Wesleys had a terrible falling-out over theological differences that divided them for many years. Whitefield was a devout Calvinist; the Wesleys were devout Arminians. Fortunately, they reconciled near the end of their lives, and John Wesley preached a warm and moving eulogy at George Whitefield's funeral.

to serve there. Rather, Paul urged Timothy to faithfully use his spiritual gifts, to boldly preach the gospel, to preach the Word of God consistently, to be faithful in prayer, to make disciples and encourage those under his care to do the same, and to govern himself and the congregation he pastored in such a way that "your progress will be evident to all" (1 Timothy 4:15). These were the goals of the leaders of the Great Awakening as well.

In this regard, the historical record is clear and compelling: the Great Awakening had a dramatic and positive impact on individual lives and families and on early American society as a whole. Millions of people became hungry for the Word of God. Millions of people renewed their commitments to live lives of greater holiness and to pray for their neighbors and their nation. As Americans rediscovered the timeless truths of the Scriptures, they became more unified as a people and more courageous in standing for what was right.

In time, this national hunger for spiritual freedom and wise, moral leadership led to the widespread desire to be a nation free from the religious, economic, and political tyranny imposed by King George III. While not every founding father was a devout Christian, many of them were, and they sought to establish a free society based firmly on Judeo-Christian principles. The Great Awakening thus created the moral climate for the Declaration of Independence and the founding of a new country, conceived in liberty, which would truly become a light to the nations. No country in the history of mankind has done more to liberate other peoples politically, economically, or spiritually than the United States of America. And all this began with the prayers and the preaching of a few faithful, prayerful men.

To be clear, neither George Whitefield nor most of the other powerful preachers of his day had political motives. Their goals were spiritual. They weren't trying to build an independence movement against the king of England. They were trying to be faithful to the King of kings and the Lord of lords. They weren't trying to build powerful political parties. They were trying to wake up a sleeping church and rediscover the power of the Holy Spirit. They were not trying to run for office. They were trying to run the race marked out for them by Christ himself. But their efforts had social and political consequences beyond their expectations. And by God's grace—and in his power and for his glory—they were remarkably successful in turning many Americans back to the Lord and setting the fledgling nation on the right track for decades to come.

Let me encourage you to study the events and the leaders of the Great Awakening for yourself. I think they will amaze you as they have me. Understanding the dynamics of the Great Awakening has inspired and encouraged me. It has given me cause for optimism that what God has done in the past to revive and restore America he could certainly do again. Even more encouraging is the fact that amazingly, this wasn't the only time America experienced a spiritual rebirth. Just a few decades later, a Second Great Awakening swept the young country in a historic way. Let us turn our attention now to this second remarkable revival as we ponder the question of whether God might be so gracious as to give us another one in our time.

CHAPTER FIFTEEN

MORE CAUSE FOR OPTIMISM: INSIDE AMERICA'S SECOND GREAT AWAKENING

NO SPIRITUAL REVIVAL LASTS FOREVER. If the church does not remain faithful in prayer and faithful to the Spirit-filled teaching of God's Word, even the children and grandchildren of those who have been greatly awakened can find themselves drifting off to sleep. Unfortunately, after the American Revolution, after the long, hard fight against the British, many Americans began drifting again from the nation's biblical moorings, and before long, the new democracy was experiencing a cultural crisis that threatened to unravel the fabric of the country.

Professor Mark Noll, the esteemed Christian historian who in 2005 was named by *Time* magazine as one of "The 25 Most Influential Evangelicals in America,"[1] described post-Revolution America in his extensive and insightful book *A History of Christianity in the United States and Canada.*

The state of Christianity after the American Revolution was not good. The tide of warfare itself had disrupted many local congregations, particularly where the fighting had been most intense—in New Jersey, New York City, the Philadelphia area, and the Carolinas. The Revolution had dealt an especially hard blow to the Episcopal church, whose ties with England made it particularly suspect. . . . Interest in religion more generally also seemed on the decline. Concern for creating a new nation, for populating the open lands west of the Appalachians, for overcoming the ravages of inflation, and for avoiding foreign entanglements left little time for church. . . . [After the Revolution,] well under 10 percent of the population belonged formally to local congregations, and many on the frontier were entirely devoid of Christian influence.[2]

Fortunately, God chose to move in a very powerful way in America in the early 1800s, and we can learn much from what became known as the Second Great Awakening.

The Second Great Awakening (1800–1850s)

As I mentioned in the previous chapter, I first became curious about this period in history back in the late 1990s, when I was working as a senior aide to Steve Forbes, editor in chief of the nation's foremost business magazine and two-time presidential candidate. During the four years I worked for Steve (1996–2000), I had the opportunity to work closely with him on two books, a small paperback titled *The Moral Basis of a Free Society* and a hardcover titled *A New Birth of Freedom*. One of the things I appreciated so much about Steve was his command of American history and his great curiosity about the Second Great Awakening. He spoke of it frequently during his 1996 campaign.

Before I joined the campaign, I remember watching Steve on C-SPAN and other networks as he suggested to audiences in Iowa and New Hampshire that America had made positive, sweeping changes in the past and that we could do so again. Such talk captured my interest. It wasn't often that I heard business leaders or presidential candidates talk about the vital importance of spiritual revivals in American history, much less our urgent need for more of them. I was impressed, and when I was asked to join his team as a communications advisor, I was honored to do so. I believed in his message and was eager to help more people hear it. I was particularly encouraged when Steve decided to embark on these two writing projects and asked me to do more research on the Second Great Awakening.

What we found—drawing on the work of Professor Noll and a range of other Christian and secular historians—was fascinating.

Following the Revolutionary War, America experienced a period of moral decline. . . . Spiritual devotion waned, and social problems proliferated. From the late 1770s until the late 1820s, per capita consumption of alcohol in America rose dramatically, to about four or five times what it is today. Everybody took a swig from the jug—teachers, preachers, children. They called it "hard cider," but it was nothing like the cider we buy at the grocery store today. In those days, it seemed everyone was in a haze by noontime. . . . The social consequences were predictable.

"Illegitimate births were rampant. . . . Thomas Paine was proclaiming that Christianity was dead—and certainly the body of faith appeared to be in a coma. Yet even as church rolls were shrinking and greed, sensuality, and family breakdown were becoming more widespread, America was about to experience a great spiritual revival."

Slowly at first, then building over the next several decades, one wave of spiritual renewal and religious rededication after another swept the country, in what historians now call America's "Second Great Awakening." In one community after another, people began to wake up from their moral and spiritual slumber as though saying, "If we're going to have a self-governing nation, it must be occupied by self-governing people." The first public health movement in America was launched not by government but by citizens such as Lyman Beecher, the founder of the American Bible Society and a pastor who went on to form the American Society for the Promotion of Temperance in 1826. This enterprise became known as the Temperance Movement—and it worked. Within one generation alcoholic consumption in America fell by two-thirds.

Soon pastors and community leaders were opening elementary and secondary schools (this was before "public" education), founding colleges and universities, setting up orphanages and homes for abandoned children, creating shelters for the poor, building hospitals, and exhorting people to stop drinking and spend more time with their families.[3]

I learned a lot in the process of working on those projects. Since then I've taken the time to look even more closely at this remarkable period of American history. I've learned that in many ways the Second Great Awakening was even more powerful and impactful on American society in the nineteenth century than the First Great Awakening had been in the eighteenth. The more I learned, the more I found myself hoping that maybe, just maybe, the Lord will bless us with a third such sweeping spiritual awakening in our times.

The Rise of Francis Asbury (1745–1816)

One of the most important figures in the Second Great Awakening was a man named Francis Asbury. Born near Birmingham, England, on August 20, 1745, as America's First Great Awakening was in full swing, Asbury was raised in a strong Christian home by parents who had been heavily influenced by the teachings of John Wesley. In 1771, after Asbury had finished his schooling, he heard Wesley urge young people in Britain to become missionaries to America. The twenty-six-year-old Asbury quickly signed up.

He didn't see much success at the beginning of his ministry. After all, the Revolutionary War was about to disrupt everything and make Americans extremely wary if not hostile toward anyone from England. In fact, soon after the war broke out, every single other Methodist missionary left America and returned to England. But not Asbury. He stayed put. He carefully navigated the dangerous political climate, built strong personal relationships with pastors throughout the colonies, faithfully planted the seeds of the Word of God, and preached the gospel. In so doing he laid the groundwork for a ministry that in time, he prayed, would bear much fruit, just as the Wesley brothers had taught him.

In reading various accounts of Asbury, several things moved me.

First, Asbury was a man deeply committed to Jesus Christ. He rose around four or five o'clock in the morning—obviously not to watch television or check his e-mail or engage in trivialities. Rather, Asbury spent at least an hour in prayer, pleading with God to give him strength and wisdom and to change the hearts of Americans wherever he preached.[4]

Second, Asbury was a man deeply committed to the Word of God. Asbury studied the Bible voraciously and read many other Christian books as well. Indeed, he wrote in his journal that his daily routine was to read at least a hundred pages to keep his mind and heart sharp and focused.[5]

Third, Asbury was a man deeply committed to preaching the gospel no matter what the cost. Over the course of his ministry as a Methodist church circuit rider, he logged more than three hundred thousand miles on his trusty horse, riding from town to town, village to village, state to state to spread the Word of God and try to save men's souls. He is said to have crossed the Appalachian Mountains more than sixty times to find and reach Americans who had never heard the gospel before.[6] During all those travels—often through blistering heat or driving rain or freezing snow (conditions that frequently left him ill)—he preached more than ten thousand sermons.[7] Though he wasn't known as a particularly fiery or charismatic speaker, he was convinced that living frugally, teaching the Bible simply, being out among the people, understanding their concerns, and communicating in a way they could understand would ultimately be effective. And it was. This life wasn't easy for him or for his wife. But Asbury was determined to be found faithful to this high calling and let nothing distract him from his mission.

Fourth, Asbury was a man deeply committed to making disciples, recruiting and training new pastors, and planting new churches that were biblically based and theologically committed to solid, orthodox Christianity. He believed that Christ had given him—and all believers—the great commission not simply to go and preach the gospel but also to make disciples. So that's what he did. He knew full well that the vast majority of towns and villages he traveled to and through didn't have a church and couldn't afford a preacher. He also knew that he couldn't personally shepherd all the people he and his allies were helping lead to Christ. So he became determined to do more than simply preach the gospel in these areas. He also wanted to help the new Christians start their own congregations with pastors who could minister to them year-round. He held training meetings. He organized and taught at regional Bible conferences. Like the apostle Paul on his missionary journeys, Asbury returned to visit new pastors in various far-flung parts of the country time and again so he could answer their questions and encourage them and help them not feel isolated and alone. He proved to be an extraordinary organizer of men as he followed (and at times improved upon) the methods that Wesley had taught him in England, for which the Methodists became so well known in their early history. On top of all this, and again following the Wesleys' lead, he dedicated himself to caring for the poor and needy and the disenfranchised in society, and he encouraged the men he trained to care for them as well.

The Impact of Francis Asbury

The impact of Asbury's approach was nothing less than astounding. Inspired by the Wesley brothers to leave England and become a Methodist missionary in America, Asbury was the model disciple. He studied the Wesley model carefully, applied it tirelessly, prayed continuously, and by the grace of God saw tremendous fruit.

Yet what impresses me most about Asbury is his keen understanding that his objective should not simply be winning converts in the colonies, as wonderful as that would be. Rather, he saw his objective as identifying, recruiting, training, and mobilizing into action future pastors, evangelists, and disciple makers. Winning more souls to Christ, he determined, would simply be a ministry of addition—useful but shortsighted. Recruiting and training more soul winners and church planters, by contrast, would be a ministry of multiplication. If he did it right and did it well, relying upon the power of the Holy Spirit and not his own human effort, Asbury realized that a ministry of multiplication could help the Methodist church not simply expand but grow exponentially over time. That was the Wesleys' theory. It was heartily embraced by Asbury. And they were right.

"Statistics can never tell a whole story," Mark Noll wrote, "but when Francis Asbury came to America in 1771, four Methodist ministers were caring for about 300 laypeople. When he died in 1816, there were 2,000 ministers and over 200,000 Methodists in the States and several thousand more in Canada devoted, as he put it, to 'the dear Redeemer . . . of precious souls.'"[8]

Many of those new Methodist pastors were saved through Asbury's preaching and were recruited and trained in part by his efforts. Such men then followed his lead and saw extraordinary results.

- By 1830, there were over 500,000 followers of Christ who had become members of the Methodist church in the United States.
- By 1840, that number had climbed to over 890,000.
- By 1850, there were more than 1.2 million professing Methodists in the U.S.
- By 1900, that number had skyrocketed to more than 4.6 million.[9]

Can we say with absolute certainty that each and every one of those was a born-again believer? We cannot, though many certainly were, and there is a rich history of people being truly converted through the Methodist church during the nineteenth century and becoming mobilized to care for the poor and needy, to start schools and orphanages, and to impact their communities in other positive ways in the name of Jesus.

Sadly, in the twentieth century many Methodist congregations embraced liberal theology and distanced themselves from the orthodox teachings of their predecessors, but that cannot be held against the movement's founders or early leaders. Indeed, we should pray for the Methodist church to experience another awakening today that would take it back to its solid biblical roots, that it might again have such a powerful effect on the American nation.

The Rise of Timothy Dwight (1752–1817)

In the last chapter, we noted the remarkable legacy of Jonathan Edwards's descendants and the key roles many of them have played in American religious, social, and political life, as well as in overseas missions. Consider briefly the story of one of those descendants, an important but generally overlooked figure in the Second Great Awakening.

Timothy Dwight, a grandson of Jonathan and Sarah Edwards on his mother's side, was born on May 14, 1752, in Northampton, Massachusetts. Raised in a deeply devoted Christian home, he gave his life to Jesus Christ at a young age. He was a brilliant boy who was homeschooled by his mother (since there were no public schools at the time) and loved to study the Scriptures. "It didn't take long for Mary Dwight to discover her eldest had an unusually quick mind," one chronicler noted. "By age four, Dwight was reading the Bible, songbooks, books on prayer, and whatever else his mother gave him. At the age of six, the precocious Dwight would overhear Latin lessons given to older boys at a local grammar school, and then steal away on his own to go over Lily's Latin Grammar. He had a remarkably absorbent mind and not infrequently surprised adults by recounting stories he had read, with all the minutiae included."[10]

Dwight attended and graduated from Yale College in New Haven, Connecticut (later expanded into Yale University). Among other subjects, he studied theology and became an ordained minister, serving as a military chaplain during the Revolutionary War. After the war, he became the pastor of a congregation in Greenfield, Connecticut, started an elementary school, was twice elected to the Massachusetts legislature, and became an outspoken opponent of slavery. Committed as he was to impacting both the church and the newly free American nation for the cause of Christ, he was also determined to impact the world for Christ. Working toward this goal, he helped start three foreign missions societies to recruit, train, send, and support evangelists, pastors, and church planters to win souls in other countries.

Despite poor health and weak eyesight, Dwight read constantly, and he loved to write. He was a poet and penned a multi-book epic titled *The Conquest of Canaan* about the Jews conquering and settling the land of Israel.

For most men, such accomplishments would have been enough, but not for a descendant of Jonathan Edwards. For Dwight, this was merely preparation for how God was going to use him next. In 1795, Dwight was elected president of Yale College, his alma mater. He wasn't entirely sure, however, that he wanted the assignment. Yale was not the school it had once been. Founded in 1701 by clergymen who wanted to train young men to make a difference for Christ, Yale had built an impressive legacy early on. Twenty-five of its graduates had served in the Continental Congress. Four had signed the Declaration of Independence. But since the end of the war, the prestigious school had drifted from its biblical moorings, and Dwight wasn't convinced it could be turned around.

"Before [President Dwight] came college was in a most ungodly state," a Yale student during this time later wrote. "The college church was almost extinct. Most of the students were skeptical, and . . . intemperance, profanity, gambling, and licentiousness were common."[11]

"Students found pleasure in nightly revelings that frequently included breaking tutors' windows and smashing bottles," another chronicler wrote. "Yale men regularly clashed with drunken townsmen in violent engagements where rocks flew and clubs flailed. Christian faith was unfashionable and reviled on campus."[12]

From 1701 to 1744, records show that on average, half of Yale's graduates went into full-time Christian ministry. By the late 1790s, however, most of the students attending Yale weren't even professing Christians.[13] The year Timothy Dwight took office, barely one in ten of the 125 students enrolled at Yale would admit to being a Christian.[14]

"To build up a ruined college is a difficult task," Dwight remarked upon being named Yale's president.[15]

Nevertheless, that's what he set out to do.

The Impact of Timothy Dwight

After much prayer and analysis of the situation on campus, Dwight concluded that the only way to change Yale was to change the minds of the students and faculty who lived and worked there. The only way to change their minds was to change their hearts. And the only way to change their hearts was for God to do it himself by bringing about a revival.

Dwight *knew* revival was possible. As a boy he had seen the effects of the Great Awakening with his own eyes. He had heard his mother's and grandfather's stories with his own ears. He had read his grandfather's books. He knew that in dark times Jonathan Edwards had trusted in the inerrancy of God's Word and the transforming power of the Holy Spirit. Dwight couldn't know for sure whether God would choose to send revival again or not. But he had faith in passages of Scripture like "You do not have because you do not ask God" (James 4:2, NIV) and "The effective prayer of a righteous man can accomplish much" (James 5:16). What's more, he believed that revivals would precede the second coming of Jesus Christ, and he wanted to be faithful in doing his part while praying for and expecting God to do his.

First, Dwight personally engaged the faculty and staff. He met with them and got to know them. He let them know who he was and where he was coming from, and he made it clear that under his leadership, Yale would now be returning to its biblical heritage. He suggested that those who supported this direction were welcome to stay, but for anyone who embraced theological heresy or European radicalism, it was time to leave. Some have suggested that Dwight unleashed a purge at Yale, firing numerous professors who refused to boldly profess their Christian faith.[16] While I have not found sufficient evidence to back up such broad claims, there is no question that Dwight did let at least one faculty member go—Josiah Meigs, professor of mathematics, who was a supporter of the antireligious elements of the French Revolution and who clashed repeatedly with Dwight on a range of issues.[17]

Second, Dwight personally engaged the students. He didn't hide from their skepticism and cynicism but directly answered them. In a class he taught to seniors, he asked the students to give him a list of all the tough questions they wanted answered that semester. "When the senior class decided to test their new instructor by suggesting they debate the question, 'Are the Scriptures of the Old and New Testament the Word of God?' Dwight, to their utter amazement, picked up the gauntlet," one chronicler noted. "With academic rigor he refuted the popular arguments against the reliability of Scripture and submitted his reasons for believing it to be the revelation of God. With a rhetorical knife sharpened by faith and years of diligent study, he cut through the seductive abstractions of the French philosophies and demonstrated to their devotees the unreasonableness of what they had embraced."[18]

Third, Dwight powerfully taught the Word of God day in and day out. In the classroom and in the college chapel, he did what few, if any, members of the faculty or administration at Yale had done in quite some time—he opened the Bible and made it the centerpiece of the students' instruction. He also began "preaching six solid months on the question of biblical authority and accuracy."[19]

Students could not refute Dwight's deep understanding of Scripture or his deconstruction of all manner of philosophical and religious heresies. He spent time with the students one-on-one and in small groups. They were generating lots of questions, but Dwight patiently answered them all. A man once asked him whether he allowed his children to read "the books of infidels." "Yes," Dwight replied, "for they must become acquainted with them sooner or later, and while I am living I can confute the arguments they use. . . . I should be unwilling to have them find these arguments unawares, with nobody to meet them."[20]

Indeed, Dwight treated his students with the same love and respect that he afforded his own children. The approach startled everyone at first, but eventually it began to work. In 1796, barely one in ten students at Yale claimed to be followers of Jesus Christ. But God was beginning to answer Dwight's prayers. "Signs of revival began to emerge as early as 1797, when a group of twenty-five students founded the Moral Society of Yale College. Members of this secret society pledged to hold one another accountable in small groups similar to the Wesleys' Holy Clubs at Oxford. . . . This stirring foreshadowed bigger outpourings to come."[21]

Dwight kept faithfully praying and teaching the Word. One by one, students were giving their lives to Christ. Dwight thanked God for each soul, but he was praying for something more dramatic. And then, suddenly, the dam broke. During the 1801–1802 school year, a true revival broke out on campus. Fully one-third of students enrolled in Yale—about 80 out of 230—prayed to receive Christ. Thirty-five of them decided to enter full-time Christian ministry. Benjamin Silliman, a student at the time, wrote to his mother to say that Yale College had become "a little temple: prayer and praise seem to be the delight of the greater part of the students, while those who are still unfeeling are awed into respectful silence."[22] Heman Humphrey, then a freshman, wrote, "The whole college was shaken. It seemed for a time as if the whole mass of the students would press into the kingdom. It was the Lord's doing, and marvelous in all eyes. Oh, what a blessed change! . . . It was a glorious reformation. It put a new face upon the college."[23]

Each year, of course, some of the spiritually strongest students would graduate, and new skeptics and cynics would arrive. But Dwight was undeterred. He kept praying and preaching and answering questions, and he saw another revival sweep the campus in 1808. Then another during the 1812–1813 academic year when nearly half the student body accepted Christ. A fourth revival came in the spring of 1815, "this one sparked by a group of students who gathered at 3:30 every morning to pray for the campus."[24]

Dwight, however, was not content simply to lead students to the Lord. He discipled them and endeavored to equip them to preach the gospel and teach the Word to the rest of the country and the world. And the Lord rewarded those efforts. Newly converted students shared the gospel with fellow students, leading many to the Lord. They gathered for prayer and Bible study. And they encouraged one another to think beyond their time at Yale on how the Lord might use them to further advance the Kingdom of God. Over the course of his tenure at Yale, Dwight saw an average of one in five graduates enter full-time Christian ministry, often as pastors or missionaries.[25]

One of his earliest converts, from the class of 1797, became one of his most fruitful disciples. Lyman Beecher, who considered Dwight his mentor, not only trusted Christ under Dwight's preaching but stayed on at Yale for another year to study theology. Upon leaving Yale, Beecher went on to become an ordained pastor, a renowned Bible teacher, an evangelist, the president of a seminary, a trainer of missionaries to reach the American West, an outspoken abolitionist, and a key figure in the Second Great Awakening. A tireless organizer seemingly cut from the same cloth as John Wesley, Beecher launched one new ministry after another. He helped found and build the American Bible Society, the American Sunday School Union, the American Tract Society, and the American Society for the Promotion of Temperance.[26]

When Dwight died on January 11, 1817, he had not seen all the fruit his ministry would eventually bear, but he had surely proven faithful to his task. "It would be impossible to adequately describe the legacy he left behind at Yale and beyond," two church historians noted. "Revival spread from Yale to Dartmouth and Princeton, though Harvard continued its slide toward Unitarianism. Yale continued to experience revival long after Dwight's death. The largest revival came in 1831, when 104 students became members of the college church, and 900 others in New Haven were converted."[27]

The Rise of Charles Finney (1792–1875)

While Timothy Dwight's influence during the Second Great Awakening was primarily in New England, and Francis Asbury's influence was primarily in the Mid-Atlantic, the South, and over the Appalachian Mountains, God also raised up men in New York State—the most populous state in the union in the 1800s and thus one of the most influential—to preach the gospel to the lost and revive the existing churches. One of the most prominent—and at times controversial—of these men was Charles Grandison Finney.

Charles Finney was born in Litchfield County, Connecticut, on August 29, 1792, but his family soon moved to Oneida County in central New York and later to the southern shores of Lake Ontario, near a town called Sackett's Harbor. "Neither of my parents were professing Christians, and among our neighbors there were very few religious people," he wrote in his autobiography. "I seldom heard a sermon, unless it was an occasional one from some traveling minister."[28]

The first time Finney became interested in the Bible was while studying to become a lawyer in the town of Adams, New York, in Jefferson County, not far from the Adirondack Mountains. Noticing how often the law of Moses or other Scriptures were cited in his law books, he bought his first copy of the Bible and began to read it eagerly, though he understood little of it at first. What bothered Finney and kept him from the faith for some time was the dullness and lethargy and even hypocrisy that he saw in the churches he attended. He met numerous ministers, for example, who didn't seem to truly believe the very Scriptures they were teaching. This troubled him greatly, and rightly so.

But there were also occasions when he misread the hearts and motives and sincerity of genuine believers, for he was not yet one himself. For a period of time, Finney attended a weekly prayer meeting that he concluded had no purpose and no impact. "On one occasion when I was in one of the prayer meetings, I was asked if I did not desire that they should pray for me," he wrote. "I told them no, because I did not see that God answered their prayers. I said, 'I suppose I need to be prayed for, for I am conscious that I am a sinner, but I do not see that it will do any good for you to pray for me, for you are continually asking, but you do not receive. You have been praying for a revival ever since I have been in Adams, and yet you do not have it. You have been praying for the Holy Spirit to descend upon you, and yet complaining of your leanness."[29]

Little did Finney know that God *was* about to answer the prayers of those nameless but faithful saints—and the prayers of many others like them around the Northeast. Indeed, a sweeping revival was coming there, too, and the Lord was going to use Finney as one of the key agents of change.

It began on October 10, 1821, when Finney himself was miraculously saved. After many months of searching the Scriptures and imploring God for insight, one night Finney's eyes were opened. "Right there the revelation of my pride was distinctly shown to me as the great difficulty that stood in the way," Finney wrote. He wept on his knees, deeply struck by "an overwhelming sense of my wickedness." Yet at that moment, a passage of Scripture he had been reading (Jeremiah 29:12-13) "seemed to drop into my mind with a flood of light," and he sensed the Lord saying directly to him, "Then shall you go and pray unto me, and I will hearken to you. Then shall you seek me and find me when you shall search for me with all your heart."[30]

What happened next stunned Finney. "I instantly seized hold of this with my heart. I had intellectually believed the Bible before, but never had the truth been in my mind that faith was a voluntary trust instead of an intellectual state. . . . I seized hold of [God's promises] with the grasp of a drowning man. . . . I remembered saying with great emphasis, 'If I am ever converted, I will preach the Gospel.'"[31]

Finney was not only saved to his great joy and relief, but he was true to his word, and the Lord used him to great effect. Immediately, acquaintances could see a change in his countenance and asked him what had changed. He told them of his salvation, and others began trusting Christ from that first day. The more people with whom Finney shared the gospel and his own experience, the more people were struck deeply by their own need for salvation, and they, too, prayed to receive Christ.

Soon Finney was leading so many people to the Lord that he decided he could no longer do the work of a lawyer but had to preach the gospel with all of his time. He realized that he had decided to become a lawyer before coming to Christ. He had never made the decision with God's wisdom or direction. Therefore, he concluded after prayer, the career wasn't from the Lord. He became convinced that he had the spiritual gift of an evangelist as described by the apostle Paul in Ephesians 4:11 and thus had to obey Paul's admonition in 2 Timothy 4:5 to "do the work of an evangelist, [and] fulfill your ministry."

The Impact of Charles Finney

Word spread rapidly that something extraordinary was happening. The power and favor of Christ was upon Finney's life, and people could see it and sense it and were moved by it. Though he had no formal training in theology, he understood the basics of the gospel, and when he shared these truths, people said yes to Jesus. "The work spread among all classes and extended itself not only through the village but also out of the village in every direction," Finney recalled. "My heart was so full that for more than a week I did not feel at all inclined to sleep or eat."[32]

Finney's parents were soon converted after he shared the message of Christ with them. Ministers began to ask him to preach, and he accepted many of those invitations. Floods of people were converted through his proclamation of the gospel.

Pastors who thought they had already been saved realized they had never truly been born again and were dramatically converted. Soon they, too, began preaching the gospel with new sincerity and conviction. People who had attended church for years but had never really believed now trusted Christ and began sharing the gospel with family, friends, and neighbors. Time after time, skeptics and cynics came to Finney's meetings to mock the young preacher, but time after time they shortly fell to their knees, weeping and begging Christ for mercy.

Finney realized that he desperately needed to know as much of the Bible as he possibly could. He later wrote, "I read my Bible on my knees a great deal during those days . . . beseeching the Lord to teach me his own mind."[33]

Finney also wrote, "I used to spend a great deal of time in prayer, sometimes literally praying 'without ceasing.' I also found it very profitable, and felt very much inclined to hold frequent days of private fasting. On those days I would seek to be entirely alone with God—and would generally wander off into the woods, or get into the meeting house [church] or somewhere away entirely by myself. . . . Whenever I fasted and let the Spirit take his course with me, and gave myself up to let him lead and instruct me, I always found it in the highest degree useful. I found I could not live without enjoying the presence of God."[34]

God heard Finney's prayers and used him even more mightily in the years ahead. Sometimes Finney would show up at a completely packed church to preach (he often spoke for up to two hours at a time) only to find that the moment he stood up to speak, people began crying and publicly confessing their sins and rededicating their lives to Jesus Christ before Finney said a word. People were not only receiving Christ as their Savior and Lord but were intensely moved by their own sinfulness and their desperate need for God's mercy and forgiveness.

Revivals swept through central and upstate New York in places like Syracuse, Rome, and Utica, and "a great revival in Rochester over the winter of 1830–31 catapulted him to national renown."[35] Rochester was one of the larger cities in western New York, with a population of approximately ten thousand at the time. Finney not only preached three times on Sundays but held revival meetings at least three other times each week. In fact, in Rochester, the outpouring of the Holy Spirit to save the unsaved and draw the already saved into a closer walk with Christ was so astounding that Finney's meetings drew hundreds of thousands of people from all over the region. Dr. Lyman Beecher, who contemporaneously chronicled the impact of the Finney revivals, observed that the ministry in Rochester "was the greatest work of God, and the greatest revival that the world has ever seen in so short a time. One hundred thousand . . . were reported as having connected themselves with churches as the results of that great revival. This is unparalleled in the history of the church."[36]

"The moral aspect of things [in Rochester] was greatly changed by this revival," Finney observed. "It was a young city, full of thrift and enterprise, but also full of sin. The inhabitants were intelligent and enterprising in the highest degree, but as the revival swept through the town and converted the great mass of the most influential people, both men and women, the change in the order, sobriety, and morality of the city was wonderful."[37]

Christianity Today has noted that "the zenith of Finney's evangelistic career was reached at Rochester, New York, where he preached 98 sermons between September 10, 1830, and March 6, 1831. Shopkeepers closed their businesses, posting notices urging people to attend Finney's meetings. . . . Crime dropped by two-thirds over the same period."[38]

Better yet, one historian noted, "the revival spread far beyond Rochester as revivalists and pastors who visited the city carried its enthusiasm and message back to the surrounding towns" and "a wave of revivals broke out from New England to Ohio as the new divinity suddenly caught hold and new measures proved an effective method for advancing them."[39] Finney preached the gospel all over the Northeast, including in New York City for a year. To train and equip pastors, evangelists, and laypeople, he also published books of his sermons and later his autobiography.

The Legacy of Charles Finney

Revival "is the renewal of the first love of Christians, resulting in the awakening and conversion of sinners to God," Finney wrote in his much-read and -discussed 1835 book, *Lectures on Revival*. "A revival of [true Christianity] is the arousing, quickening, and reclaiming of the more or less backslidden church and the more or less general awakening of all classes, and insuring attention to the claims of God. It presupposes that the church is sunk down in a backslidden state."[40]

In order to train a future generation of pastors and lay leaders and affect the moral and spiritual climate of the entire nation, Finney accepted the position of president of Oberlin College in Ohio in 1851. Like Francis Asbury, Finney took a long-term view. He didn't simply want to win souls; he wanted to win, build, and send pastors and fellow soul-winners throughout the United States. Also like Asbury, Finney cared deeply about the poor and needy in society, and he encouraged his students to do so as well. What's more, he believed women should receive better education, and Oberlin was the first college in the U.S. to admit women into its classes.[41]

At Oberlin, Finney also became known for advocating the abolition of slavery. He and his students helped lay the groundwork for the North's moral opposition to slavery that would change the future of the nation just nine years later. Tragically, the people of the South resisted such desperately needed moral changes as the abolition of slavery and the restoration of freedom and justice to African Americans. Southern states began to secede from the Union upon the election of Abraham Lincoln in 1860, eventually resulting in a war that brought tremendous devastation on the country. Neither Finney nor the other revivalists can be directly blamed for the Civil War. Their desire, shared by millions of other Americans in the North and the South, was to see a peaceful process of national reform and renewal.

Finney was not perfect, of course, and he was by no means everyone's cup of tea. His critics have accused him, for example, of being too emotional and theatrical in his preaching in the early years of his ministry, and this is a fair criticism. That said, he seems to have matured over time and was somewhat less emotional in his later preaching and teaching, to the point where some later criticized him for not being passionate enough in his preaching.

As noted previously, Finney was not a trained theologian. But this should by no means be a disqualifier. Many men and women who have been used powerfully by the Lord have not had formal theological training. Yet some believed Finney was not careful enough with his theology and his teaching of the Scriptures. Others saw Finney as an outright heretic. Both charges he vehemently denied.

While there are a number of theological areas in which one could take issue with Finney, let me note one here, as it is particularly relevant to whether we will see a Third Great Awakening. While Finney spoke often about the power of the Holy Spirit and wrote extensively about the role of the Holy Spirit in changing lives, he firmly believed that employing certain methods of ministry could bring about a revival no matter what. Whereas the Wesleys and Asbury taught that ministers should use certain methods based on biblical principles with the hope that the Lord would unleash revivals, Finney taught with conviction that if believers followed certain principles and took certain steps, God would, in turn, pour out his Holy Spirit, and a revival would ensue. "[Revival] is not a miracle," he argued vigorously, "or dependent on a miracle. . . . It consists entirely in the *right exercise* of the power of nature. It is just that, and nothing else. . . . It is a purely philosophical result of the right use of the constituted means—as much so as any other effect produced by the application of means. There may be a miracle among its antecedent causes, or there may not. The apostles employed miracles, simply as a means by which they arrested attention to their message, and established its divine authority. But the miracle was not the revival."[42]

I don't believe this teaching is scripturally sound. Revivals and awakenings cannot be created by man. Only God can bring them about. There are certainly things that the Scriptures tell all believers to do to serve the Lord and seek to win a community and bless a nation. We'll discuss these in the next chapter. Nowhere in Scripture, however, do we see that human actions guarantee a revival, much less a Great Awakening. Our test is our faithfulness to the Word, not the results that we see. Pastors and missionaries who faithfully preach the gospel in a community or a country for years but see little fruit will be rewarded in heaven for their faithful obedience to the Lord and his Word, not for their visible results. As the apostle Paul wrote to the church in Corinth, "I planted, Apollos watered, but God was causing the growth. So then neither the one who plants nor the one who waters is anything, but God who causes the growth. Now he who plants and he who waters are one; but each will receive his own reward according to his own labor" (1 Corinthians 3:6-8). We do our part, God does his, and only he decides whether to cause much growth or a little, to unleash a revival or an awakening or not.

That said, I don't think Finney should be condemned or dismissed for believing that his methods would always cause revivals. He took certain actions, and they did bear much fruit. Many people did come under the conviction of sin. Many people did repent and give their hearts, souls, and minds to Christ. Nearly everything Finney did seemed to result in revival. So perhaps he can be forgiven for believing that other believers in other times and places would see the same results if they took the same actions.

Not surprisingly, then, Finney is widely regarded by historians as one of the key players in the Second Great Awakening. In the end, an estimated half million souls were converted through his preaching.[43] Indeed, one historian has described Finney as having had "a greater impact on the public life of antebellum America than any of the nation's politicians."[44]

Bottom Line

Like the First Great Awakening before it, the Second Great Awakening was not a panacea. It did not save every soul or solve every social ill. No revival ever has or will. Men and women always have the freedom to reject the Word of God and the mighty demonstration of his Holy Spirit. Take Judas Iscariot, for example. The Bible describes Judas as walking with and serving alongside Jesus for years. He saw Christ heal the sick and raise the dead. Yet Judas never actually received Jesus as his Messiah and Savior but betrayed him instead. Sadly, it happens. People reject Christ for all sorts of reasons, even in the midst of Great Awakenings.

The good news is this: the historical evidence is clear and compelling that many Americans found salvation during these periods, and

American society as a whole was dramatically impacted and improved by both of these revivals. One piece of observable evidence in this regard is the explosive growth in the number of church congregations that were established in the wake of both Great Awakenings. Thomas S. Kidd, the historian and author of *The Great Awakening: The Roots of Evangelical Christianity in Colonial America*, noted that "as part of the stunning evangelical Protestant boom during that period, the total number of Baptist churches in America rose from about 150 in 1770 to just more than 12,000 in 1860."[45] Mark Noll, in his aforementioned book *A History of Christianity in the United States and Canada*, wrote, "Particularly in the southern and new western states, Baptists became leaders in evangelizing the frontier population. By 1812, there were close to 200,000 Baptists in the United States. . . . By 1850, the total exceeded 1,000,000. By that time, nearly three-fourths of them were also cooperating in national missionary ventures."[46] Likewise, Kidd's research concluded that "in 1770, Methodists had a paltry 20 churches in America. By 1860, that number had swelled to just under 20,000."[47]

And it wasn't just white Americans who were coming to faith and filling the churches. African Americans were coming to Christ in unprecedented numbers during this same period as well.[48]

What's more, Noll found that "the revivals of the Second Great Awakening increased interest in missionary outreach," moving the Baptists to send out more than one hundred missionaries into foreign lands in the early years of the 1800s.[49]

At the same time, Christians during this period sought to put their faith into action to improve their neighborhoods and communities and the nation as a whole. They persuaded millions of children to enroll in Sunday school programs to learn about the Bible and pray for their nation. They opened orphanages and soup kitchens to care for the poor and needy. They started clinics and hospitals to care for the sick, elderly, and infirm. They founded elementary and secondary schools for girls as well as boys. They established colleges and universities dedicated to teaching both the Scriptures and the sciences. They led social campaigns to persuade Americans to stop drinking so much alcohol and to abolish the evil of slavery. These Christians didn't expect the government to take care of them. They believed it was the church's job to show the love of Christ to their neighbors in real and practical ways. They were right, and they made America a better place as a result—not perfect, but better.

"Asbury and Finney were representatives of the most visible religious movements between the Revolution and the Civil War," Noll concluded in his history of American Christianity. "They were both charismatic figures. . . . They were both great communicators. . . . They both had broad visions of Christian society . . . defining Christian social responsibilities as clearly as they defined personal spiritual duties. Together with like-minded leaders of only slightly less influence, they established the revival and voluntary society as the foundations of American Protestant faith."[50]

Such history is worth examining. I encourage you to study the leaders and dynamics of the Second Great Awakening more closely for yourself and discuss what you learn with family, friends, and neighbors. I think you will be deeply encouraged, as I have been, that God has shown tremendous grace and mercy to America during dark times in the past.

CHAPTER SIXTEEN

WILL AMERICA EXPERIENCE A THIRD GREAT AWAKENING?

★ ★ ★ ★ ★ ★ ★ ★ ★ ★ ★ ★ ★ ★ ★ ★

FOR ME, THE CENTRAL QUESTION of our time for Americans is this: Will God in his grace and mercy decide to allow the American people to experience a Third Great Awakening?

If so, may this spiritual renaissance begin immediately, for we are desperate for his help. If not, then I believe our days are numbered and a terrible implosion is coming. There is no more middle ground, in my view. It is one or the other.

Unfortunately, I have absolutely no idea which way God will decide. I wish I did and could help prepare you for one outcome or the other. But as much as I long and pray for a Third Great Awakening, I simply don't know how this intense drama is going to play out.

So for me, the second-most important question of our time for Americans is this: How will we invest our time, talent, and treasure now, before either revival or implosion comes?

In a moment, I will endeavor to lay out the approach my family and I are taking, in the hope that it will be helpful to you as well. First, however, I need to acknowledge that some people believe they do know for certain what is coming. While working on this book, I attended an event to pray and fast for our country. One of the speakers proclaimed with great conviction that America will soon experience a Third Great Awakening. His comment caught me off guard. The young man on the platform wasn't simply asking God to bring about revival; rather, he was asserting to the audience that such a revival was a foregone conclusion, that we could bank on it. The audience erupted with wild applause, but I was troubled. *Is the speaker correct?* I wondered. *Can we truly rest assured that God is going to save our country from economic, spiritual, and cultural implosion?*

I have pondered and prayed over these questions for months. I have carefully studied the Scriptures and wrestled with a variety of passages. Unfortunately, I have to say that I remain as uncomfortable today as I was then by what this gentleman said to the audience and the way he said it, projecting an assurance that suggested he was speaking with scriptural authority. As we have noted, nowhere in Scripture is America specifically mentioned. Thus, nowhere in Scripture are we promised such a sweeping spiritual and moral revival. We can hope for revival in America, we can pray for revival—indeed, we absolutely should—but we cannot assert that it is a done deal. There is simply no biblical basis for doing so.

Some Americans—including many at that prayer-and-fasting event—point to 2 Chronicles 7:14 as a direct promise of another revival in America. In that passage, the Lord says, "If my people, who are called by my name, will humble themselves and pray and seek my face and turn from their wicked ways, then I will hear from heaven, and I will forgive their sin and will heal their land" (NIV). Some believe that so long as they and their congregations ask God for a Third Great Awakening, this passage obligates God to grant their request. I wish that were the case, but we must be honest with the text. The entire seventh chapter of 2 Chronicles involves a series of very specific promises to—and warnings for—the Jewish people in the nation of Israel. We certainly should ask the Lord to apply the same principles to the United States. We certainly should humble ourselves, pray, seek Christ's face, turn from our wicked ways, and ask God to hear us and forgive our sin and heal our land. And the Lord may very well decide to have mercy on us and rescue us as a nation, because the Bible tells us that by nature he is slow to anger and abounding in loving-kindness (Exodus 34:6). But we must remember that this passage is not a specific promise to us as Americans, and thus the Lord is under no obligation to say yes just because we ask.

Revivals are not man-made phenomena. Yes, God historically has used men and women to accomplish his will. And historically he has blessed nations that have turned to him in repentance en masse. But God is holy, and he is sovereign, and the Scriptures teach us that his ways are not our ways and his thoughts are much higher than our thoughts (Isaiah 55:9). He alone knows the end from the beginning. If God chooses to pour out his Holy Spirit on our nation once again in such a powerful and dramatic way, then to God be the glory. What a blessing that would be! But if God in his sovereignty decides that it is too late for America and chooses not to pour out his Holy Spirit on our nation in a Third Great Awakening, then to God be the glory as well. We cannot dictate outcomes. Rather, we can trust him to do the right thing and faithfully obey him day in and day out, come what may. The Lord is not a vending machine. We don't put our prayer quarters in and get out whatever treat we ask for. God always answers our prayers, but sometimes his answer is no.

Do I hope that in the twenty-first century America experiences a revival—or a series of revivals—as dramatic as the awakenings of the eighteenth and nineteenth centuries? Absolutely. Am I praying that we see such a revival soon? Every day. Am I fasting for God to move in his great power to rescue our country? More than ever in my life. Am I calling other Americans to fast and pray that we experience a Third Great Awakening? Indeed I am. That is, after all, the point of this book. I hope you will join in praying daily for such an outpouring of God's love and redemption on our needy country.

Our challenges are too large for political and business leaders alone to solve. To be sure, Washington, Wall Street, and Main Street have critical roles to play in our nation's recovery, and I wish them Godspeed in making the fundamental economic and fiscal reforms this country so desperately needs. But we need more than mere tax reforms to save us. We need more than spending and entitlement reforms in Washington. We need more than better jobs and stronger economic growth and truly balanced budgets. These are crucial to our survival, but by themselves they are insufficient. What we urgently need is a national U-turn. We require a wholesale national turning from our current path of pride, materialism, narcissism, selfishness, unkindness, and vulgarity. We need to turn away from violence against the unborn and rampant pornography and the assault on traditional marriage and the family. All of us as Americans need to turn away from our sins and plead for the grace and mercy and forgiveness of Jesus Christ. We need a renewed national hunger for the Word of God. We need once again to make a solemn national commitment to walk in the power of the Holy Spirit from this day forward.

At this point, nothing less than a Third Great Awakening will save us. These are not normal times. We are not facing normal problems. We dare not continue with business as usual. We cannot keep tinkering around the edges and procrastinating and living in denial. We are in mortal danger as a nation. We are on the verge of seeing God's hand of favor removed from us forever. We are on the brink of facing God's fair but terrifying judgment. Yet some deny God even exists. Others concede God exists but deny that we really need him.

Some give lip service to being a "Christian nation" but deny Christ's power, refusing to live holy, faithful, fruitful lives.

And now the hour is late. The clock is ticking. God certainly can save America. He has the power, and he has done it in the past, but he has made us no promises—and we dare not assume that because America has been such an exceptional nation in the past, she will forever remain so. How then should we live as we face the unknown?

What We Should Expect from the Church

A weakened country needs a strong and revitalized church.

There are an estimated 340,000 church congregations in the United States. That's an average of 6,800 per state. That's about one congregation for every 900 people. Imagine how rapidly America would change if all of these 340,000 congregations were healthy, strong, brightly shining lighthouses, as God intended.

What if they were all faithfully teaching the Word of God book by book, chapter by chapter, verse by verse so the people of God would know the whole counsel of God? What if they were truly helping people repent of their sins, purify their hearts, and heal from their emotional and spiritual wounds? What if they were all actively assisting those recovering people to be able to turn around and care for others who are needy and suffering? What if they were all training their people to share the gospel with their friends and neighbors? What if every pastor was modeling the kind of personal one-on-one and small-group discipleship that Jesus and Paul modeled? What if they were training and equipping young people in the Word of God and in their spiritual gifts and helping them plant new congregations in the U.S. and around the world? What if they were truly caring for the poor and needy in their communities and in countries around the globe, not in lieu of sharing the gospel but as part of fulfilling the great commission? What if they were teaching their congregations to bless Israel and her neighbors in the name of Jesus and to show unconditional love and unwavering support to both the Jewish and Palestinian people?

This is what we should expect and pray for in the American church—that she would respond to the shakings God has been sending our way and get back to teaching and obeying the whole counsel of God.

We can't know whether renewed devotion and obedience to Christ will move the Father's heart to unleash an outpouring of the Holy Spirit as he has done in our nation's history. But we can know for certain that if the church remains sluggish or asleep, we will one day have to answer before the Lord, face-to-face, for our failings.

Whether you're a pastor or a layperson, let me once again encourage you to carefully study the First Great Awakening and the Second Great Awakening. What were our spiritual forefathers doing then that we should be doing today? Are there any lessons you could draw from the last two chapters and begin applying right now in your own life, your own family, your own congregation?

I would also encourage you to spend time studying—and teaching others about—other periods of tremendous evangelism, pastoral training, church planting, and moral reform in American history, particularly those from the twentieth century. Consider how powerfully God moved through the ministries of men like Dwight L. Moody (1837–1899), Billy Sunday (1862–1935), Lewis Sperry Chafer (1871–1952, founder of Dallas Theological Seminary in 1924), Billy Graham (whose evangelistic crusades worldwide spanned from 1949 to 2005), Dawson Trotman (1906–1956, founder of the Navigators ministry in 1933), Bill Bright (1921–2003, founder of Campus Crusade for Christ in 1951), Dr. James Dobson (founder of Focus on the Family in 1977), Chuck Swindoll (chancellor of Dallas Theological Seminary, with more than seventy books published), Chuck Smith (a leader in the "Jesus Movement" of the 1970s and founder of Calvary Chapel, which has planted more than 1,200 congregations worldwide), and many others. While God didn't unleash full-scale Great Awakenings through these men, he certainly effected amazing miracles through them, and we have much to learn from their accomplishments. Indeed, their ministries may very well have planted the seeds that will turn into the greatest spiritual awakening in the history of the United States.

Most of all, I would encourage you to study the Scriptures afresh with an eye toward examples of national prayer, fasting, and revival. Study the stories of Joel, Nehemiah, Ezra, and Josiah, for example, a prophet, governor, priest, and king of Israel respectively, all of whom God used to call his people to wholesale national repentance and a renewed hunger for the Word of God and moral reforms.

In the book of Joel (admittedly my favorite book of the Bible), the Lord spoke through the Old Testament prophet to the entire nation of Israel and "all inhabitants of the land" (Joel 1:2). He told them that just as a severe natural disaster (a locust plague) had shaken them in the past, so too a time of severe and unprecedented traumas was coming upon them and upon the world in the future. Joel told anyone listening to "the word of the LORD" to "sound an alarm" because the "day of the LORD is coming; surely it is near" (Joel 1:1; 2:1).

How, then, were the spiritual leaders, ministers, and elders of the time supposed to respond? And what does this mean for us today? Joel made it crystal clear in the second chapter:

- **Blow a trumpet in Zion, and sound an alarm** (v. 1). That is, wake up the people and call them to action, remind them that the Lord is coming soon, and urge them to make a pure relationship with Christ their top priority.
- **Consecrate a fast** (v. 15). Urge people to stop doing normal things; urge them to make serving God more important than eating food or reading e-mails or being entertained or anything else.

- **Proclaim a solemn assembly and gather the people**
  (vv. 15-16). Gather the children and the nursing infants and
  the brides and the bridegrooms. Encourage people to spend
  more time with the Lord in their homes as individuals and
  families, but don't stop there. Bring the people together for
  a special event or a series of events—not entertainment but
  serious self-reflection, prayer, fasting, repentance, and time
  in the Word. Invite everyone to come; everyone needs time
  to get right with Jesus, not just the grown-ups.
- **Sanctify the congregation** (v. 16). *Sanctify* means to set
  someone or something aside for sacred and holy purposes,
  to free something from sin, to purify it. Here's one idea for
  illustrating sanctification for your congregation or small
  group: Encourage people to make a list of things they are
  doing that God doesn't want them to be doing. Have them
  write down on the bottom of that list that they promise to
  ask for God's help to repent of such things and not do them
  anymore. Have them sign the list and write "1 John 1:9" over
  the list. Then have them tear up, shred, or burn the list as
  an act of prayerful repentance. Find other ways to encourage
  your congregation to sanctify themselves from sin.
- **Assemble the elders and urge the Lord's ministers to weep
  and ask the Lord to spare his people** (vv. 16-17). Focus on
  leaders; spend time in prayer and fasting and repentance with
  and for them. If you're a leader, set a godly model, and ask
  people to follow.
- **Return to the Lord with all your heart, with fasting, with
  weeping, with mourning; rend your hearts and not your
  garments** (vv. 12-13). These are not supposed to be typical,
  run-of-the-mill prayer and praise meetings; this is a call to
  get on our faces and beg and plead with the Lord to have
  mercy on us as individuals, as families, and as a nation.

This is supposed to be serious time with the Lord. Think differently about your services; consider radically changing your schedule; give people time to talk to the Lord and listen to him; give people time and space to get on their knees—or on their faces. Maintain order, and don't let things get out of hand, but take this issue of mourning and weeping very seriously, and make sure your pastoral staff and counselors and elders and ushers are ready to comfort people and pray with people and mourn with people—and have lots of Kleenex ready.

· **Return to the Lord, because he is gracious and compassionate, slow to anger, abounding in loving-kindness, and relenting of evil** (v. 13). Encourage people to remember how wonderful and loving and forgiving the Lord is. Don't let people simply dwell on their sinfulness; teach people the stories of the First and Second Great Awakenings to remind them that God has saved us before and can do so again.

For all of 2010 and for nearly half of 2011, I studied the book of Joel. Not every day, of course. But I read it dozens of times. I also read commentaries about it. I listened to several pastors preach on it (though not many do). The more I chewed on it, the more the Lord taught me.

May I encourage you to spend several months studying the book of Joel? It's short—only three chapters—but it is powerful. May I encourage you to meditate on those three critical chapters, comparing those passages with other passages throughout the Scriptures, especially those that call entire nations back to repentance, prayer, and fasting? If you're a pastor or church leader, may I also encourage you to take your congregation through the book of Joel? There is a message there that is relevant for our time. There are warnings there that we dare not ignore. There is a sense of urgency that we need to share. This is a book that is near and dear to the heart of the Father. There is a fallen world that is not listening and a church that by and large is not proclaiming. True, the promises spoken of by Joel are specifically for the nation of Israel. But like 2 Chronicles 7:14, the book of Joel contains godly principles we should seek to put into practice. May we commit in our hearts today to apply the lessons from the book of Joel while we still can.[1]

What We Should Expect from Ourselves

What, then, should we expect from ourselves?

The church cannot be healthy and strong unless believers are walking closely, purely, and powerfully with Christ, right? That means that ultimately, revival begins with you and me. Let's not be fearful about the state of the church or angry about the failings of her members or leaders. Rather, let's start beseeching the Lord to have mercy on us, to purify us, to heal us, to shake us and wake us up while there is still time.

My friend Anne Graham Lotz said many things at the 2011 Epicenter Conference in Jerusalem that caught Lynn's and my attention. But the point that captured us most was when Anne cited the famed British evangelist Gypsy Smith. "Do you really want to see a revival begin?" Smith used to ask his audiences. When the people said yes, Gypsy replied, "Then go back to your home and draw a circle around you on the floor. Then get down on your knees in the middle of the circle and ask God to convert everybody inside that circle. When you do that, and God answers, you are experiencing the start of revival."

If we want to see our churches and our nation experience revival again, we first need to experience personal revival. To that end, here are nine steps the Bible instructs each of us to take to get right with God.

1. Reject Fear

Paralyzing fear and anxious despondency are not God's will for our lives.

No matter what is going on all around us, born-again believers in Jesus Christ must not succumb to fear. Why? Because Christ commanded us not to fear. Indeed, well over three hundred times throughout the Old and New Testaments, God's people are commanded, "Do not be afraid" or "Fear not" or a similar variation. As Jesus said in John 14:1, for example, "Let not your heart be troubled" (KJV). Some of you think that line was coined by Sean Hannity. But it wasn't. It was a command from Christ. Jesus told us that he is God. He's in charge. He's preparing a place for us in heaven, and he's coming back for us. He promised never to leave us or forsake us. He promised to always be with us. We need to believe him. We need to take him at his word.

How can we avoid being consumed by fear? The apostle Paul gave us godly counsel: "Be anxious for nothing, but in everything by prayer and supplication with thanksgiving let your requests be made known to God. And the peace of God, which surpasses all comprehension, will guard your hearts and your minds in Christ Jesus. Finally, brethren, whatever is true, whatever is honorable, whatever is right, whatever is pure, whatever is lovely, whatever is of good repute, if there is any excellence and if anything worthy of praise, dwell on these things" (Philippians 4:6-8).

Don't fixate on the dangers and threats and anxiety producers in your life. Instead, fix your mind on Christ. Bring all your cares and concerns to him. Dwell on the truths in the Bible about who God is, how much he loves you, how much he has done for you, the promises he has made to you, and the reality of his imminent return. In fact, it would be a great thing to memorize this passage in Philippians so you can recall it every time fear threatens to paralyze you again. I, too, get attacked often by flashes of fear and anxiety. And every time I do,

I try to go back to these and similar reassuring words from Scripture and fix my eyes and heart on Christ and his love.

2. Resist Anger

Losing a job, a car, a home, a business, a lifetime of savings, your health, or a loved one doesn't just produce fear. It can produce anger—anger at your boss, at the politicians in Washington, at one political party or another, at Wall Street, at the rich, at the poor, at other countries, at other races, at a family member or neighbor, and even at God. Be very careful about this, especially in turbulent and difficult times.

Anger, in and of itself, is not necessarily sinful. Whenever God is angry—and he does get angry—it is righteous anger. That is, it is anger at evil and injustice. With God, however, anger never turns into sin. He always deals with it appropriately and righteously. The problem with us is that our anger most often turns quickly into sin. Sometimes we become justifiably angry at something terrible that someone says or does, but more often than not we express that anger in sinful ways. We lash out verbally or even physically.

That's why the apostle Paul urged us in Ephesians 4:26, "Be angry, and yet do not sin." Don't let something sinful that another person has done cause you to be sinful too.

Paul also says in Ephesians 4:26-27, "Do not let the sun go down on your anger, and do not give the devil an opportunity." In other words, don't go to sleep angry. Don't let a problem fester or build up, lest it explode later. Start dealing with the problem immediately—first and foremost in your own heart. Hold your tongue, and plead with the Lord to cool you down, to drain away all the angry emotions, to give you a calm heart and a level head. And then, when you're calm again, begin to talk the problem through with the person who offended you, and start to work the problem out.

Now is not the time to become engulfed in anger. Now is the time to once again read about and meditate on the fruit of the Spirit in Galatians 5 and ask the Lord to develop within us "love, joy, peace, patience, kindness, goodness, faithfulness, gentleness, self-control."

3. Rekindle Your Love for Jesus

Personal revival doesn't come from being obsessive about a new list of dos and don'ts. Rather, it comes from a deep, personal friendship with Jesus Christ.

In the book of Revelation, Jesus said these words to the church in the city of Ephesus: "I know your deeds and your toil and perseverance, and that you cannot tolerate evil men, and you put to the test those who call themselves apostles, and they are not, and you found them to be false; and you have perseverance and have endured for My name's sake, and have not grown weary. But I have this against you, that you have left your first love. Therefore remember from where you have fallen, and repent and do the deeds you did at first; or else I am coming to you and will remove your lampstand out of its place—unless you repent" (Revelation 2:2-5).

Christ didn't tell that struggling church to stop doing the right things. To the contrary, he urged them to keep doing the things they were commanded in the Scriptures to do. But Jesus missed *them*. The people in that congregation were working so hard at working hard that they weren't abiding with Jesus. They weren't really enjoying fellowship with him. They weren't telling him they loved him. They weren't slowing down to listen to him. They weren't reflecting on how amazing and awesome and beautiful and powerful and majestic he is. They had gotten into a ministry rut. They were doing the right things, and probably for the right reasons, but they had left their first love.

They had fallen in love with ministry and out of love with Jesus. And it grieved him. He wanted them to learn to love him all over again.

How is your friendship with Jesus?

4. Repent of Your Sins and Recommit Yourself to Holiness

What was John the Baptist's message when he was trying to get the people ready for the first coming of the Messiah? "Repent, for the kingdom of heaven is at hand" (Matthew 3:2).

What was Jesus' message when he began his earthly ministry? "Repent, for the kingdom of heaven is at hand" (Matthew 4:17).

What was the apostle Peter's message in his first sermon in Jerusalem on the Day of Pentecost? "Repent, and each of you be baptized in the name of Jesus Christ for the forgiveness of your sins; and you will receive the gift of the Holy Spirit" (Acts 2:38).

What was Jesus' message to the sleeping church at Sardis in the book of Revelation? "So remember what you have received and heard; and keep it, and repent. Therefore if you do not wake up, I will come like a thief, and you will not know at what hour I will come to you" (Revelation 3:3).

The Bible directly uses the word *repent* or *repented* or *repentance* more than seventy times. The message is clear.

Now is the time to become doers of the Word, not hearers only. If you are not a born-again follower of Christ, why not take time right now to confess your sins to him? To repent means to turn around spiritually. Once you have turned toward Jesus, ask him by faith—trusting the promises in the Bible—to come into your life to forgive you, to save you, to adopt you into his family, to fill you with his Holy Spirit, and to start showing you how to be his disciple and walk with him and love him and serve him daily. This is the most important decision you will ever make, and Christ is waiting for you to say yes to him.

If you are already a born-again believer, now is the time to ask the Lord to show you—gently and mercifully, but clearly—areas of unconfessed sin in your life. Look at these areas squarely, though it's painful. Then ask Christ to forgive you and cleanse you by the blood he shed on the cross. Ask him to give you the strength to turn away from your sins and walk with him more purely than you ever have before. And remember this beautiful promise: "If we confess our sins, He is faithful and righteous to forgive us our sins and to cleanse us from all unrighteousness" (1 John 1:9).

5. Recommit Yourself to the Study of God's Word

If Jesus delivered a letter to your mailbox, wouldn't you open it? If he sent you an e-mail or a text message or posted a note on your Facebook wall, wouldn't you read it? You would if you really loved him, right?

When was the last time you read through Psalm 119? Have you ever noticed the following verses?

- "Revive me according to Your word" (Psalm 119:25).
- "Turn away my eyes from looking at vanity, and revive me in Your ways" (Psalm 119:37).
- "Behold, I long for Your precepts; revive me through Your righteousness" (Psalm 119:40).
- "This is my comfort in my affliction, that Your word has revived me" (Psalm 119:50).
- "Consider how I love Your precepts; revive me, O LORD, according to Your lovingkindness" (Psalm 119:159).

Including these five, the psalmist asks God eleven times in this psalm to revive him by the Word of God. Is it possible that we grow weaker when we avoid reading the Bible or when we read just a few verses quickly or sporadically, but that we grow stronger and are revived when we immerse ourselves in the Word of God and meditate on it, memorize it, chew on it, savor it?

In the first chapter of John, we learn that Jesus Christ is the Word of God. The more time, therefore, we spend in the Bible, the more time we are listening to the heart of Jesus. Didn't Jesus also say in John 6:48, "I am the bread of life"? Didn't Jesus say in John 6:51,

"I am the living bread that came down out of heaven; if anyone eats of this bread, he will live forever; and the bread also which I will give for the life of the world is My flesh"? Isn't it possible that we are slowly but certainly starving ourselves when we rush through our day without partaking of the Bread of Life?

While I was working on this book, I had the joy of leading a man in another city to faith in Jesus Christ. He was so excited by his newfound faith at first. Every day for weeks we spent between an hour and an hour and a half studying the Gospel of John together. He would ask many questions, and I would point him back into the Scriptures to find the answers. He was growing rapidly. Then he had to do some travel for work, and so did I. When we reconnected, I asked him if he was continuing to study and savor God's Word every day. He admitted that over time he had gotten too busy. I certainly understood, and I told him that for years I struggled to be disciplined and faithful to study the Bible on a daily basis. But rather than let him get discouraged, I suggested he let me help him.

I reminded him that if he really loved Jesus, he would obey him by spending more time listening to him. He readily agreed, so I gave him a thirty-day challenge. He and I promised each other that for the next thirty days, we would both spend at least forty-five minutes at the beginning of our day reading and studying the Bible and praying to the Lord. Then we would e-mail each other as a way of keeping each other accountable. We'd let each other know that we had finished our morning devotions and share a few nuggets of what God had taught us that day. We'd also share prayer requests. They wouldn't be long e-mails, just quick and to the point. He agreed, and we made the commitment. My friend ended up reading all of John, all of Acts, and most of the book of Romans. We continue to e-mail each other, and we call when we can.

It's not a foolproof system, but may I encourage you to find someone with whom you can take the thirty-day challenge? Be honest with each other if you miss a day or two. Forgive each other, and get back on schedule.

When the thirty days are over, evaluate how you both are doing spiritually. Then consider keeping each other accountable for another thirty days, and another thirty after that.

I highly recommend that you have a plan for your Bible reading. Rather than randomly opening the Bible each day and reading whatever page you open up to, pick a book of the Bible and work your way through it day by day. Take notes in a journal. Look up cross-references. Look up words you're not clear about. Underline verses that grab your attention. Discuss what you're reading and learning with family members, friends, and colleagues. Ask the Lord to reveal to you what he is saying. Take special note of commands the Lord gives you through his Word, and be sure to obey those right away—that is, don't just be a hearer of the Word; be a doer of God's Word, and he will bless you as you do.

May I suggest that you don't merely begin your day reading the Word of God? Have a Bible with you at work, in your car, or in your backpack, briefcase, or purse. Take a moment at lunch or on a coffee break to pull it out. Maybe do your main study in the morning, but sometime during the rest of the day, read a psalm, or a chapter of Proverbs. And spend some time reading the Bible in the evening, too, before you go to bed.

I would also recommend having a time of Bible study, discussion, and prayer with your children each day. In our family, we call this time "devotions," and we have them from 8 to 9 a.m. each weekday. Since I'm an author and Lynn is homeschooling the kids, our schedule is a little more flexible than most in the mornings. Other families we know have their devotions right after dinner or earlier in the morning. Whenever you do it, the point is to find the time and stick with it. We pick a book of the Bible and read through a chapter or so each morning and discuss it together. The kids have actually loved it much more than I originally expected them to. They have lots of questions, and that's been fun for Lynn and me. We take turns praying for family members, friends, neighbors, missionaries, and ministry partners around the world. We pray for the peace of Jerusalem and for people we know in Israel and the rest of the epicenter. It has been great for our family life as well as our spiritual growth, and it's particularly important for Dad to be centrally involved. Sure, there are times I'm traveling or otherwise unable to participate, and Lynn leads devotions in my absence. But I try to make it a top priority because I believe kids (and especially boys) need to see their fathers stepping up and showing consistent spiritual leadership inside the home as well as outside.

Psalm 1 describes a man who is committed to immersing himself in the Word of God. It calls such a man "blessed" and says that his "delight is in the law of the LORD, and in His law he meditates day and night. He will be like a tree firmly planted by streams of water, which yields its fruit in its season and its leaf does not wither; and in whatever he does, he prospers" (Psalm 1:1-3). May you be richly blessed as you press into God's Word this year more than ever before.

6. Rediscover the Power of Prayer and Fasting

Are you wondering what God's will is for your life?

Fortunately, the apostle Paul tells us the answer in one sentence: "Rejoice always; pray without ceasing; in everything give thanks; for this is God's will for you in Christ Jesus" (1 Thessalonians 5:16-18).

Could it be any clearer?

First, rather than worry, we are to rejoice in who God is, how much he loves us, how much we love him, what he has done in his Word, and what he promises to do for all believers in the future.

Second, we are to pray always. That doesn't mean nonstop talking to God. It does mean keeping up a running dialogue with the Lord, just as we would with our husband or wife when we first fell in love and got married. Why? Because that's how we communicate to God that we really love him and care about what he thinks. Are we praying every day for personal revival? Are we praying every day for God to bring a powerful spiritual revival to our spouse and our children? Are we praying daily for a revival in our church and community and for a spiritual awakening to spread across the United States? If not, why not? Shouldn't this be our hearts' cry at this critical moment? What are we waiting for?

Third, we need to thank the Lord a whole lot more than we do. Often we're grumbling or complaining in our prayers or asking for a laundry list of things we need or want. Of course we're encouraged to bring our requests to the Lord, but we should make sure we begin by thanking the Lord for the answers to all the other prayers we've prayed—including the times he told us "no" and the times he told us, "Yes, but wait." Sometimes the "no" answers to prayer in my life have been the most wonderful, because the Lord was protecting me from something I thought was right or good but wasn't. What have you thanked God for today?

Many believers get bogged down over prayer. They say they don't have the time to pray or the interest to pray. Take a moment and think of how that sounds to the Lord, who died on the cross for you to pay for your sins and rose again from the dead to rescue you out of hell. You and I don't have time for him? We're not interested in talking or listening to him?

Would your husband or wife believe you really loved them if you never talked to them and never listened to them? Would your children believe you really loved them if you never conversed with them? What about the Lord? Do you think he really believes you love him if you never spend time talking to him in prayer? Your Father in heaven wants you to listen to him by reading his Word, and he wants to listen to you as you share what is on your heart through prayer.

One of the great things Lynn and I have discovered is praying specifically for things that the Bible tells us to pray for. This is what we're trying to teach our four sons to do in their prayer lives too. Let me give you two examples:

- In Ephesians 5:18, we are commanded to "be filled with the Spirit," meaning we should be constantly filled and refilled with the wisdom and the power of the Holy Spirit.
- In Ephesians 6:10-11, we are commanded to "be strong in the Lord and in the strength of His might" and to "put on the full armor of God, so that you will be able to stand firm against the schemes of the devil."

At first glance, it might seem like the Lord is commanding us to do two important things but then not telling us how to do them. The Bible tells us we receive the Holy Spirit immediately when we are born again. How then can we be constantly filled and refilled with God's Holy Spirit, whom we cannot see, and thus be continually operating in his love and wisdom and power and kindness? The Bible tells us that the enemy, known as Satan or the devil, and his forces will continually attack and seek to destroy us. How then can we put on a spiritual helmet and breastplate and other armor we cannot see?

Actually, the Bible does tell us how, immediately after these commands. The apostle Paul writes in Ephesians 6:18, "With all prayer and petition, pray at all times in the Spirit." In other words, if you want to be filled with the Holy Spirit, begin each day asking the Lord to fill you with his Holy Spirit, and ask him several more times throughout the day. Do you want to be suited up in the full armor of God as you head out the door to school or work or anywhere else each day? Ask for the power and protection of the Holy Spirit, and you shall receive it. That's what Lynn and I do with our sons each day during devotions, and God has proven himself time and time again to be a prayer-hearing and a prayer-answering God, a wonder-working God!

Isn't that what Christ said? "So I say to you, ask, and it will be given to you; seek, and you will find; knock, and it will be opened to you. For everyone who asks, receives; and he who seeks, finds; and to him who knocks, it will be opened. Now suppose one of you fathers is asked by his son for a fish; he will not give him a snake instead of a fish, will he? Or if he is asked for an egg, he will not give him a scorpion, will he? If you then, being evil, know how to give good gifts to your children, how much more will your heavenly Father give the Holy Spirit to those who ask Him?" (Luke 11:9-13).

Also, be specific when you pray. Pray in a way that is definable and measurable so that you'll really know when God has answered. For example, don't simply pray, "Lord, please bless my sister." How would you know if that prayer was answered? Instead, pray for something specific. "Lord, please open the eyes of my sister's heart so that she will see that you love her and sent your Son, the Lord Jesus Christ, to rescue her. Please bless her by persuading her to give her life to you so that she will spend eternity with you in heaven and so I'll get to spend it with her as well." Will you know when your sister (or whoever) prays to receive Christ? I suspect you will.

Likewise, don't get fixated on praying merely for your basic needs. I don't mean that you shouldn't pray for those things, but let me encourage you not to pray *only* for those things. As Jesus told his disciples in Matthew 6:31-33, "Do not worry then, saying, 'What will we eat?' or 'What will we drink?' or 'What will we wear for clothing?' For the Gentiles eagerly seek all these things; for your heavenly Father knows that you need all these things. But seek first His kingdom and His righteousness, and all these things will be added to you." Try praying, "Lord, would you open the door for me to share the gospel with someone this week who doesn't know you?" Or try praying, "Lord, would you show me a specific person I can invite to church this week and encourage to pray to receive Christ as Savior?" Or how about, "Lord, our family has never been on a short-term missions trip, but would you show us where you would like us to go and then provide the funds to get us there?"

Aim higher. Seek first the Kingdom of God and his righteousness, and he will take care of all your other needs.

Also, be sure you're practicing the spiritual discipline of fasting—skipping a meal (or even a day or more of meals) or some other activity you normally do and devoting that time to prayer. The prophet Joel called on the people of God to fast while they prayed and repented of their sins and turned their hearts back to God. Actually, most of the prophets called the people to fasting. The apostles fasted and taught other followers of Christ to do the same. Jesus himself said, "Whenever you fast, do not put on a gloomy face as the hypocrites do, for they neglect their appearance so that they will be noticed by men when they are fasting. Truly I say to you, they have their reward in full. But you, when you fast, anoint your head and wash your face so that your fasting will not be noticed by men, but by your Father who is in secret; and your Father who sees what is done in secret will reward you" (Matthew 6:16-18).

Clearly, Jesus expected his disciples to fast. He didn't say, "*If* you fast." He said, "*Whenever* you fast." It's important to tell God through fasting that spending time with him is more important to us than eating, entertaining, being entertained, or engaging in any other activity. Denying ourselves for a time things that are basic and important to us so that we can tune out all distractions and talk to God and listen carefully to his Word is a vital part of a healthy relationship with Christ. Be sure to talk to your doctor for advice on fasting in the context of your own unique medical history, and ask your pastor for his wisdom and input. But don't put off fasting. We need to obey the Lord in this spiritual discipline now more than ever, for the Bible is clear that fasting is an essential element in personal and national revival.

7. Recommit Yourself to a Local Congregation That Is Committed to Teaching and Obeying the Bible

Right after three thousand people from all over the Roman Empire repented of their sins and received Jesus Christ as their Savior and Lord in Jerusalem on the Day of Pentecost, what did all those believers do next? The book of Acts tells us they were baptized and then began forming church congregations in homes and wherever else they could gather.

> They were continually devoting themselves to the apostles'
> teaching and to fellowship, to the breaking of bread and
> to prayer. Everyone kept feeling a sense of awe; and many
> wonders and signs were taking place through the apostles.
> And all those who had believed were together and had all
> things in common; and they began selling their property
> and possessions and were sharing them with all, as anyone
> might have need. Day by day continuing with one mind in
> the temple, and breaking bread from house to house, they
> were taking their meals together with gladness and sincerity
> of heart, praising God and having favor with all the people.
> And the Lord was adding to their number day by day those
> who were being saved.
>
> ACTS 2:42-47

This passage tells us six things about the churches those early believers were establishing:

- They were studying the Word of God together and listening to the teaching of wise men who were familiar with the commands of Scripture and had walked with Jesus.
- They were spending time worshiping the Lord and encouraging fellow believers.

- They were taking Communion, or what's known as "the Lord's Supper," together. That is, they were taking time to formally remember and give thanks for Christ's sacrifice on the cross on their behalf.
- They were praising God and lifting up their concerns and needs to him.
- They were sharing their possessions with one another and even selling property in order to have the financial resources available to share with those in need.
- They were spending time together, sharing meals and fellowship with one another.

As a result, not only did the believers feel "a sense of awe" at the goodness and majesty of God, but the Lord blessed them with "many wonders and signs." And not only did they enjoy a favorable reputation in the community, but the Lord blessed them further by bringing newcomers to their fellowship daily.

Are you a member of a solid, Bible-believing, Bible-teaching church? Good! Ask the Lord how he wants you to serve there, grow there, and invest your time, talent, and treasure there. How can you serve and encourage your pastor and the staff? How can you welcome new people and make them feel at home? What nonbelievers do you know whom you can invite to attend the next church service with you? What skill or spiritual gift do you have that you could use to encourage and strengthen the other believers in that congregation? When the Lord shows you, follow his lead.

If you're not in such a church, don't grumble or complain. Just ask the Lord to help you find one, and then prayerfully start looking. Seek a congregation that is theologically solid and personally loving and warm. Look for a place where the pastor and the people have a heart to strengthen the body of Christ and reach out to the lost. If the Lord gives you such a place, get involved and see how you can learn and grow and make a positive difference.

Don't expect to find a perfect congregation. They don't exist. All congregations are made up of sinners just like you and me. Don't let yourself be discouraged if you can't find a congregation that feels "just right." Ask the Lord to put you where he wants you, even if it's a fellowship that seems less than ideal, and trust him to guide you one step at a time. Maybe God wants you to join there to pray for that congregation's revival. Or maybe he wants you to become friends with a particular couple or single person or a group of young people whom you can encourage in Christ and who can encourage you in turn.

The Scriptures are clear that apostasy will rise in the last days, and thus more and more congregations will turn away from the Lord. Therefore, we must be on guard against attending a church that is teaching false doctrines and willfully and publicly disobeying the teachings of the Bible. But we must also guard against letting the perfect become the enemy of the good. Too many Christians in America are giving up on going to church at all. Too many have let themselves become discouraged because they haven't found congregations that truly welcome them or teach the Scriptures as deeply as they wish. Too many have given up entirely on being in fellowship with other Christians.

Too many others have become overly critical of worship styles and preaching styles and decorating styles and all kinds of other things and have given up attending church for these reasons. Still others are attending church on Sunday morning but are not getting involved in small-group Bible studies, home fellowship groups, local outreaches, foreign missions, or other areas of service. Yet the Lord specifically commands us to be proactively involved in the local church—and to be committed to building close personal relationships with local believers. As the writer of the book of Hebrews put it, "Let us consider how to stimulate one another to love and good deeds, not forsaking our own assembling together, as is the habit of some, but encouraging one another; and all the more as you see the day drawing near" (Hebrews 10:24-25).

8. Reach Out to the Unsaved and Share the Gospel

Have you ever taken the opportunity to share the gospel message of salvation with someone who didn't know the Lord Jesus? When was the last time?

Have you helped a person pray to receive Jesus Christ as their personal Savior and Lord? When was the last time?

I have found that few things in life are more exciting and more satisfying than being used by the Lord to help people become adopted into God's Kingdom. Sadly, however, I find that many Christians are hoping to slip into heaven incognito—wearing sunglasses, as it were, hoping no one notices that they haven't ever led a single person to the Lord. Too many Christians think they have no responsibility to share the gospel, even when people all around them are lost and headed for hell if they don't repent and receive Christ. We have to turn this around. We have to help each other become faithful to the Lord in telling others the Good News about our great Savior!

Many Christian parents take seriously the importance of sharing the gospel with their own children, and many have the joy of helping their kids pray to receive Christ. That's a wonderful thing. But too many have the view that they don't have a responsibility to share Christ with anyone else. Such thinking is unbiblical and urgently needs to change.

Many people are nervous about sharing the gospel because they're afraid of being rejected or humiliated. Yet people rarely hesitate to share with others the details of something they're excited about, whether it's a sports team, a new workout routine, a store they recently discovered, etc. We share what we're passionate about. If we're passionate about Jesus, why wouldn't we want to share him with the people we care about? Of course, not everybody is Billy Graham or Luis Palau. Not everyone has the spiritual gift of evangelism. Not everyone has been given a personality that allows them to share Christ with strangers as though it's second nature. But that doesn't mean the obligation just goes away.

Jesus said, "Go into all the world and preach the gospel to all creation" (Mark 16:15). The apostle Paul told us, "How then will they call on Him in whom they have not believed? How will they believe in Him whom they have not heard? And how will they hear without a preacher [somebody telling them]? How will they preach unless they are sent?" (Romans 10:14-15). The Lord Jesus is calling you to tell others about him. Do you love him enough—and do you love others enough—to start obeying Christ today?

Ask God to provide opportunities for you to share the gospel with someone, and he'll do it. He knows your personality—he created you, after all! He knows what you're comfortable with and what makes you nervous. He will give you the words to say if you trust him and obey him. Engage your Facebook friends in discussions about the gospel. E-mail an old friend and start a spiritual conversation. Invite a neighbor family over for dinner and get to know their spiritual background. Invite them to come to church with you and then go out for lunch afterward and engage them in conversation about the sermon.

If you've read and enjoyed any of my fiction books, you might consider giving one of them to an unsaved family member, friend, coworker, or neighbor for a birthday or Christmas or Hanukkah present. I've been so encouraged by the number of people I hear from who do this because the gospel is shared clearly in each of my books. Many people have told me that they used to be terrified to share the gospel with others but now they give one of my books because "it's like a gospel tract woven into a *New York Times* bestselling novel." Others have told me, "Your books are good icebreakers for spiritual conversations." Indeed, it's been exciting to hear from people—and occasionally meet them in person—who have prayed to receive Christ as their Savior after reading my books. Hopefully these and other tools can be useful in helping you start sharing your faith as well.

Does your church offer a class on how to share your faith? Take it. Is there a conference nearby on practical evangelism? Attend it. And don't go alone. Bring your spouse or some close friends—maybe even your kids, if they are old enough. Together, set a goal of how many people you want to share Christ with each week or month. Then pray together, and keep each other accountable to reach your goals.

When Lynn and I were first married, I set a personal goal of sharing the gospel with one person per month—just twelve people per year. I told Lynn about it and prayed earnestly for opportunities. Sometimes God graciously opened an obvious door in a conversation, and the gospel came up naturally. Other times, God required me to take a risk and begin asking someone spiritual questions, hoping it would lead to an opportunity to share Christ. As the end of the month drew near, I would often get anxious if I hadn't shared with anyone yet. But setting the goal and taking it seriously helped me press forward and try to obey the great commission even when it was difficult. Eventually, through my books and blog and speaking opportunities across the U.S. and around the world, God has given me the opportunities to share the gospel with millions of people. I look back and wonder why I set my initial goal so low! But at least I was taking baby steps, and as God helped me be faithful in a few things, eventually he helped me be faithful in more things. The same dynamic will be true for you, if you determine in your heart to be obedient.

9. Reach Out to a Younger Believer and Make a Disciple

In Matthew 28:19-20, the passage commonly known as the great commission, the Lord Jesus Christ told his disciples to go make more disciples. "Go therefore and make disciples of all the nations," Jesus declared, "baptizing them in the name of the Father and the Son and the Holy Spirit, teaching them to observe all that I commanded you; and lo, I am with you always, even to the end of the age."

In 2 Timothy 2:2, the apostle Paul told Timothy to do exactly what Jesus said to do—reach out to younger believers and make disciples. "The things which you have heard from me in the presence of many witnesses, entrust these to faithful men who will be able to teach others also."

Christianity is not a solo sport. It's about building strong, healthy teams of fully devoted followers of Jesus Christ whom God can use to change the world. It's about older believers taking younger believers under their wings to love them, help them grow in faith, and help them reproduce that faith in the lives of other, younger believers.

Lynn and I were deeply fortunate to have several older, wiser believers come into our lives and truly care for us and teach us and model for us a more godly, biblical path. For us, this began in college when we were both involved in Campus Crusade for Christ and some CCC staff personally discipled us. We were also blessed by our college pastor, T. E. Koshy, and his dear wife, Indira, who showed a special love toward us and invested deeply in our spiritual growth. They taught us how to live our faith and how to share our faith. They modeled lives of prayer and fasting and compassion for the poor and the needy and for immigrants and refugees. They sent us out on ministry projects, encouraged our successes, and helped us correct our mistakes. We were forever marked by their care for us, and we've tried to pass along what we've learned to younger believers we've encountered along the way.

Jesus, of course, set the supreme model. He prayerfully recruited a team of young men. He invested in them. He cared for them like family, loving them with an everlasting, sacrificial love. He led them on spiritual adventures. He modeled a life of intense prayer. He let them see supernatural answers to their prayers. He gave them assignments—to feed the hungry, care for the sick, comfort the brokenhearted, and preach the good news of the Kingdom of Heaven. He treated them like sons or younger brothers, correcting their mistakes, praising their successes, and marking their progress. And then he told them to go invest in others. He told them to make disciples. He told them to build warm and loving and nurturing communities of believers. And in the process he ignited the greatest spiritual revolution the world has ever seen.

The problem is that nearly two thousand years later, remarkably few Christians are able to point to a single disciple they have made or are in the process of making. Indeed, many would be hard-pressed even to define what is meant by the phrase "make disciples."

Jesus came to make disciples. Therefore, it isn't enough to win men and women to Christ, though obviously that is an essential first step. We must also build people up in Christ. We must also *invest* in them until they are fully devoted followers of Jesus, able to help others come to Christ and become fully devoted followers as well. This requires training Christian leaders—vocational ministers as well as lay leaders and volunteers—to see themselves as investors. After all, the key to Christ's definition of *success* in ministry is that we produce *successors*, disciple makers who produce still more disciple makers.

How is it possible, then—for all the emphasis in the church these days on world missions and on winning souls to Christ worldwide—that so many Christians have missed the centrality of personal, intentional discipleship in God's plan and purpose for his people? How is it that we have more and more *seeker churches* but so few *investor churches*—churches committed to helping Christians achieve a healthy balance of evangelism *and* discipleship in their daily walks with the Lord?

And it's not just "baby" Christians—young and inexperienced in the ways of God—who are not being discipled or beginning to learn the importance of discipling others. Far too often it is *mature* believers within the church—those who have known Christ for quite some time and whose lives may be busier than ever with ministry activity—who don't seem to understand the centrality of discipleship. Indeed, in Lynn's and my experience, we find that many pastors and church leaders have never been personally discipled and have yet to discover how exciting and transforming and fulfilling it is to be discipling their staffs and teaching them how to disciple laypeople and particularly young people.

How about you? How would you answer these two simple questions?

- Who is investing in you?
- Whom are you investing in?

Let us not get to heaven and be stunned and saddened—mortified, even—when Christ welcomes us with open, loving arms and then asks us to show him our disciples, and we have no one to show him and nothing to say. Making disciples was a big deal to Jesus. If we really love him, making disciples should be a big deal to us, too.

Bottom Line

If you and I are faithful in these nine areas, are we guaranteed that God will give America a Third Great Awakening? Honestly, the answer is no.

But let's ask the question another way: If you and I are too lazy or too proud or too busy or too self-absorbed to obey the Lord in these nine areas, why should God give America a Third Great Awakening?

America is on the brink of collapse. We desperately need God's mercy. Without his grace, we will implode. It's not a matter of *if* but *when.* Thus, now is the time we must urgently ask the Lord to give us a sweeping series of spiritual revivals in every part of our nation that will culminate in a Third Great Awakening. Whether God decides to say yes is up to him. But let us not compound our many national sins by failing to get on our faces before him and implore him to pour out his Holy Spirit and save us from disaster.

Let us get serious once again as individuals, families, and church congregations about turning our hearts fully back to the Lord so that on the day we stand before Jesus Christ, we will hear him say, "Well done, my good and faithful servant. You have been faithful in handling this small amount, so now I will give you many more responsibilities. Let's celebrate together!" (Matthew 25:21, NLT).

CHAPTER SEVENTEEN

CAN AMERICA AGAIN BE A SHINING CITY ON A HILL?

FOR JOHN WINTHROP (1588–1649), one of our nation's Founding Fathers, though he died more than a century before the Revolution, America had a special place in the world and a special mission from God. One of the key figures in helping to establish the Massachusetts Bay Colony, Winthrop served as governor of the settlement for twelve of its first twenty years. In his famous address in 1630 to passengers aboard the ship *Arbella*, bound for the New World, Winthrop called on his Christian brothers and sisters to aim high and think big.

> For we must consider that we shall be as a city upon a hill. The eyes of all people are upon us. So that if we shall deal falsely with our God in this work we have undertaken, and so cause him to withdraw his present help from us, we shall be made a story and a byword through the world.[1]

Winthrop was referencing the New Testament, quoting from the words of Jesus to his disciples. "You are the light of the world," Jesus told them. "A city set on a hill cannot be hidden; nor does anyone light a lamp and put it under a basket, but on the lampstand, and it gives light to all who are in the house" (Matthew 5:14-15). Winthrop believed that followers of Christ were to radiate the light that Christ himself put in their hearts. We are to reflect his holiness, his love, his kindness and compassion for others, his justice, and his mercy. Christ did not expect his disciples to be perfect, and he doesn't expect perfection of us, either. He knows our perfection cannot and will not come until the Resurrection and the Rapture. But he does expect us to be different from the dark and fallen world. He does expect us to stand out, to be distinct and thus attractive to the lost. When people look to Christ's followers, they should find Christ, his Word, and his life-changing Holy Spirit. Winthrop thus challenged the believers on the *Arbella* to set their feet on the fresh soil of the New World with the intention of building a society that radiated, reflected, and represented Jesus Christ. And overwhelmingly, those on the *Arbella* agreed.

They were not alone. Many Americans from the days of the Massachusetts Bay Colony and beyond saw America as not just another country, not just some new nation-state among many. To them, America was something special both for those who lived here and for others around the world. To them, America was a new Garden of Eden or a new Jerusalem, at least metaphorically speaking. They agreed with Governor Winthrop. They saw America as a shining city on a hill, and they committed their lives to making that dream come true for themselves, their children, their grandchildren, and the world.

Winthrop, Kennedy, and Reagan

Over time, the concept of America as a shining city on a hill became less about Christ's calling for his followers and the unique and powerful role of the church in this world and more a generalized expression of American political, cultural, and economic exceptionalism.

John F. Kennedy, the Massachusetts Democrat, for example, referenced Winthrop's famous line in an address to the Massachusetts General Court on January 9, 1961, as president-elect of the United States.

I have been guided by the standard John Winthrop set before his shipmates on the flagship *Arbella* three hundred and thirty-one years ago, as they, too, faced the task of building a new government on a perilous frontier. "We must always consider," he [Winthrop] said, "that we shall be as a city upon a hill—the eyes of all people are upon us." Today the eyes of all people are truly upon us, and our governments, in every branch, at every level—national, state, and local—must be as a city upon a hill, constructed and inhabited by men aware of their great trust and their great responsibilities. For we are setting out upon a voyage in 1961 no less hazardous than that undertaken by the *Arbella* in 1630. We are committing ourselves to tasks of statecraft no less awesome than that of governing the Massachusetts Bay Colony, beset as it was then by terror without and disorder within. History will not judge our endeavors . . . merely on the basis of color or creed or even party affiliation. Neither will competence and loyalty and stature, while essential to the utmost, suffice in times such as these. For of those to whom much is given, much is required.[2]

Likewise, Ronald Reagan, the California Republican, loved to reference Winthrop's line and did so repeatedly throughout his political career and particularly during his presidency. In fact, in his farewell address to the nation, broadcast from the Oval Office on January 11, 1989, President Reagan said:

> The past few days when I've been at that window upstairs, I've thought a bit of the "shining city upon a hill." The phrase comes from John Winthrop, who wrote it to describe the America he imagined. What he imagined was important because he was an early Pilgrim, an early freedom man. He journeyed here on what today we'd call a little wooden boat; and like the other Pilgrims, he was looking for a home that would be free. I've spoken of the shining city all my political life, but I don't know if I ever quite communicated what I saw when I said it. But in my mind it was a tall, proud city built on rocks stronger than oceans, windswept, God-blessed, and teeming with people of all kinds living in harmony and peace; a city with free ports that hummed with commerce and creativity. And if there had to be city walls, the walls had doors, and the doors were open to anyone with the will and the heart to get here. That's how I saw it, and see it still. And how stands the city on this winter night? More prosperous, more secure, and happier than it was eight years ago. But more than that: after two hundred years, two centuries, she still stands strong and true on the granite ridge, and her glow has held steady no matter what storm. And she's still a beacon, still a magnet for all who must have freedom, for all the pilgrims from all the lost places who are hurtling through the darkness, toward home.[3]

Reagan offered a powerful and beautiful image of America's role in the world. Sadly, that was a different era. Today America no longer seems to be standing "strong and true." Her light is dimming, her impact fading, her magnetism weakening amid so many storms and self-inflicted wounds. America's enemies sense opportunities in our vulnerabilities. They are convinced we are doomed. But many Americans also fear we are on the road to decline and that this decline could be permanent. Others fear our situation is worse than a matter of mere decline. They believe they can hear the ice cracking beneath us. They fear that if major and fundamental economic, spiritual, and moral changes are not made immediately, America is heading for implosion. Some Americans go even further. They believe the implosion of America is not merely a possibility but an outright certainty.

How about you? Do you believe America can still be a shining city on a hill? If so, how have you chosen to be engaged in the battle to save this country? Or have you decided it's too late and no longer worth the fight? If that's the case, are you just planning to watch from the sidelines and do nothing to help?

I admit that in my darker moments I worry we have crossed the Rubicon and there is no way back. But I refuse to succumb to the pessimism in my DNA. As I write this, America is not finished—not yet. America has not imploded—not yet. So I refuse to give up. I choose to believe there is hope. I choose to pray that God will save this country. So long as there is still time, I choose to press on and do everything I can possibly do—or more precisely, everything the Lord directs me to do and gives me permission to do—to preserve this great nation and to mobilize people to work together and pray together to turn this ship around before it really is too late. I'm not blind to the enormity and gravity of the challenges we face. But neither am I blind to the power and might of our God. The Bible says "nothing will be impossible with God" (Luke 1:37). I believe that, and that is what gives me hope.

In the previous chapter, we examined what we should expect from the church and from ourselves in a prayerful, principled, passionate pursuit of a Third Great Awakening. Now let us consider what we should expect from government and what role—if any—we should play in pushing our government to help the nation get back on the right track. After all, while our local, state, and national political leaders cannot save us or solve all our problems, they can be either a great help or a terrible hindrance.

What Should We Expect from Government?

First and foremost, we should consider the role of government through the third lens of Scripture. The Bible is clear that God created government as a legitimate earthly institution with certain limited functions. These functions are to protect innocent human life and liberty, establish and enforce justice, and defend a nation from foreign and domestic threats. Scripture also makes clear that government leaders are subordinate to God. They are not authorized to give people rights or to arbitrarily take them away. Rather, they are supposed to protect people's God-given rights from all those who would seek to threaten those rights. Clearly, not every government on earth has played this role throughout history, but this is the role government is supposed to play.

While the Old Testament laid out a theocratic system of government for the nation of Israel during a certain period of her history, never in the New Testament do we see God telling Christians to seek to build a theocracy or impose one on any other country. What's more, nowhere does Scripture indicate that government can save us or solve all our problems or take care of all our needs, and we shouldn't expect it to. Other divinely ordained institutions—including marriage, the family, the church, and even business—have specific roles to play in society. The government isn't supposed to do their jobs; nor should it make their jobs more difficult. Instead, government is supposed to protect these other essential institutions and create a climate of safety and liberty where these institutions can flourish and thrive.

The apostle Paul summarized God's perspective on the healthy, responsible role of government this way:

> Every person is to be in subjection to the governing authorities.
> For there is no authority except from God, and those which
> exist are established by God. Therefore whoever resists
> authority has opposed the ordinance of God; and they who
> have opposed will receive condemnation upon themselves. For
> rulers are not a cause of fear for good behavior, but for evil.
> Do you want to have no fear of authority? Do what is good
> and you will have praise from the same; for it is a minister of
> God to you for good. But if you do what is evil, be afraid; for
> it does not bear the sword for nothing; for it is a minister of
> God, an avenger who brings wrath on the one who practices
> evil. Therefore it is necessary to be in subjection, not only
> because of wrath, but also for conscience's sake. For because of
> this you also pay taxes, for rulers are servants of God, devoting
> themselves to this very thing. Render to all what is due them:
> tax to whom tax is due; custom to whom custom; fear to
> whom fear; honor to whom honor.
>
> ROMANS 13:1-7

Many of the American Founding Fathers were devout Christians who sought to apply biblical principles in the formation of our federal government. "It is impossible to rightly govern the world without God and the Bible," said George Washington, our first president and a strong follower of Christ.[4] John Adams, our second president and also a Christian, put it this way: "The general principles, on which the fathers achieved independence, were the only principles in which that beautiful assembly of young gentlemen could unite. . . . And what were these general principles? I answer, the general principles of Christianity."[5]

Even those founders who weren't Christians were nevertheless steeped in—and deeply influenced by—the teachings of Scripture and highly respectful of Christianity and its critical role in fashioning American life. As Thomas Jefferson, the author of the Declaration of Independence and a deist, once wrote to a friend, "The Christian religion, when divested of the rags in which they [some corrupt clergy members] have enveloped it, and brought to the original purity and simplicity of its benevolent institutor, is a religion of all others most friendly to liberty, science, and the freest expansion of the human mind."[6] Jefferson also famously wrote, "God who gave us life gave us liberty. And can the liberties of a nation be thought secure when we have removed their only firm basis, a conviction in the minds of the people that these liberties are of the gift of God? That they are not to be violated but with his wrath?"[7]

The founders purposefully designed our system of government with such biblical principles in mind. They weren't trying to impose a theocracy; they were notably trying to prevent one. They understood that mankind is sinful by nature and that therefore government must set and enforce rules to limit people's abuses of others' rights and property. As James Madison, the father of our Constitution, explained, "If men were angels, no government would be necessary."[8]

Likewise, the founders understood that power corrupts and absolute power corrupts absolutely. Therefore they also believed that government's role and power must be limited and must include a system of checks and balances to prevent any one branch or party or person from becoming too powerful and abusing the rights of the very people they were sworn to protect. "I am . . . a mortal enemy to arbitrary government and unlimited power," Benjamin Franklin said. "I am naturally very jealous for the rights and liberties of my country; and the least appearance of an encroachment on those invaluable privileges is apt to make my blood boil exceedingly."[9]

Time and time again, the men involved in forming our system of government drew from and pointed to the Bible. Professor Donald S. Lutz of the University of Houston once did a fascinating study on the influence of the Bible on our founders and the political system they established. Lutz reviewed "916 pamphlets, books, and newspaper essays" written during the period 1760–1805. The sample, he noted, included "virtually all the pamphlets and essays from the 1780s by Federalists and Antifederalists concerning the Constitution." In those documents, Lutz counted 3,154 references to 224 individuals. He found that far and away the largest number of citations—34 percent—came directly from the Bible or from sermons quoting the Bible.[10]

What, then, should we expect of the American federal government at this point in our history? It's not rocket science. We should rediscover and vigorously reassert the basic principles of government that our Founding Fathers established in our principal documents, while obviously correcting for their unfortunate mistakes, such as not protecting the civil and political rights of all Americans, including women and minorities. We should, therefore, expect our leaders to:

- Once again honor the Declaration of Independence, which holds that "all men are created equal, that they are endowed by their Creator with certain unalienable rights, that among these are life, liberty, and the pursuit of happiness."[11]
- Truly preserve, protect, and defend the Constitution of the United States.
- Get back to respecting the Tenth Amendment, which asserts that "the powers not delegated to the United States by the Constitution, nor prohibited by it to the States, are reserved to the States respectively, or to the people."[12]

In other words, Washington needs to get focused once again on what the Constitution directs the federal government to do and stop wasting precious time and money monkeying around with everything else. To be precise, Washington needs to make these basic principles its top priorities:

- Protect the sanctity of innocent life from conception to natural death.
- Protect traditional marriage between one man and one woman, the building block of human civilization.
- Protect the American people from all threats, both foreign and domestic, that would threaten our lives, liberties, and property.
- Strengthen our military and care for our troops.
- Protect our borders and defend American sovereignty.
- Establish justice, protect our civil rights, punish criminals (especially violent ones), and appoint wise and sensible federal judges and Supreme Court justices who will uphold the Constitution, not legislate from the bench.
- Protect Americans' freedom to save, invest, start small businesses, grow those businesses, create jobs, and provide for their families.
- Create the proper conditions for economic growth and innovation. This can be done in part by making tax rates as low as possible and by radically simplifying the federal tax code; this also means setting fair rules and vigorously enforcing those rules—but not trying to use federal power to solve every problem through legislation and regulation.
- Balance the federal budget by limiting the size and scope of government, cutting waste and duplication, returning key responsibilities back to the states, and reforming federal entitlement programs.
- Get out of debt.
- Maintain a sound and stable currency.
- And don't make promises you can't or won't keep.

Given the mess that we are in, will it be easy to reassert the principles espoused by our Founding Fathers? No, it won't. It will take men and women of deep conviction, character, and courage to get us back on the right track. But one thing is certain: we have no hope unless we try.

A Spiritual and Political Journey

For as long as I can remember, I have had a fascination with American politics, and I have long wrestled with the question of just what role—if any—a Christian should play in politics. Should believers stick to preaching and teaching the Word of God, sharing the gospel, and making disciples, and steer clear of all things political? Should we avoid altogether the political process of electing our leaders and advocating certain policies because it's a "dirty game"? Or should we engage in the political arena to protect our God-given rights and advance our biblical values? Should we actively resist the onslaught of secular humanism in our schools, our courts, our legislatures, and in the White House even if it's a hard, brutal, no-holds-barred battle for the heart and soul of America?

These are challenging questions. And given that the stakes are now so high, never has it been more important for Christians in America to wrestle with them and come to solid, defensible conclusions.

Let me take a few moments here to share some of my own story, in the interest of full disclosure and so you can get a sense of how I've drawn my conclusions.

In the fourth grade, I did a book report on *All the President's Men* by Bob Woodward and Carl Bernstein and found myself disgusted by the corruption inside the administration of President Richard Milhous Nixon. Sometime around then, I remember chastising my only living grandmother when I learned that she had voted for Nixon in 1968 and then again for his reelection in 1972. "How could you do that, Grammie?" I asked. "How could you vote for Nixon when he was such a crook?" She, of course, like many Republicans, hadn't known in 1972 that Nixon was guilty of crimes against the Constitution. She didn't imagine that Nixon would face impeachment and leave office in disgrace. She believed at the time that the charges were being trumped up by Nixon's enemies. What's more, she deeply disagreed with the liberal policies of George McGovern, the Democrats' nominee, and feared for where McGovern would take the country. But she didn't try to defend herself to me that day. She just smiled and gave me a hug and told me to go back outside and play.

With the notable exception of my Republican-voting Grammie, I like to joke that my family were "Democrats going back to the Bolsheviks." My mother was literally a "bra-burning, tree-hugging, liberal Democrat" in the 1960s and early 1970s. My father was also a liberal Democrat, as were his Jewish parents and his Jewish grandparents (who escaped from Russia) before them.

My parents both came to faith in Jesus Christ in 1973. But they didn't suddenly decide to bolt out of the Democratic Party. They, like millions of evangelical Christians, voted for Jimmy Carter in 1976. They were repulsed by Watergate and were looking for an honest leader in Washington. They were attracted to Carter's willingness to openly describe himself as a "born-again Christian."

But over the next few years, they became deeply disappointed by Carter's failed economic policies and disastrous foreign policies. By 1980, my parents ended up voting for a Republican presidential candidate—Ronald Reagan—for the first time in their lives. They voted again for Reagan in 1984, two of millions of "Reagan Democrats"— a movement made up largely of disaffected evangelical Protestant Christians and blue-collar Catholics who not only favored Reagan's pro-growth, pro-freedom economic and military policies but who could no longer abide by the Democratic Party's increasingly far-left agenda of support for abortion on demand, capitulation to the gay-rights movement, and timidity in the face of the evil Soviet Empire. My parents went on to vote for George H. W. Bush in 1988 and actually reregistered as Republicans in the early 1990s, during what became known as the "Republican Revolution" to take control of Congress from the Democrats.

What I eventually noticed in my parents' journey was that a person's political views are often lagging indicators of his or her spiritual views. Yes, my parents had had a radical change of spiritual beliefs in 1973 when they stopped being agnostics and accepted Jesus Christ as their Savior. But that didn't immediately translate into changed political views. It took time for them to reconsider their worldview through the third lens of Scripture, and longer still to wrestle through whether—and how—to apply their newly developing core spiritual convictions to the political issues of the day. However, the deeper they went in their faith, the more determined they became to find candidates who better represented their values. They had numerous and strong disagreements with the old, establishment, country-club elements of the Republican Party and various GOP candidates. But as time went by, they felt increasingly more at home with the millions of evangelical ex-Democrats who were forming the conservative, pro-life, pro-family, pro-freedom, Reaganite base of the new Republican Party. Not all followers of Jesus Christ have drawn the same political conclusions, of course, but clearly millions have. This has had a dramatic, transformative impact on the American political scene in recent decades as more Christian conservatives have been elected to public office and more conservative judges have been appointed to the bench.

My parents, however, were way ahead of me. In 1975, I prayed to receive Christ as my Savior. For the next decade or so, I grew as a new Christian, but I can't say I was as deeply serious about my faith as I should have been. Then, in my junior year of high school, God began to shake my personal world in an effort to wake me up and draw me closer to him. Our church experienced a severe split over some important theological issues. My family left the church, and as a result I rarely saw any of the closest friends I'd had growing up. During this time I didn't have a girlfriend. I didn't have a best friend. I was anxious about college and my future, and I began to slip into a depression in the fall of 1983. As I lost emotional altitude, my grades started slipping, and I began withdrawing from my family. I became angry with God and doubtful that Christianity was either real or relevant.

And then, completely unexpectedly, I had a powerful and very personal experience with Jesus Christ in January 1984. God shook me to my core and made it clear to me that he wasn't happy with the shallowness of my relationship with him. One bitterly cold winter night, I was essentially yelling at the Lord in the privacy of my room. I was bitter and confused. "You say that you promise love and joy and peace and hope and happiness, and I don't have any of it," I told God. "So either all this Christianity stuff is a joke, or I totally don't get it."

It wasn't the first time I'd had such a blow-up session with God, but it was to be the last. Suddenly I heard the Lord speak directly back to me. Whether it was audible or not I cannot say, but it might as well have been, because the message was loud and clear. "Joel, do you ever really study my Word?" God asked me. Stunned, I thought about it for a few moments and finally had to say no. Obviously I had read the Bible from time to time in my life, but the blunt truth was I had never been serious about knowing the Scriptures for myself. Then God said, "Joel, do you ever spend time talking to me in prayer?" Immediately I was deeply ashamed of myself. Again I had to say no. Of course I had said prayers now and then, but I had never been serious about talking to—or listening to—the Lord.

At that point, God lowered the boom. "Then, Joel, why would you expect to experience my blessings when you don't even really know me?" Then the transmission, as it were, ceased.

But rather than be further depressed by my obvious shallowness and disobedience, I was electrified. Christ had spoken directly to me! In his mercy, he hadn't punished me for expressing my emotions and directing my blunt questions to him. On the contrary, he kept his word. As Jeremiah 29:11-13 says, "'For I know the plans I have for you,' declares the LORD, 'plans to prosper you and not to harm you, plans to give you hope and a future. Then you will call on me and come and pray to me, and I will listen to you. You will seek me and find me when you seek me with all your heart" (NIV).

God had just shown me what I was doing wrong. He had revealed to me the reason for my discouragement and depression and had shown me how to change. I had been ignoring the basics of the faith, and as a result, God had allowed me to experience the emptiness and sadness of being distant from him. But these were simple enough changes to make, and from that point forward, I became voracious about studying the Bible (starting with John's Gospel) and spending long hours with the Lord in prayer. That's when my own personal revival began, in the winter of my junior year of high school.

Suddenly my faith really started to take off. My parents and I changed churches and began attending a congregation where the young people were passionate about knowing Christ and making him known and where the leaders actively taught us how to live not in our own meager strength and wisdom but in the power of the Holy Spirit. That summer I went on a missions trip to Los Angeles with other high school and college students to share the gospel with people from all over the world who were attending the Olympics. I was terrified but at the same time exhilarated.

That fall, as I began my senior year, I sensed God leading me to start a small prayer and evangelism group at my high school. Again it was terrifying, but that small group (which we called "Christ for Life") saw God open up all kinds of doors to share Christ, and we saw kids get saved.

The following year, in the fall of 1985, I entered Syracuse University as a freshman and joined a student ministry called Campus Crusade for Christ (now called "Cru"). I developed many lifelong friendships and was discipled by a CCC staffer and later by my pastor, T. E. Koshy, the evangelical chaplain at SU. I also became active in sharing my faith with dozens of students on campus and on a summer missions trip to the Soviet Union.

Still, I had not yet wrestled through how my newly developing biblical worldview could or should affect my political views. I still thought of myself as a liberal Democrat. I wasn't paying attention to the fact that my parents had become increasingly conservative Reagan Democrats. So when the 1988 presidential campaign rolled around—the first election I was old enough to participate in—I registered as a Democrat. I voted for Al Gore in the New York primary. A friend and I went down to the Syracuse War Memorial to heckle Republican vice presidential candidate Dan Quayle. In November I voted for Michael Dukakis for president in the general election. I look back at all this now and grimace. But at the time I couldn't imagine voting for a Republican. I considered the Republicans enemies of the poor, intellectually vapid, and bereft of any serious, thoughtful ideas for moving the country forward.

This is the first time I've ever told this story in print. Indeed, I've rarely spoken of it in public. My purpose isn't to try to persuade you to become a partisan Republican operative. It is, as I mentioned earlier, simply to let you know where I came from and where I am today.

It was actually on my honeymoon in the summer of 1990 that my sweet bride challenged me on the disconnect between my spiritual convictions and my political views. "Aren't you pro-life?" she asked me.

"Yes, of course," I answered.

"Then how could you vote for Dukakis, who essentially supports abortion on demand?" she replied.

We argued about this and dozens of other issues. She couldn't understand my reasoning. I couldn't believe she didn't agree with me! How had we failed to discuss politics all the time I was courting her and during our engagement?

Still, I loved Lynn dearly and respected her greatly. Therefore, I carefully listened to her. Within days, I reluctantly (dare I say, begrudgingly) came to the conclusion that she was right and I was wrong. It was time for me to connect my faith to my political beliefs. I needed to start voting for people who shared my convictions and values on as many issues as possible, not simply vote for or against a particular political party because that's what my family had done in the past or because I didn't like certain elements in the history of one party or another.

In 1990, Lynn and I moved to Washington, DC, and were fortunate enough to get jobs working with and for leaders whose pro-life, pro-family, and limited-government values we shared and whose constitutionally based conservative ideas to protect life, liberty, and American security and sovereignty we genuinely wanted to promote. We were excited to find principled, compassionate, and intellectually vigorous leaders who consistently put their deeply held moral convictions ahead of partisan politics and were working hard to shape both the ideas and the image of a Republican party that desperately needed a more positive, forward-looking approach to governance.

After a brief stint at the Japanese embassy, Lynn wound up working for Beverly LaHaye, founder and then president of Concerned Women for America—an evangelical pro-family organization—organizing their national conventions and special events. I worked as an administration assistant at the Heritage Foundation, the nation's premier conservative think tank. Later I worked as a policy analyst for Jack Kemp and Bill Bennett at Empower America, a conservative grassroots organization, and after that as research director for Rush Limbaugh's newsletter and radio show. Later still I worked as a senior advisor to Steve Forbes on both of his GOP presidential campaigns (1996 and 2000) and, between campaigns, for his nonprofit grassroots organization, Americans for Hope, Growth, and Opportunity. I learned a great deal from these mentors, and while I didn't always agree with every idea they had or tactical decision they made, I was deeply impressed by the passion and creativity they brought to what they called the "war of ideas."

What Role—If Any—Should Christians Play in Politics?

Having now lived and worked in Washington, DC, for more than two decades and having had the opportunity to work inside the world of policy and politics as a follower of Christ, I have come to several conclusions about what role all Americans—and particularly Christians—should play in the political arena. I hope these ideas will be helpful as you come to your own convictions.

1. Christians need to pray faithfully and consistently for wisdom and direction for our national leaders.

We may not always be happy with what our leaders are doing and saying, but we need to pray for them anyway. Failing to do so is disobedience to God. As the apostle Paul instructed Timothy and the church he pastored in Ephesus, "First of all, then, I urge that entreaties and prayers, petitions and thanksgivings, be made on behalf of all men, for kings and all who are in authority, so that we may lead a tranquil and quiet life in all godliness and dignity" (1 Timothy 2:1-2). Paul told the church in Rome to "render to all what is due them: tax to whom tax is due; custom to whom custom; fear to whom fear; honor to whom honor" (Romans 13:7).

The apostle Peter reinforced this message.

> Be careful to live properly among your unbelieving
> neighbors. Then even if they accuse you of doing wrong,
> they will see your honorable behavior, and they will give

honor to God when he judges the world. For the Lord's sake, respect all human authority—whether the king as head of state, or the officials he has appointed. For the king has sent them to punish those who do wrong and to honor those who do right. It is God's will that your honorable lives should silence those ignorant people who make foolish accusations against you. For you are free, yet you are God's slaves, so don't use your freedom as an excuse to do evil. Respect everyone, and love your Christian brothers and sisters. Fear God, and respect the king.

I PETER 2:12-17, NLT

The Christians who founded this great country certainly were men and women of prayer. Indeed, because of the First Great Awakening, many of our nation's early leaders had become deeply faithful in praying and fasting. They most definitely prayed for God to protect and guide those in authority. But they also prayed that God would remove tyrants and unfit men from leadership and replace them with new leaders who had great wisdom and sound judgment to govern the struggling nation. Should we do any less today?

2. Christians need to exercise their right to vote and mobilize others to vote as well.

We are not slaves of an empire. By God's grace, we are free people and citizens of the greatest democratic republic in the history of mankind. Very few people in history have had a say in who got elected in their countries and what values and policies those leaders would defend and advance, but we have that very privilege. How dare we ignore and squander it? We should take this right seriously. As Jesus said, "From everyone who has been given much, much will be required" (Luke 12:48).

Over the past four decades, the number of Americans of voting age who describe themselves as born-again Christians has risen from 50 million to more than 80 million. While such Christians do not have the numbers to dominate American politics, we can play a decisive role. But we cannot have any influence on the direction of our country if we don't get involved. So if we want to help our government fundamentally change direction—if we're committed to doing everything possible to avoid an economic and cultural implosion—we need to be serious, focused, and involved in the political process.

What does this mean for you if you're a Christian? At the very least you should register to vote and then go to the polls to vote your conscience. Encourage others to register to vote too. Become informed on the issues, and help educate your friends. Pay close attention to what the candidates are saying and what their records are. Study all candidates carefully. Don't make any rash decisions. Weigh all the elements—a candidate's character, history, marriage, experience, voting record, views on the issues, speeches, statements, articles, ads, advisors, and allies. Don't expect candidates to be perfect. Remember that campaigns are about choices. You will be presented with flawed candidates. That's a given. So you must carefully choose the least flawed, most principled, most experienced, and most effective candidates during primaries and during general elections. Don't ignore a candidate's moral failures. Don't ignore unorthodox religious views. Don't ignore that uneasy feeling you have in your gut that you can't explain but that you sense is trouble. Study hard, and weigh everything carefully. Patiently ask God for wisdom. And don't simply pray; fast as well.

When you find a candidate you like and can trust, ask the Lord whether he would have you help that candidate with your time, your talent, or your treasure. The Lord doesn't call every believer to get actively involved in a campaign beyond voting, but some he does. Do only what the Lord tells you to do, no more but no less. And when the time comes, vote—and mobilize others to vote—and then trust the Lord with the results. As the prophet Daniel told us, ultimately it is the Lord who "removes kings and establishes kings" (Daniel 2:21). So don't let yourself become depressed if your candidate loses. God is still in control. And don't gloat if your candidate wins. Keep your eyes on Jesus Christ, the King of kings and the Lord of lords.

Not all Christians are going to agree on every issue or every candidate, of course. But consider how much impact Christians could make in reshaping the fundamental direction of the White House, the Congress, the federal courts, and the Supreme Court (as well as local and state government) if we unified behind leaders who share and represent our values. Consider a few facts:

- In 1976, 35 percent of voting-age Americans (about 50 million people) described themselves as "born again," according to a Gallup poll.[13]
- That same year, fully 50 percent of self-described born-again Christians voted for Democrat Jimmy Carter, playing a critical role in helping Carter win the presidency over the Republican incumbent Gerald Ford.[14]
- By 1980, the number of self-described born-again Christians in America had increased to 39 percent, according to Gallup.[15]
- That same year, born-again Christians broke against Carter, voting almost two-to-one (61 percent to 34 percent) for Republican candidate Ronald Reagan and playing a key factor in Reagan's victory.[16]
- In 1984, Reagan won 78 percent of the Christian vote in his landslide victory over Democrat Walter Mondale, who received only 22 percent.[17]
- Republican George H. W. Bush won a stunning 81 percent of the evangelical vote in 1988 as part of his lopsided victory over Democrat Michael Dukakis, who received only 18 percent.[18]

- However, when born-again Christian support for George H. W. Bush declined significantly in 1992—he secured only 59 percent of this critical voter bloc—Bush ended up losing the presidency to Democrat Bill Clinton, who received 21 percent (Independent Ross Perot siphoned off the remainder of born-again Christian voters).[19]

- In 1996, Bill Clinton increased his share of the evangelical vote to 43 percent, which helped him defeat Bob Dole, who secured only 49 percent—the lowest percentage for any Republican in two decades.[20]

- By 2000, the number of voting-age Americans who described themselves as born again had increased to 45 percent (about 87 million people).[21]

- That same year, Republican George W. Bush, a devout and outspoken evangelical Christian, won 57 percent of the born-again Christian vote (which was far more than Dole but actually less than his father, George H. W. Bush) and only very narrowly defeated Democrat Al Gore, who received 42 percent.[22]

- In 2004, George W. Bush specifically and heavily courted Christians and won 62 percent of the self-described born-again Christian vote and defeated Democrat John Kerry, who secured only 38 percent.[23]

- In 2008, Republican candidate John McCain was faring poorly among Christians for much of the election cycle. His numbers improved after he named Sarah Palin, a devout and outspoken evangelical, to the ticket, but not enough to defeat Democrat Barack Obama. In the end, McCain won 57 percent of the born-again vote, while Obama won 41 percent.[24]

- In 2010, a stunning 77 percent of self-described born-again Christians voted for Republican candidates running for the House of Representatives, while only 19 percent voted for

Democrat candidates, resulting in a landslide victory for the GOP in which they picked up sixty-three congressional seats and won back control of the House.[25]

How will the American government be shaped in the future? Christians could play a key role in answering this question. But one thing is certain: disunity will destroy us. Jesus said, "If a house is divided against itself, that house will not be able to stand" (Mark 3:25). If in coming elections Christians are divided between candidates who share our biblical principles and constitutional convictions, who practice what they preach, and on the other hand candidates who are opposed to our principles or who flip-flop on them or cannot be trusted for other reasons, then elections will be won by candidates who do not share our values. In turn, we will lose the opportunity to turn this ship of state around.

But if Christians register to vote en masse and unite behind serious, substantive, pro-life, pro-marriage, pro-growth, pro-defense candidates who truly use the Constitution as their guide, then we have a real chance to put solid candidates in office and empower them to make the reforms we so desperately need to rescue our country from the abyss.

3. Some Christians need to run for elected office, serve in some other governmental capacity, or serve as advisors to national leaders who are affecting the future of our country.

God doesn't call all Christians to such roles, but he calls some, and these are high and honorable callings.

The Bible is filled with examples of people whom the Lord called to work not only in godly governments but in ungodly ones as well. Joseph was called to serve in the Egyptian government and eventually rose to the equivalent of the Egyptian prime minister, second in power only to the pharaoh himself. In that position, God used Joseph to save Egypt and Israel and other nations from a terrible famine. Daniel was called by God to serve in the Babylonian and Persian governments, advising leaders at the highest levels but always keeping his true allegiance to God. Shadrach, Meshach, and Abednego also worked for the Babylonian government, ultimately acting as provincial governors while maintaining their faith in the God of Abraham, Isaac, and Jacob. Queen Esther and the wise Mordecai faithfully served the leaders of the Persian Empire and helped save the Jewish people because they were in the right place at the right time, doing the Lord's will with fasting and prayer. And of course, David and Solomon and Josiah and others served as kings of Israel, while many other faithful men and women of God served in various government and military roles at God's direction.

What if such men and women had refused to obey the Lord by serving in government? Imagine how much more evil would have been done in their time, how many lives would have been lost or harmed. We should not go into politics or government life if God is not calling us. God will not bless our efforts if we do. But if he calls us and we refuse to serve, we dishonor him and cede the playing field to those who oppose our biblical values and will fight against them.

Again, consider the founders of our country. Many were devout believers. Some were pastors. They entered the political arena after much prayer and after concluding God was directing them to serve their country in this manner. We should do no less.

Christians who do run for office, of course, should always be careful to respect people of all faiths as well as those who embrace no faith. They should also conduct themselves in office with the highest moral and ethical standards, setting an example of which the nation can be proud.

Sometimes God calls people to play a role in government or in the political arena for a season, not for a lifetime. Make certain you listen carefully to God's voice and step off the political stage when he tells you to. After much prayer and Bible study, Lynn and I were certain we were called to live and work in Washington, DC, beginning in 1990. We didn't make a lasting difference on our capital or our country as we hoped, but we sought to be faithful. Then, when God told us to change our focus and serve him in other ways, we again sought to follow Christ's lead. We still live in the Washington area and will until the Lord moves us, but we're not immersed in the political world as we once were. As King Solomon once wrote, "There is an appointed time for everything. And there is a time for every event under heaven" (Ecclesiastes 3:1).

4. Some Christians need to stay completely away from the political arena.

As I noted above, not all Christians are called to get directly involved in politics and government. Those who are not should be very careful to remain faithful to the specific responsibilities entrusted to them by God and not get tempted into political activity. They should certainly pray for their leaders, vote, help others register to vote, and encourage others to get to the polls on Election Day. These are basic civic responsibilities, after all, and pastors and others in ministry should set a good example in this area for those they oversee. But while some pastors and ministry leaders should publicly endorse a candidate or be actively engaged in political campaigns when the Lord directs them, those who haven't been called should avoid such activities at all costs, even though the law permits a wider degree of political involvement for clergy members than most people realize. Rather, they should stay focused on preaching and teaching the Bible, sharing the gospel, making disciples, shepherding their flock, and counseling those in need. A shepherd, after all, needs to be able to care for Democrats, Republicans, Independents, and the unaffiliated. A partisan reputation could severely hinder some believers from effectively exercising their spiritual gifts and divine callings.

The apostle Paul could have organized political opposition to the Roman government in addition to preaching the gospel and planting churches. But that's not what God told him to do. Likewise, consider this passage, John 6:15: "So Jesus, perceiving that they were intending to come and take Him by force to make Him king, withdrew again to the mountain by Himself alone." Jesus Christ certainly came to earth to be the King of kings and the Lord of lords, but not by some human political process. That was not the Father's will for his life, so he avoided it at all costs.

Remember, ultimately we are called to serve the Kingdom of God, not to help build kingdoms on earth. The key is prayer and fasting and seeking the specific will of God. What is he calling you to do? This is no time for indecision or cowardice. The fate of the country hangs in the balance. Are you supposed to be like Nehemiah, a strong follower of the Lord who was called to serve as governor of Judah, the political leader of the people? Nehemiah oversaw the rebuilding of the walls of Jerusalem, organized the people to defend themselves from multiple enemies, and administered numerous civil reforms. Or are you supposed to be like Ezra, another strong follower of the Lord, who was called to serve as a priest and the spiritual leader of the people? Ezra taught the Word of God, leading the people in prayer and repentance, and administered the religious reforms of his day. Each of us must come to a deep conviction of our role and then be "all in." We must know the Lord's will and then obey him with more passion and determination than ever before in our lives.

5. Christians must not become addicted to partisanship.

I have met too many Christians over the years who have become completely obsessed with winning political battles at all costs. They have allowed their utter devotion to a political party to trump their essential commitment to Christ. It's not pretty.

Even if we're called into political activity, we must maintain balance and perspective. Now is no time to become angry with people who disagree with you politically or to treat political opponents unkindly. Yes, the stakes are high. Yes, the fate of our country hangs in the balance. But Jesus told us to love our neighbor and love our enemies. He commanded us to show kindness and gentleness to everyone we encounter. So fight hard—and clean—for your beliefs, your values, and your team. But don't get addicted to partisanship. Don't become nasty and petty, even if others do. It's not worth it. It's not Christlike. And it won't work.

Also, remember that one political party may represent your values better than another, but it cannot save you. Politics isn't the ultimate answer. Don't imagine for one moment that just by winning an election, the enormous problems facing our nation will suddenly be solved overnight. It's not going to happen that way. The battles are going to intensify. The opposition will increase. If Washington can be turned around at all, it will only happen amid enormous political combat, day by day, week by week, year by year. It's not for the faint of heart. It is warfare by nonlethal means. That's precisely what our founders intended. And if history is any guide, the opposition doesn't always fight fair.

If you're hoping for your political party to take over Washington and make everything all better just because they control all the levers of power, forget it. It's a pipe dream. Lynn and I have seen it all in this town. We've seen Democrats control everything—the White House, the House of Representatives, and the Senate. We've seen the Republicans control everything. We've seen the government split between Democrat and Republican control. We've seen the budget balanced for a few years, then spin wildly out of control all over again. We must pray and work hard with the hope that God will have mercy and allow our elected national leaders to make things better. But never forget this basic truth: politicians are going to let you down, so brace yourself for disappointment.

Take our democracy seriously, but don't put all your emotional eggs in the political basket. Don't become obsessed with the political process. Don't become fixated on political change as though your hope is in the Republican Party or the Democratic Party or some other party, rather than Jesus Christ, our soon-coming King.

There was a point in my life when I was becoming a bit too enthralled with partisan politics. I knew that God was directing me to be engaged in the political arena for a season, but I didn't always maintain a proper balance and perspective. Often I had to make course corrections. For example, at one point while I was working as the deputy campaign manager for a Republican presidential contender, Lynn was discipling a young woman who was a relatively new Christian and an outspoken Democrat. She became agitated anytime I talked about my candidate or his issues, and Lynn suggested that I cool it by not talking about politics when the young woman was around. She was right. Helping that young woman grow in her faith in Christ was far more important than trying to persuade her to change her party or her vote.

People say, "Never talk about religion or politics." My career has actually been about doing both. But my experience with that young woman helped me rethink how to navigate these tricky waters. I resolved not to talk much about politics with the young men I have discipled over the years. If they bring up political topics, I am happy to answer some of their questions, but even then I've tried to be circumspect. Most of these young men were hungry to know God, not hungry to become Republicans. Good for them. I can't say I always found the right balance. But with God's help and Lynn's encouragement, I've tried.

Today, I like to say that I've gone through "political detox"—I'm out; I'm clean! People usually laugh when I say it, but I'm serious. What I mean is that I have asked God to help me not be addicted to political partisanship. I no longer work professionally for political campaigns. I no longer work as an activist for a particular political party or movement. And I try hard to limit my partisan comments. I still have deeply held views on policies and politics, of course, and I believe God has given me the freedom both to speak out on issues and to provide private advice and counsel to national and international leaders who seek it. But I went through "political detox" for a very specific reason. I don't want to do or say anything that could distract people here at home or abroad from the message God has given me to communicate concerning the importance of preaching the gospel and making disciples in fulfillment of the great commission, the urgent need for a Third Great Awakening, the importance of Bible prophecy, God's heart for Israel and her neighbors, and the increasingly close return of Jesus Christ.

God gave me a season in politics. Now he has given me a different calling, and it is one that I seek to take very seriously. How about you?

Bottom Line

As John Winthrop finished his message to the pilgrims on the *Arbella* on that dramatic voyage, he not only spoke of creating a shining "city upon a hill" but also warned them in no uncertain terms what could happen if they did not stay close to Christ in the New World.

> If our hearts shall turn away, so that we will not obey, but shall be seduced, and worship other gods, our pleasure and profits, and serve them; it is propounded unto us this day, we shall surely perish out of the good land whither we pass over this vast sea to possess it. Therefore let us choose life, that we and our seed may live, by obeying his voice and cleaving to him, for he is our life and our prosperity.[26]

How we need to hear and heed Governor Winthrop's message today. For our nation is in grave danger. That's why God is shaking us—to wake us up and get us to change course before it's too late.

Can America once again be a shining city on a hill? I don't know for certain, but I hope so. As a person who deeply loves America, it is my earnest prayer that this nation can once more be good and thus once more be great. And as a person who much more deeply loves Jesus Christ, I believe with all my heart that if we are to avoid implosion as a nation, we must repent of our sins and turn to Christ—personally and nationally.

Will you join me in that endeavor? Will you pray with me for our nation, for the church, and for a Third Great Awakening? Will you examine your own heart and seek your own personal revival? Will you work to engage your church and your culture with the truths of Scripture? Will you ask God to show you whether he wants you to be involved in political change, and if so, how? Our founders devoted their lives, their fortunes, and their sacred honor to creating a nation that would protect life, liberty, and the pursuit of happiness. What are you and I willing to devote to saving this country?

We must not kid ourselves. The evidence suggests we may very well be aboard the *Titanic*, heading for icebergs and inexplicably increasing our speed toward disaster. So many on board are unaware of the dangers fast approaching and not concerned in the slightest. We haven't hit the icebergs yet, but if we don't make a sharp turn fast, we soon will, and we will sink. Who will serve as our captain and crew going forward? Will they understand the gravity of the threat and have the wisdom, courage, and speed to take appropriate action before it is too late? What is our role as passengers? Are we to succumb to decadence, indulging ourselves in amusements and entertainment and alcohol with no regard for our own safety or the safety of others aboard? Or will we rise up, sound the alarm, and take action while we still can?

As you make your decision and I make mine, let us also remember the dangers that lie ahead even if we are successful. Remember, the First and Second Great Awakenings didn't ultimately spare the American people from the fast-approaching Revolutionary War of the eighteenth century or the Civil War of the nineteenth century. Devastating, life-altering conflicts were coming. But God knew they were coming and wanted Americans to be spiritually and morally ready for great pain, hardship, and sacrifice. Would a Third Great Awakening spare us from wars and other traumas, whether from Middle Eastern Radicals, Asian tyrants, terrorist forces, or other forces, natural or supernatural? No, I don't believe it would. But we need such an awakening and sweeping government reforms anyway. For only then will we as the American people be prepared for anything and everything that lies ahead.

Now is the time for brave hearts and bold actions. Now is the time to be "joyful in hope, patient in affliction, faithful in prayer" (Romans 12:12, NIV).

To be candid, I don't believe we can be certain of earthly success if we follow a course such as I've laid out in this book, but we can certainly be assured of utter disaster if we do not. If you and I will put everything on the line, then I pray America may still have time to change direction and receive God's grace.

As John Winthrop urged his fellow passengers, I urge all of us: let us choose life by obeying God's voice and clinging to him, for he is our life, our prosperity, and our ultimate hope.

Now is the time. Let us choose wisely.

Recommended Reading

Mark A. Noll, *The Rise of Evangelicalism: The Age of Edwards, Whitefield and the Wesleys* (IVP Academic, 2003)

Mark A. Noll, *A History of Christianity in the United States and Canada* (Eerdmans, 1992)

Arnold A. Dallimore, *George Whitefield: God's Anointed Servant in the Great Revival of the Eighteenth Century* (Crossway, 1990)

Richard L. Bushman, ed., *The Great Awakening: Documents on the Revival of Religion, 1740-1745* (University of North Carolina Press, 1989)

Thomas S. Kidd, *The Great Awakening: A Brief History with Documents* (Yale University Press, 2007)

John Wigger, *American Saint: Francis Asbury and the Methodists* (Oxford University Press, USA, 2009)

Charles G. Finney, *The Autobiography of Charles G. Finney* (Bethany House, 1977)

William G. McLoughlin, Jr., *Modern Revivalism: Charles Grandison Finney to Billy Graham* (Wipf and Stock, 2005)

Collin Hansen and John Woodbridge, *A God-Sized Vision: Revival Stories That Stretch and Stir* (Zondervan, 2010)

George Barna, *Futurecast: What Today's Trends Mean for Tomorrow's World* (Tyndale House, 2011)

David Kinnaman and Gabe Lyons, *unChristian: What a New Generation Really Thinks about Christianity . . . and Why It Matters* (Baker Books, 2007)

David Platt, *Radical: Taking Back Your Faith from the American Dream* (Multnomah, 2010)

Anne Graham Lotz, *Expecting to See Jesus: A Wake-Up Call for God's People* (Zondervan, 2011)

Gregg Matte, *I AM Changes Who i Am: Who Jesus Is Changes Who I Am; What Jesus Does Changes What I Am to Do* (Regal, 2012)

Bill Bright, *The Coming Revival: America's Call to Fast, Pray, and "Seek God's Face"* (Thomas Nelson, 1995)

Billy Graham, *Just As I Am: The Autobiography of Billy Graham* (HarperCollins, 1997)

Charles Swindoll, *The Church Awakening: An Urgent Call for Renewal* (FaithWords, 2010)

Francis Chan, *Crazy Love: Overwhelmed by a Relentless God* (David C. Cook, 2008)

Jim Cymbala, *Fresh Wind, Fresh Fire* (Zondervan, 1998)

Chuck Smith and Tal Brooke, *Harvest* (Word for Today, 2005)

Acknowledgments

OVER THE YEARS, I have been very fortunate to work with such a great publisher. The folks at Tyndale House are the best in the business. They have become dear friends, and I am very grateful for our partnership. Very special thanks to Mark Taylor, Jeff Johnson, Ron Beers, Karen Watson, Jeremy Taylor, Jan Stob, Cheryl Kerwin, Dean Renninger (for his always-amazing covers), and the rest of the phenomenal Tyndale team. It's a joy to work together.

Thanks to Scott Miller, my amazing agent and good friend at Trident Media Group.

Thanks to my loving family—my mom and dad, Len and Mary Jo Rosenberg; June "Bubbe" Meyers; the entire Meyers family; the Rebeizes; the Scomas; and the Urbanskis.

Thanks to my dear friends Edward and Kailea Hunt, Tim and Carolyn Lugbill, Steve and Barb Klemke, Fred and Sue Schwien, Tom and Sue Yancy, John and Cheryl Moser, Jeremy and Angie Grafman, Nancy Pierce, Jeff and Naomi Cuozzo, Lance and Angie Emma, Lucas and Erin Edwards, Chung and Farah Woo, Dr. T. E. Koshy and family, and all our teammates and allies who work with or for the Joshua Fund and November Communications, Inc.

Most of all, thanks to my best friend and awesome wife, Lynn—

you are more than I could have ever hoped for, dreamed of, or imagined—and thanks to our four wonderful sons and prayer warriors: Caleb, Jacob, Jonah, and Noah. I love doing life with all of you, and I will love you guys forever!

About the Author

JOEL C. ROSENBERG is a *New York Times* bestselling author with more than 2.5 million copies in print. His books include *The Last Jihad, The Last Days, The Ezekiel Option, The Copper Scroll, Dead Heat, Epicenter, Inside the Revolution, The Twelfth Imam,* and *The Tehran Initiative.* He is the cofounder and president of the Joshua Fund, a nonprofit organization whose mission is to mobilize Christians "to bless Israel and her neighbors in the name of Jesus, according to Genesis 12:1-3," whose methods include providing humanitarian relief to the poor and needy in the Middle East. As a communications strategist, he has worked with some of the world's most influential leaders in business, politics, and media. He has been interviewed on hundreds of radio and TV programs, including ABC's *Nightline*, CNN, FOX News Channel, History, and MSNBC. He has been profiled by the *New York Times*, the *Washington Times*, *World* magazine, and the *Jerusalem Post*. He has addressed audiences all over the world, including Israel, Iraq, Jordan, Egypt, Turkey, Russia, Philippines, France, Germany, and Belgium, and has spoken at the White House, the Pentagon, the U.S. Capitol, and the European Union Parliament.

The first page of his first novel—*The Last Jihad*—puts readers inside the cockpit of a hijacked jet, coming on a kamikaze attack into an American city, which leads to a war with Saddam Hussein over weapons of mass destruction. Yet it was written months before 9/11 and published before the actual war with Iraq. *The Last Jihad* spent eleven weeks on the *New York Times* hardcover fiction bestseller list, reaching as high as #7. It raced up the *USA Today* and *Publishers Weekly* bestseller lists, hit #4 on the *Wall Street Journal* list, and hit #1 on Amazon.com.

His second thriller—*The Last Days*—opens with the death of Yasser Arafat and a U.S. diplomatic convoy ambushed in Gaza. Two weeks before *The Last Days* was published in hardcover, a U.S. diplomatic convoy was ambushed in Gaza. Thirteen months later, Yasser Arafat was dead. *The Last Days* spent four weeks on the *New York Times* hardcover fiction bestseller list, hit #5 on the *Denver Post* list, and hit #8 on the *Dallas Morning News* list. Both books were optioned by a Hollywood producer.

The Ezekiel Option centers on a dictator rising in Russia who forms a military alliance with the leaders of Iran as they feverishly pursue nuclear weapons and threaten to wipe Israel off the face of the earth. On the very day it was published in June 2005, Iran elected a new leader who vowed to accelerate the country's nuclear program and later threatened to "wipe Israel off the map." Six months after it was published, Moscow signed a $1 billion arms deal with Tehran. *The Ezekiel Option* spent four weeks on the *New York Times* hardcover fiction bestseller list and five months on the Christian Booksellers Association bestseller list, reaching as high as #4. It won the 2006 Gold Medallion award from the CBA as the year's best novel.

In *The Copper Scroll*, an ancient scroll describes unimaginable treasures worth untold billions buried in the hills east of Jerusalem and under the Holy City itself—treasures that could come from the Second Temple and whose discovery could lead to the building of the Third Temple and a war of biblical proportions. One month after it was released, *Biblical Archaeology Review* published a story describing the real-life, intensified hunt for the treasures of the actual Copper Scroll. *The Copper Scroll* spent four weeks on the *New York Times* hardcover fiction bestseller list, two weeks on the *Wall Street Journal* bestseller list, two weeks on the *Publishers Weekly* hardcover fiction list, and several months on the CBA bestseller list. It won the 2007 Logos Bookstores Best Fiction Award.

In *Dead Heat*, America is in the midst of a heated presidential election when the Secret Service learns of a catastrophic terrorist plot to assassinate one of the candidates. U.S. forces attempt to stop the terrorists before millions lose their lives, but events threaten to spin out of control. *Dead Heat* debuted at #4 on the *New York Times* hardcover bestseller list. It also became a *USA Today*, *Wall Street Journal*, *Publishers Weekly*, and CBA hardcover bestseller.

Epicenter: Why the Current Rumblings in the Middle East Will Change Your Future, Joel's bestselling nonfiction title, explains why the eyes of the nations are increasingly riveted on the State of Israel and gives readers ten future headlines before they happen. It explains what is happening in the Middle East and how it will impact our world by examining geopolitical and economic trends, as well as examining events through the "third lens" of the Bible. It contains exclusive interviews with top political, military, intelligence, business, and religious leaders in Israel, Iran, Iraq, and Russia. It also contains previously classified documents from the CIA, Pentagon, and White House. *Epicenter* is available in hardcover and a *2.0* updated and expanded softcover edition. *Epicenter* appeared on the *New York Times* political bestseller list, as well as the CBA and *Publishers Weekly* religion lists. It also appeared on the Top 100 list in *Christian Retailing* and won the 2007 Retailers Choice Award from *Christian Retailing*.

Inside the Revolution: Why the Followers of Jihad, Jefferson, and Jesus Are Battling to Dominate the Middle East and Change the World explores the growing tensions within the Muslim world three decades after the Islamic Revolution in Iran. A national bestseller in 2009, it describes the Radicals, the Reformers, and the Revivalists, explaining in detail who each group is, why they matter, what they want, and how far they are willing to go to get it. An updated paperback edition was released in 2010.

The Twelfth Imam and *The Tehran Initiative* are the first two political thrillers in a new trilogy and were released in 2010 and 2011, respectively. Both were *New York Times* bestsellers and widely acclaimed as the best of Joel's novels. They focus on David Shirazi, a CIA operative of Iranian descent, who is sent undercover deep inside Iran to disrupt or destroy Iran's nuclear weapons program without sparking a new war in the Middle East. The series also considers these questions: What if an American president, well-meaning though he might be, miscalculates on Iran? What if he waits too long to take decisive action to neutralize the Iranian nuclear threat, and Tehran suddenly emerges with the Bomb? What would Iran do then? What would Israel do? What would the U.S. do? The novels also consider how Shiite End Times theology could be driving Iranian foreign policy and what might happen if someone claiming to be the Islamic messiah known as the "Twelfth Imam" or the "Mahdi" were to emerge in the Middle East. How would that reshape events and potentially set into motion the apocalypse?

Joel is an evangelical Christian with a Jewish father and Gentile mother. He was raised in Fairport, New York, graduated from Syracuse University in 1989, and studied at Tel Aviv University. He and his wife, Lynn, have been married since 1990 and have four sons. They live just outside of Washington, DC.

www.joelrosenberg.com
www.joshuafund.net

Endnotes

CHAPTER ONE: A COMING IMPLOSION?

1. Judd Greg (R-NH), interview by Greta Van Susteren, "America on Track for Economic Implosion?" Fox News, September 16, 2010, http://video.foxnews.com/v/4340596/america-on-track-for-economic-implosion/.

2. Aaron Task, "Rubin Warns of Bond Market 'Implosion': U.S. in 'Terribly Dangerous Territory,'" Yahoo News, November 17, 2010, http://finance.yahoo.com/tech-ticker/update-rubin-warns-of-bond-market-%22implosion%22-u.s.-in-%22terribly-dangerous-territory%22-535621.html?tickers=C,TBT,TLT,UUP,FXI,EWH,EWS. For more on the event itself, see the press release issued by the Concord Coalition, http://www.prnewswire.com/news-releases/senator-kent-conrad-to-receive-concord-coalition-award-and-discuss-americas-fiscal-outlook-107269293.html.

3. David Walker, interview by Steve Kroft, "U.S. Heading for Financial Trouble?" *60 Minutes*, CBS News, March 4, 2007 (updated July 8, 2007), http://www.cbsnews.com/stories/2007/03/01/60minutes/main2528226.shtml.

4. Task.

5. See Nicholas Ballasy, "Ryan: Debt on Track to Hit 800 Percent of GDP; 'CBO Can't Conceive of Any Way' Economy Can Continue Past 2037," CNS News, April 6, 2011, http://cnsnews.com/news/article/rep-ryan-obama-s-budget-path-do-nothing.

6. See Dana Bash and Deidre Walsh, "Behind the Scenes: How the GOP Is Selling Its Budget Plan to Itself," CNN, March 18, 2011, http://www.cnn.com/2011/POLITICS/03/17/gop.budget.plan/.

7. Louis Jacobson, "Paul Ryan Says CBO Model of Economy Self-Destructs Due to Rising Deficits in 2037," PolitiFact.com, March 21, 2011, http://www.politifact.com/truth-o-meter/statements/2011/mar/21/paul-ryan/paul-ryan-says-cbo-model-self-destructs-due-rising/.

8. See Nancy Gibbs and Michael Duffy, *The Preacher and the Presidents: Billy Graham in the White House* (New York: Center Street/Hachette Book Group USA, 2007), p. 48.

9. Ibid., p. 52.

10. Ibid., p. 108.

11. Winston Churchill, "Sinews of Peace," (address to Westminster College, Fulton, Missouri, March 5, 1946), http://www.americanrhetoric.com/speeches/winstonchurchillsinewsofpeace.htm.

CHAPTER TWO: AMERICA'S RISING ANXIETY

1. Robin Wright, *Sacred Rage* (New York: Touchstone, 1985, 2001), p. 257. Bin Laden made the statement in a May 1998 interview on ABC News.
2. Alireza Jafarzedeh, *The Iran Threat* (New York: Palgrave Macmillan, 2007), p. 25.
3. Steve Stalinsky. "The Iranian Threat: Ayatollah Ali Khamenei," *New York Sun*, February 9, 2005.
4. "Ahmadinejad Says Israel Will Soon Disappear," Agence France-Presse, June 2, 2008; see also, "Ahmadinejad: Iran, Japan Should Be Prepared for a World without U.S.," Islamic Republic News Agency, June 4, 2008.
5. "President Ahmadinejad: U.S. Collapse Imminent," Fars News Agency, June 4, 2011, http://english.farsnews.com/newstext.php?nn=9003143193.
6. See "Ahmadinejad Says Israel, U.S. Will 'Collapse' in Near Future," Haaretz, June 4, 2011, http://www.haaretz.com/news/international/ahmadinejad-says-israel-u-s-will-collapse-in-near-future-1.365843.
7. "Satisfaction with the United States," Gallup, http://www.gallup.com/poll/1669/general-mood-country.aspx.
8. Frank Newport, "Americans' Satisfaction at All-time Low of 9%," Gallup, October 7, 2008, http://www.gallup.com/poll/110983/americans-satisfaction-alltime-low.aspx. Also see Gallup data: "Satisfaction with the United States," http://www.gallup.com/poll/1669/general-mood-country.aspx.
9. The poll was taken September 19–22, 2008. See NBC News/*Wall Street Journal* historical polling data at www.pollingreport.com/right.htm.
10. The poll was taken December 11–14, 2008. See ABC News/*Washington Post* historical polling data at www.pollingreport.com/right.htm.
11. Dana Blanton, "Fox News Poll: 79% Say U.S. Economy Could Collapse," FoxNews.com, March 23, 2010, http://www.foxnews.com/politics/2010/03/23/fox-news-poll-say-economy-collapse/.
12. Specifically, 78 percent said they were dissatisfied, while 20 percent said they were satisfied. The poll was taken June 9–12, 2011. See Lydia Saad, "U.S. Satisfaction Dips to 20% in June," Gallup, June 16, 2011, http://www.gallup.com/poll/148070/satisfaction-dips-june.aspx and Gllup historical polling data at www.pollingreport.com/right.htm.
13. Specifically, 39 percent of Americans feared a permanent decline of the American economy in June 2011, up from just 28 percent in October 2010. The polls were taken on June 24–28, 2011, and October 21–26, 2010, respectively. See *New York Times*/CBS News poll, http://s3.documentcloud.org/documents/213045/nytcbspoll.pdf.
14. Specifically, 48 percent of Americans believe a Great Depression is coming. See "CNN Poll: Obama Approval Rating Drops as Fears of Depression Rise," *Political Ticker* (blog), June 8, 2011, http://politicalticker.blogs.cnn.com/2011/06/08/cnn-poll-obama-approval-rating-drops-as-fears-of-depression-rise/.
15. An NBC News/*Wall Street Journal* poll in November 2011 found that 73 percent of Americans believed the country was on the wrong track. See http://msnbcmedia.msn.com/i/MSNBC/Sections/NEWS/A_Politics/November_Poll.pdf. An ABC News/

Washington Post poll in September 2011 found that 77 percent of Americans believed the country was on the wrong track. Only 20 percent believed the country was on the right track. The poll was taken August 29–September 1, 2011. See "Obama's Approval Ratings Skid to New Low; Economic Stewardship in Question," *The Washington Post*, September 5, 2011, http://www.washingtonpost.com/obamas-approval-ratings-skid-to-new-low-economic-stewardship-in-question/2011/09/05/gIQACwxH5J_graphic.html. A Reuters/Ipsos poll taken in August 2011 found 73 percent of Americans believing the country was on the wrong track. See Steve Holland, "Most Americans Say U.S. on Wrong Track: Poll," Reuters, August 10, 2011, http://www.reuters.com/article/2011/08/10/us-usa-poll-idUSTRE7794EX20110810.

16. See Keith Olbermann, "Beginning of the End of America," MSNBC, October 19, 2006, http://www.msnbc.msn.com/id/15321167/ns/msnbc_tv-countdown_with_keith_olbermann/t/beginning-end-america/.

17. See Glenn Beck, "Beck insists audience 'must not allow' health care bill to pass, warns it would mean 'the end of America as you know it,'" video, Media Matters for America, from *The Glenn Beck Program*, Premiere Radio Networks, November 19, 2009, http://mediamatters.org/mmtv/200911190012.

18. Former VP Gore was speaking on threats to American democracy; see "Text of Gore Speech at Media Conference," Associated Press, October 6, 2005, http://www.legitgov.org/transcript_gore_media_conference_071005.html. With regards to the planet facing an emergency, see Al Gore's Nobel Prize acceptance speech, Oslo City Hall, December 10, 2007, http://nobelprize.org/nobel_prizes/peace/laureates/2007/gore-lecture_en.html.

19. See Charles Krauthammer, comments on *Fox News All-Stars*, Fox News Channel, June 8, 2011, quoted in "Krauthammer's Take," *The Corner* (blog), National Review Online, http://www.nationalreview.com/corner/269140/krauthammers-take-nro-staff.

20. See Noel Sheppard, "Paul Krugman: The American Dream Is Dying," NewsBusters, September 26, 2009, http://newsbusters.org/blogs/noel-sheppard/2009/09/26/paul-krugman-american-dream-dying#ixzz1Oj9ALtky.

21. See Peggy Noonan, "A Separate Peace: America Is in Trouble—and Our Elites Are Merely Resigned," *Wall Street Journal*, October 27, 2005, http://www.peggynoonan.com/article.php?article=289.

22. See Chalmers Johnson, *Nemesis: The Last Days of the American Republic*, (New York: Metropolitan Books, Henry Holt and Company, 2006), p. 71.

23. See Thomas Sowell, *Dismantling America: And Other Controversial Essays*, (New York: Basic Books, Perseus Books Group, 2010), pp. vii–viii.

24. See Cullen Murphy, *Are We Rome? The Fall of an Empire and the Fate of America*, (New York: Mariner Books, Houghton Mifflin Company, 2007), p. 197.

25. See Pat Buchanan, "Pat Puchannan: Overextended U.S. Empire Is Coming Down," video, Real Clear Politics Video, from *Morning Joe*, MSNBC, July 6, 2011, http://www.realclearpolitics.com/video/2011/07/06/pat_buchanan_overextended_us_empire_is_coming_down.html.

26. See "Health Care Law Signals U.S. Empire Decline?" CNBC, March 24, 2010 http://finance.yahoo.com/news/Health-Care-Law-Signals-US-cnbc-4091862289.html?x=0&.v=1.

27. See Thomas L. Friedman, "The Earth Is Full," *New York Times*, June 7, 2011, http://www.nytimes.com/2011/06/08/opinion/08friedman.html?_r=1.

28. See Rick Newman, "9 Signs of America in Decline," *U.S. News & World Report*, October 26, 2009, http://money.usnews.com/money/blogs/flowchart/2009/10/26/9-signs-of-america-in-decline.

29. See Alfred W. McCoy, "How America Will Collapse (by 2025)," Salon.com, December 6, 2010, http://www.salon.com/news/feature/2010/12/06/america_collapse_2025.

30. See Fareed Zakaria, "Are America's Best Days Behind Us?" *Time*, March 14, 2011, http://www.time.com/time/nation/article/0,8599,2056610,00.html#ixzz1PNPJ3xm5.

31. See Ray B. Williams, "Why America Is In Decline," *Psychology Today*, March 13, 2011, http://www.psychologytoday.com/blog/wired-success/201103/why-america-is-in-decline.

32. See John Barry and Tara McKelvey, "Gates Says U.S. at Risk of Losing Global Supremacy," *Newsweek*, June 19, 2011, http://www.thedailybeast.com/newsweek/2011/06/19/the-defense-rests.print.html.

33. Naomi Wolf. *The End of America: Letter of Warning to a Young Patriot* (White River Junction, VT: Chelsea Green, 2007), p. 19.

34. Ibid., pp. 1, 14, 151, 152.

35. Mark Steyn. *After America: Get Ready for Armageddon* (Washington, DC: Regnery Publishing, 2011), p. 2.

36. Ibid., p. 4.

37. Ibid., p. 5.

38. Ibid., pp. 6, 22. See also Steyn's conclusion on pp. 347–349.

39. Fareed Zakaria, *The Post-American World: Release 2.0* (New York: Norton, 2011), pp. 1–2.

40. Ibid., pp. 4–5.

41. Ibid., p. 3.

42. Ibid., pp. 241–242.

43. Ibid., p. 243.

CHAPTER THREE: THE CASE OF THE OPTIMISTS

1. The phrase "leading from behind" comes from an unidentified advisor to President Obama, quoted in *New Yorker* magazine. For a link to the original reference and some of the controversy ignited by the remark, see Ryan Lizza, "Leading from Behind," *New Yorker*, April 27, 2011, http://www.newyorker.com/online/blogs/newsdesk/2011/04/leading-from-behind-obama-clinton.html. See also Charles Krauthammer, "The Obama Doctrine: Leading from Behind," *Washington Post*, April 28, 2011, http://www.washingtonpost.com/opinions/the-obama-doctrine-leading-from-behind/2011/04/28/AFBCy18E_story.html and William Kristol, "A Leader from Behind," *Weekly Standard*, May 9, 2011, http://www.weeklystandard.com/articles/leader-behind_558488.html.

2. Barack Obama, "President Barack Obama: Why I'm Optimistic," *Smithsonian*, August 2010, http://www.smithsonianmag.com/specialsections/40th-anniversary/President-Barack-Obama-Why-Im-Optimistic.html.

3. Ibid.

4. William J. Bennett, *The Index of Leading Cultural Indicators: American Society at the End of the Twentieth Century* (New York: Broadway Books, 1999), pp. 5–6.

5. William J. Bennett, *A Century Turns: New Hopes, New Fears* (Nashville: Thomas Nelson Publishers, 2009), p. 275.

6. Larry Kudlow, "Never Sell America Short," National Review Online, September 18, 2008, http://www.nationalreview.com/articles/225720/never-sell-america-short/larry-kudlow.

7. Larry Kudlow, "No 'End of the World' Stock Market Trade," National Review Online, April 12, 2011, http://www.nationalreview.com/kudlows-money-politics/264529/no-end-world-stock-market-trade.

8. Joseph S. Nye, "The Misleading Metaphor of Decline," *Wall Street Journal*, February 14, 2011, http://online.wsj.com/article/SB10001424052748704358704576118673650278558.html.

9. Charles Wolf Jr., "The Facts about American 'Decline,'" *Wall Street Journal*, April 13, 2011, http://online.wsj.com/article/SB10001424052748704415104576251292725228886.html.

10. Walter Russell Mead, "The Future Still Belongs to America," *Wall Street Journal*, July 2, 2011, http://online.wsj.com/article/SB10001424052702304450604576419700203110180.html.

11. See Thomas Jefferson et al., Declaration of Independence, July 4, 1776, transcription of the original document at the National Archives, http://www.archives.gov/exhibits/charters/declaration_transcript.html.

12. Washington Irving, *George Washington: A Biography* (New York: Doubleday, 1976; abridgement of original book published in five volumes from 1856 to 1859), p. 202.

13. Ibid., p. 202.

14. Ibid., p. 203.

15. Doris Kearns Goodwin, *Team of Rivals: The Political Genius of Abraham Lincoln* (New York: Simon & Schuster, 2005), pp. 143–144.

16. Ibid., p. 307.

17. Ibid., p. 156.

18. Ibid., p. 374.

19. Ibid., p. 347.

20. Ibid., p. 481.

21. Ibid., p. 673.

22. "Gettysburg," CWSAC Battle Summaries, Heritage Preservation Services of the National Park Service, http://www.nps.gov/hps/abpp/battles/pa002.htm.

23. See Abraham Lincoln, "Gettysburg Address," November 19, 1863, http://avalon.law.yale.edu/19th_century/gettyb.asp.

24. Goodwin, p. 346.

25. Amity Shlaes, *The Forgotten Man: A New History of the Great Depression* (New York: Harper Perennial, 2008), p. 15.

26. Ibid., p. xiii (timeline).

27. Ibid., p. xiv (timeline).

28. See "Timeline: A Selected Wall Street Chronology," "The Crash of 1929," *American Experience*, PBS, http://www.pbs.org/wgbh/americanexperience/features/timeline/

crash/2/; David Goldman, "Great Depression vs. 'Great Recession,'" CNN Money, http://money.cnn.com/news/storysupplement/economy/recession_depression/.

29. Goldman.

30. Shlaes, p. 144.

31. "The suicide rate in the United States rises when the economy slumps, and falls when economic times improve. And this has been the case at least since the Great Depression, which started with the stock market crash of 1929, the CDC says in a new study. 'Knowing suicides increased during economic recessions and fell during expansions underscores the need for additional suicide prevention measures when the economy weakens,' James Mercy, PhD, of the CDC's Injury Center's Division of Violence Prevention, says in a news release. 'It is an important finding for policy makers and those working to prevent suicide.' . . . The largest increase in the overall suicide rate occurred in the Great Depression of 1929–1933, surging from 18 per 100,000 people in 1928 to 22.1 per 100,000, an all-time high, in 1932, the last full year of the Great Depression. That four-year period witnessed a record increase of 22.8 percent compared to any other four-year period in U.S. history. The suicide rate fell to its lowest point in the year 2000." Bill Hendrick, "Suicides Go Up When Economy Goes Down," WebMD, April 14, 2011, http://www.webmd.com/depression/news/20110414/suicides-go-up-when-economy-goes-down.

32. Franklin Delano Roosevelt, "First Inaugural Address," March 4, 1933, http://www.bartleby.com/124/pres49.html.

33. Shlaes, p. 392.

34. See online historical charts for the Dow, including Yahoo! Finance, http://finance.yahoo.com/q/ta?s=%5EDJI&t=my&l=on&z=l&q=l&p=&a=&c= and StockCharts.com,http://stockcharts.com/freecharts/historical/djia1900.html.

35. William Grimes, "Christopher Lasch Is Dead at 61; Wrote about America's Malaise," *New York Times*, February 15, 1994, http://www.nytimes.com/1994/02/15/obituaries/christopher-lasch-is-dead-at-61-wrote-about-america-s-malaise.html.

36. Christopher Lasch, *The Culture of Narcissism: American Life in an Age of Diminishing Expectations* (New York: W. W. Norton & Company, 1979), p. xiii.

37. Ibid., pp. 3–4.

38. Kevin Mattson, *"What the Heck Are You Up To, Mr. President?": Jimmy Carter, America's "Malaise," and the Speech That Should Have Changed the Country* (New York: Bloomsbury USA, 2009); Steven Hayward, *The Real Jimmy Carter* (Washington, DC: Regnery Publishing, 2004); and Jonathan V. Last, "Malaise Forever: A Review of *The Real Jimmy Carter*," *Claremont Review of Books*, Spring 2005, http://www.claremont.org/publications/crb/id.977/article_detail.asp.

39. Jimmy Carter, "Crisis of Confidence," nationally televised address, July 15, 1979, transcript at "Primary Resources," *American Experience*, PBS, 2002, http://www.pbs.org/wgbh/americanexperience/features/primary-resources/carter-crisis/.

40. Jimmy Carter, "Report to the American People on Energy," nationally televised address, February 2, 1977, transcript at Miller Center, University of Virginia, http://millercenter.org/president/speeches/detail/3396.

41. Carlos Lozada, review of Kevin Mattson, *"What the Heck Are You Up To, Mr. President?" Washington Post*, July 10, 2009, http://www.washingtonpost.com/wp-dyn/content/article/2009/07/10/AR2009071002343.html.

42. Ronald Reagan, *An American Life: The Autobiography* (New York: Simon & Schuster, 1990), p. 227.

43. Dinesh D'Souza, *Ronald Reagan: How an Ordinary Man Became an Extraordinary Leader* (New York: Free Press, 1997), p. 89.

44. See Table 5.24, "Retail Motor Gasoline and On-Highway Diesel Fuel Prices, 1949-2009," U.S. Energy Information Agency, http://www.eia.gov/emeu/aer/txt/ptb0524.html.

45. See Jad Mouawad, "Oil Prices Pass Record Set in '80s, but Then Recede," *New York Times*, March 3, 2008, http://www.nytimes.com/2008/03/03/business/worldbusiness/03cnd-oil.html/.

46. Robert D. Hershey Jr., "How the Oil Glut Is Changing Business," *New York Times*, June 21, 1981, http://www.nytimes.com/1981/06/21/business/how-the-oil-glut-is-changing-business.html.

47. "Ronald Reagan TV Ad: 'It's morning in America again,'" YouTube video, posted by "avmorgado," November 12, 2006, http://www.youtube.com/watch?v=EU-IBF8nwSY; text of the ad available at *Wikipedia*, s.v. "Morning in America," http://en.wikipedia.org/wiki/Morning_in_America. (Sites last accessed January 12, 2012.)

48. Reagan, *An American Life*, p. 317.

49. D'Souza, p. 110.

50. Ibid.

51. Ronald Reagan, "Radio Address to the Nation on Proposed Natural Gas Deregulation Legislation," February 26, 1983; see transcript at The American Presidency Project, University of California, Santa Barbara, http://www.presidency.ucsb.edu/ws/index.php?pid=40982#ixzz1VExHrorg.

CHAPTER FOUR: THE THIRD LENS

1. For more on this important topic, I would recommend an excellent resource: John F. Walvoord, *Every Prophecy of the Bible* (David C. Cook, 1990, 1999, 2011). Walvoord was one of the most respected scholars of prophecy in the twentieth century. Before his passing in 2002, Walvoord served on the faculty of Dallas Theological Seminary (DTS) for half a century. He was the president of DTS from 1952 to 1986, and he later served as chancellor.

CHAPTER FIVE: SIGNS OF THE TIMES

1. Survey for Joel C. Rosenberg, "American Attitudes toward Bible Prophecy," National Omnibus Survey, conducted by McLaughlin & Associates on February 13, 2006, of 1,000 likely voters. Margin of error +/- 3 percent. For detailed survey results, see Joel C. Rosenberg, *Epicenter: Why the Current Rumblings in the Middle East Will Change Your Future* (Carol Stream, IL: Tyndale House Publishers, 2006), Appendix 2, pp. 303–305.

2. See "WWI Casualties and Death Tables," resource for *The Great War and the Shaping of the 20th Century*, PBS, http://www.pbs.org/greatwar/resources/casdeath_pop.html.

3. The 46-million figure comes from British historian Martin Gilbert, though he himself acknowledges the number could be significantly higher. See Martin Gilbert, *The Second World War: A Complete History* (New York: Henry Holt & Company,

1989), p. 746. American historian Gerhard L. Weinberg believes the number of total deaths worldwide was at least 60 million. See Gerhard L. Weinberg, *A World at Arms: A Global History of World War II* (Cambridge, U.K.: Cambridge University Press, 1994), p. 894.

4. See "Historic World Earthquakes," U.S. Geological Survey, accessed September 2, 2011, http://earthquake.usgs.gov/earthquakes/world/historical_mag_big.php.

5. See "Earthquakes with 50,000 or More Deaths," U.S. Geological Survey, accessed September 2, 2011, http://earthquake.usgs.gov/earthquakes/world/most_destructive.php.

6. See "Historic World Earthquakes," U.S. Geological Survey.

7. The deadliest quake in all of recorded human history occurred in AD 1556 in China. See "Earthquakes with 50,000 or More Deaths," U.S. Geological Survey.

8. See "Earthquakes with 50,000 or More Deaths," U.S. Geological Survey.

9. Nancy Gibbs and Michael Duffy, *The Preacher and the Presidents: Billy Graham in the White House* (New York: Center Street/Hachette Book Group USA, 2007), p. vii.

10. The *JESUS* Film Project, "History," accessed on September 1, 2011, http://www.jesusfilm.org/aboutus/history.

11. See Lawrence O'Donnell, *The Last Word*, video segment discussing Glenn Beck and the End Times, March 17, 2011, http://www.msnbc.msn.com/id/21134540/vp/42141858#42141858 and Jonathon M. Seidl, "Wacky MSNBC Segment: Lawrence O'Donnell Begs for Viewers While Blasting Beck & Bible," The Blaze website, March 18, 2011, http://www.theblaze.com/stories/wacky-msnbc-segment-lawrence-odonnell-begs-for-viewers-while-blasting-beck-god/.

12. Gershom Gorenberg, *The End of Days: Fundamentalism and the Struggle for the Temple Mount* (New York: The Free Press, 2000, updated by Oxford University Press in 2002), pp. 1–4, 223.

13. Bill Moyers, On Receiving Harvard Medical School's Global Environmental Citizen Award," speech, Harvard University Center for Health and the Global Environment, New York City, December 1, 2004, http://www.commondreams.org/views04/1206-10.htm.

14. Kevin Phillips, *American Theocracy: The Peril and Politics of Radical Religion, Oil, and Borrowed Money in the 21st Century* (New York: Viking Books, 2006), pp. vii, 252.

15. Nicholas Guyatt, *Have a Nice Doomsday: Why Millions of Americans Are Looking Forward to the End of the World* (New York: Harper Perennial, 2007), p. 63.

16. Ibid., pp. 18, 91–92.

CHAPTER SIX: THE SIGNIFICANCE OF THE REBIRTH OF ISRAEL

1. Clark Clifford (with Richard Holbrooke), *Counsel to the President: A Memoir* (New York: Random House, 1991), p. 3.

2. Ibid., p. 3.

3. Ibid., p. 4.

4. Ibid.

5. Ibid., p. 5.

6. Ibid., p. 10.

7. Ibid., pp. 10–14.

8. Ibid., p. 14.

9. For example, in his 1997 book, *Harry S. Truman and the Founding of Israel* (Westport, CT: Praeger Publishers), Michael T. Benson of the University of Utah wrote, "The role President Truman may or may not have played in lining up votes supporting partition is still a matter of considerable controversy. Even vocal critics of Truman's alleged 'arm-twisting' concede that if the president *did* give the order to step up lobbying efforts days before the U.N. vote, no records of such an injunction can be found anywhere" (p. 105).

10. David McCullough, *Truman* (New York: Touchstone/Simon & Schuster, 1992), pp. 601–602.

11. For more details on the Partition Plan, including the full text of the resolution and the list of countries voting for and against, see the website of Israel's Ministry of Foreign Affairs, http://www.mfa.gov.il/MFA/Peace%20Process/Guide%20to%20 the%20Peace%20Process/UN%20General%20Assembly%20Resolution%20181.

12. Clifford and Holbrooke, p. 15.

13. Ibid., p. 22.

14. Truman gave this speech to the Columbia Scholastic Press Association in March 1952. The speech was cited by Samuel W. Rushay Jr., "Harry Truman's History Lessons," *Prologue*, Spring 2009, http://www.archives.gov/publications/ prologue/2009/spring/truman-history.html.

15. Billy Graham, *Just As I Am: The Autobiography of Billy Graham* (New York: HarperCollins, 1997). See the introduction for Graham's description of President Truman.

16. Clifford and Holbrooke, pp. 7–8.

17. Benjamin Netanyahu, "Address at Auschwitz Death Camp," January 27, 2010; see transcript at Israeli Ministry of Foreign Affairs website, http://www.mfa.gov.il/MFA/Government/Speeches+by+Israeli+leaders/2010/Address_ PM_Netanyahu_at_Auschwitz_27-Jan-2010.htm.

CHAPTER SEVEN: ARE WE LIVING IN THE LAST DAYS?

1. Tim LaHaye, *Understanding Bible Prophecy for Yourself* (Eugene, OR: Harvest House Publishers, 2009), p. 94.

2. Thomas Ice, "Imminence and the Rapture: Part I," accessed December 29, 2011, http://www.pre-trib.org/data/pdf/Ice-%28Part1%29ImminenceandT.pdf. As part of his definition, Ice cited Gerald B. Stanton, *Kept from the Hour: Biblical Evidence for the Pretribulational Return of Christ*, 4th edition (Miami Springs, FL: Schoettle Publishing Co., [1956], 1991), p. 108.

3. Justin Berton, "Biblical Scholar's Date for Rapture: May 21, 2011," *San Francisco Chronicle*, January 1, 2010, http://www.sfgate.com/cgi-bin/article. cgi?f=/c/a/2010/01/01/BA8V1AV589.DTL&type=printable; see also Guy Adams, "U.S. Preacher Warns End of the World Is Nigh: 21 May, around 6 p.m., to Be Precise," *Independent*, March 27, 2011, http://www.independent.co.uk/news/world/ americas/us-preacher-warns-end-of-the-world-is-nigh-21-may-around-6pm-to-be-precise-2254139.html.

4. Jay Kernis, "Camping Prepares for Judgment Day," *In the Arena* (blog), CNN, May 17, 2011, http://inthearena.blogs.cnn.com/2011/05/17/ harold-camping-prepares-for-judgment-day-may-21-2011/.

5. See Annalyn Censky, "Doomsday Church: Still Open for Business," CNN Money, May 19, 2011, http://money.cnn.com/2011/05/19/news/economy/may-21-end-of-the-world-finances-harold-camping/index.htm.

6. Jesse McKinley, "An Autumn Date for the Apocalypse," *New York Times*, May 23, 2011, http://www.nytimes.com/2011/05/24/us/24rapture.html?_r=1.

7. See David Morgan, "Rapture Predictor Harold Camping Suffers Stroke," CBS News, June 13, 2011, http://www.cbsnews.com/stories/2011/06/13/national/main20070762.shtml; see also Angela Woodall, "Doomsday Herald Harold Camping's Radio Show Goes Off the Air at the End of the Month," *Oakland Tribune*, June 23, 2011, http://www.mercurynews.com/top-stories/ci_18331982.

8. Harold Camping, *1994?* (New York: Vantage Press, 1992), p. 532.

9. Edgar C. Whisenant, *88 Reasons Why the Rapture Will Be in 1988* (Nashville: World Bible Society, 1988), p. 3.

10. Ibid., pp. 48, 50.

11. Ibid., p. 69.

12. Edgar Whisenant and Greg Brewer, *The Final Shout: Rapture Report 1989* (Nashville: World Bible Society, 1989), p. ii.

13. Ibid., p. 1.

14. Hal Lindsey and C. C. Carlson, *The Late Great Planet Earth* (Grand Rapids: Zondervan, 1970), p. 54.

15. Hal Lindsey, *The 1980s: Countdown to Armageddon* (New York: Bantam Books, 1982), p. i.

16. See Gary Wilburn, "The Doomsday Chic," *Christianity Today*, January 27, 1978.

17. Hal Lindsey, *Planet Earth 2000 A.D.: Will Mankind Survive?* (Palos Verdes: Western Front Ltd, 1994, 1996), sixth page of his unnumbered introduction.

18. Ibid., pp. 307–308.

CHAPTER EIGHT: WHAT HAPPENS TO AMERICA IN THE LAST DAYS?

1. For more details on the prophecies of Ezekiel 38–39, including historical research that helps us identify Russia as Magog and the modern-day identity of Russia's allies, please see my book *Epicenter: Why the Current Rumblings in the Middle East Will Change Your Future* (Carol Stream, IL: Tyndale House Publishers, 2006).

2. E. G. White, *America in Prophecy* (Jemison, AL: Inspiration Books East, Inc., 1888, republished in 1988), pp. 410–411.

3. Herbert W. Armstrong, *The United States and Britain in Prophecy* (Worldwide Church of God, 1942), pp. 3–4.

4. S. Franklin Logsdon, *Is the U.S.A. in Prophecy?* (Grand Rapids, MI: Zondervan Publishing House, 1968), pp. 11, 13.

5. Thomas Ice and Timothy Demy, *The Truth about America in the Last Days* (Eugene, OR: Harvest House Publishers, 1998), p. 9.

6. David R. Reagan, *America the Beautiful? The United States in Bible Prophecy* (McKinney, TX: Lamb & Lion Ministries, 2003, 2006, 2009), pp. 76–78.

7. Michael D. Evans, *The American Prophecies: Ancient Scriptures Reveal Our Nation's Future* (New York: Warner Faith, 2004), p. 5.

8. Terry James, *The American Apocalypse: Is the United States in Bible Prophecy?* (Eugene, OR: Harvest House Publishers, 2009), p. 19.

9. Mark Hitchcock, *The Late Great United States: What Bible Prophecy Reveals about America's Last Days* (Colorado Springs, CO: Multnomah Books, 2009).

10. David Wilkerson, *America's Last Call* (Lindale, TX: Wilkerson Trust Publications, 1998), p. 17.

11. A. P. Watchman, *Reaping the Whirlwind: The Imminent Judgment of Babylon America* (Xulon Press, 2010), pp. 246, 268.

12. Hitchcock, *The Late Great United States*, p. 15.

13. Jeffrey Gettleman, "Babylon Awaits an Iraq Without Fighting," *New York Times*, April 18, 2006.

14. Ali Abdul Ameer Allawi (Iraqi finance minister), interview with the author, April 26, 2006.

15. Joel C. Rosenberg, "U.S. to Help Rebuild City of Babylon in Iraq," *Flash Traffic* (blog), February 14, 2009, http://flashtrafficblog.wordpress.com/2009/02/14/us-to-help-rebuild-city-of-babylon-in-iraq/. See also Khalid al-Ansary, "Babylon's Future Written in its Ruins," Reuters, February 11, 2009, http://uk.reuters.com/article/2009/02/11/us-iraq-babylon-idUKTRE51A0MM20090211.

16. See Steven Lee Myers, "A Triage to Save the Ruins of Babylon," *New York Times*, January 2, 2011, http://www.nytimes.com/2011/01/03/arts/03babylon.html?_r=2; Joel C. Rosenberg, "Iraqi Efforts to Rebuild Babylon & Draw Tourists to Hebrew Prophet Ezekiel's Tomb Focus of *New York Times* Article, Videos This Week," *Flash Traffic* (blog), January 6, 2011, http://flashtrafficblog.wordpress.com/2011/01/06/iraqi-efforts-rebuild-babylon-draw-tourists-to-hebrew-prophet-ezekiels-tomb-focus-of-new-york-times-articles-videos-this-week/.

17. Myers, "A Triage to Save the Ruins of Babylon." See also Steven Lee Myers, Stephen Farrell, Shiho Fukada, "A Tour of Iraq's Ancient Sites," *New York Times*, January 2, 2011, http://atwar.blogs.nytimes.com/2011/01/02/a-tour-of-iraqs-ancient-sites/?ref=arts.

18. For more detail on why some authors and teachers have argued these points and why they are incorrect, I recommend Mark Hitchcock, *The Late Great United States* (Colorado Springs, CO: Multnomah Books, 2009), pp. 11–33.

CHAPTER NINE: THE FINANCIAL IMPLOSION SCENARIO

1. Dana Blanton, "Fox News Poll: 79% Say U.S. Economy Could Collapse," FoxNews.com, March 23, 2010, http://www.foxnews.com/politics/2010/03/23/fox-news-poll-say-economy-collapse/.

2. Specifically, 48 percent of Americans believe a Great Depression is coming. See "CNN Poll: Obama Approval Rating Drops as Fears of Depression Rise," *Political Ticker* (blog), June 8, 2011, http://politicalticker.blogs.cnn.com/2011/06/08/cnn-poll-obama-approval-rating-drops-as-fears-of-depression-rise/.

3. See Steve Holland, "Most Americans Say U.S. on Wrong Track: Poll," Reuters, August 10, 2011, http://www.reuters.com/article/2011/08/10/us-usa-poll-idUSTRE7794EX20110810.

4. See Ciera Lundgren, "Bowles: 'These Deficits Are Like a Cancer,'" CBS News, September 13, 2011, http://www.cbsnews.com/8301-503544_162-20105714-503544.html; see also Dan Balz, "Obama's Debt Commission Warns of Fiscal 'Cancer,'" *Washington Post*, July 12, 2010, http://www.washingtonpost.com/wp-dyn/content/article/2010/07/11/AR2010071101956.html.

5. Michael Crowley, "Deficit Dilemma: Will Washington Finally Tackle the Sacred Cows?," *Time*, December 2, 2010, http://www.time.com/time/politics/article/0,8599,2034358,00.html#ixzz1Xw37VXIh.

6. Testimony of Professor Simon Johnson to the Senate Budget Committee, February 9, 2010, http://baselinescenario.com/2010/02/09/revised-baseline-scenario-february-9-2010/.

7. Nouriel Roubini, "A Presidency Heading for a Fiscal Train Wreck," *Financial Times*, October 28, 2010, http://www.ft.com/intl/cms/s/0/dd140d16-e2c2-11df-8a58-00144feabdc0.html#axzz1XJFgtU82; see also "U.S. On Track for 'Fiscal Train Wreck': Roubini," Reuters, October 29, 2010, http://www.reuters.com/article/2010/10/29/us-roubini-idUSTRE69S0ZJ20101029.

8. Testimony of Alice Rivlin to the Senate Budget Committee, March 15, 2011, http://www.brookings.edu/testimony/2011/0315_senate_budget_rivlin.aspx.

9. Stuart Butler, et al, "Saving the American Dream: The Heritage Plan to Fix the Debt, Cut Spending, and Restore Prosperity," The Heritage Foundation, Special Report #91, May 10, 2011, http://www.heritage.org/Research/Reports/2011/05/Saving-the-American-Dream-The-Heritage-Plan-to-Fix-the-Debt-Cut-Spending-and-Restore-Prosperity.

10. Paul Ryan, interview by Evan Harris, "Rep. Paul Ryan on Budget Work: 'I Sleep Well at Night,'" ABC News, April 30, 2011, http://abcnews.go.com/ThisWeek/rep-paul-ryan-budget-work-sleep-night/story?id=13499775.

11. David Brody, "Speaker Boehner to NRB Tonight: National Debt Is a 'Moral Threat' to America," *The Brody File* (blog), CBN News, February 27, 2011, http://blogs.cbn.com/thebrodyfile/archive/2011/02/27/speaker-boehner-to-nrb-tonight-national-debt-is-a-moral.aspx.

12. "Employment Situation Summary," Bureau of Labor Statistics, Department of Labor, September 2, 2011, http://www.bls.gov/news.release/empsit.nr0.htm.

13. Dan Levy and Prashant Gopal, "Foreclosure Filings in U.S. May Jump 20% from Record 2010 As Crisis Peaks," http://www.bloomberg.com/news/2011-01-13/u-s-foreclosure-filings-may-jump-20-this-year-as-crisis-peaks.html.

14. Les Christie, "Foreclosures Up a Record 81% in 2008," CNN Money, January 15, 2009, http://money.cnn.com/2009/01/15/real_estate/millions_in_foreclosure/index.htm.

15. Lynn Adler, "U.S. 2009 Foreclosures Shatter Record despite Aid," Reuters, January 14, 2010, http://www.reuters.com/article/2010/01/14/us-usa-housing-foreclosures-idUSTRE60D0LZ20100114.

16. Corbett B. Daly, "Home Foreclosures in 2010 Top 1 Million for First Time," Reuters, January 13, 2011, http://www.reuters.com/article/2011/01/13/us-usa-housing-foreclosures-idUSTRE70C0YD20110113.

17. Leah Schnurr, "Foreclosure Filings Hit Four-Year Low in 2011," Reuters, January 12, 2012, http://www.reuters.com/article/2012/01/12/us-usa-housing-realtytrac-idUSTRE80B08H20120112.

18. John Gittelsohn and Kathleen M. Howley, "U.S. Home Prices Face 3-Year Drop as Inventory Surge Looms," Bloomberg, September 15, 2010, http://www.bloomberg.com/news/2010-09-15/u-s-home-prices-face-three-year-drop-as-inventory-surge-looms.html.

19. Floyd Norris, "For Home Prices, It's Back to At Least 2004," *New York Times*, July 1, 2011, http://www.nytimes.com/2011/07/02/business/02charts.html.

20. Charles Riley, "Fed: Household Down 23% in 2 Years," CNN Money, March 28, 2011, http://money.cnn.com/2011/03/24/pf/financial_crisis_outcome/index.htm.

21. See chart, "Annual Business and Non-business Filings by Year (1980–2009)," American Bankruptcy Institute, http://www.abiworld.org/AM/AMTemplate.cfm ?Section=Home&CONTENTID=63164&TEMPLATE=/CM/ContentDisplay. cfm; also, John Hartgen, "Consumer Bankruptcy Filings Increase 9 Percent in 2010," American Bankruptcy Institute, January 3, 2011, http://www.abiworld. org/AM/Template.cfm?Section=Home&TEMPLATE=/CM/ContentDisplay. cfm&CONTENTID=62756.

22. Richard McCormack, "The Plight of American Manufacturing," *The American Prospect*, December 21, 2009, http://prospect.org/cs/ articles?article=the_plight_of_american_manufacturing.

23. Blake Ellis, "Food Stamp Use Rises to Record 45.8 Million," CNN Money, August 4, 2011, http://money.cnn.com/2011/08/04/pf/food_stamps_record_high/index.htm.

24. See Office of Management and Budget, "Fiscal Year 2012 Historical Tables: Budget of the U.S. Government," p. 5, http://www.whitehouse.gov/sites/default/files/omb/budget/fy2012/assets/hist.pdf.

25. Ibid.

26. Ibid., p. 22.

27. See Congressional Budget Office, *The Budget and Economic Outlook: Fiscal Years 2010 to 2020*, January 2010, Table F-1, "Historical Budget Data: Revenues, Outlays, Deficits, Surpluses, and Debt Held by the Public, 1970 to 2009, in Billions of Dollars," http://cbo.gov/ftpdocs/108xx/doc10871/AppendixF.shtml#1096834.

28. Ibid., Table F-2, "Revenues, Outlays, Deficits, Surpluses, and Debt Held by the Public, 1970 to 2009, as a Percentage of Gross Domestic Product."

29. Ibid., Table F-1.

30. Ibid., Table F-2.

31. Cited by Katrina Trinko, "Obama: Not Always a Fan of Upping Debt Ceiling," National Review Online, January 3, 2011, http://www.nationalreview.com/ corner/256199/obama-not-always-fan-upping-debt-ceiling-katrina-trinko.

32. See Congressional Budget Office, *The Budget and Economic Outlook*, Table F-1, http://cbo.gov/ftpdocs/108xx/doc10871/AppendixF.shtml#1096834.

33. See "Debt Position and Activity Report," U.S. Department of the Treasury, November 30, 2011, http://www.treasurydirect.gov/govt/reports/pd/pd_ debtposactrpt_1111.pdf.

34. See Patrick Tyrrell, "U.S. Debt Now Surpasses 2010 GDP," *The Foundry* (blog), Heritage Foundation, August 5, 2011, http://blog.heritage.org/2011/08/05/ us-debt-now-surpasses-2010-gdp/; see also "U.S. Debt Reaches 100 Percent of Country's GDP," FoxNews.com, August 4, 2011, http://www.foxnews.com/ politics/2011/08/04/us-debt-reaches-100-percent-countrys-gdp/.

35. Andrew Malcolm, "New National Debt Data: It's Growing about $3 Million a Minute, Even During His Vacation," *Top of the Ticket* (blog), *Los Angeles Times*, August 23, 2011, http://latimesblogs.latimes.com/washington/2011/08/obama-national-debt.html.

36. One trillion seconds is 31,688 years; see "Billions & Trillions," DefeatTheDebt. com, Employment Policies Institute, http://www.defeatthedebt.com/ understanding-the-national-debt/millions-billions-trillions/.

37. Ibid.

38. Ibid. There are about 500 billion stars in the Milky Way; see April Holladay, "Seeing the Milky Way and Counting Its Stars," Jnuary 2, 2006, *USA Today*, http://www.usatoday.com/tech/columnist/aprilholladay/2006-01-02-milky-way_x.htm.

39. Ibid.

40. Ibid.

41. See Paul Ryan, "The Democrats' Spending Spree," House Budget Committee fact sheet, February 3, 2011, http://budget.house.gov/UploadedFiles/spendingspree.pdf.

42. See Paul Wiseman, "U.S. Downgrade Raises Anxiety, If Not Interest Rates," Associated Press, August 6, 2011; see also George E. Condon Jr., "What a Week: Afghan Deaths, S&P, and Debt Limit Debate Challenge Obama," *National Journal*, August 6, 2011, http://www.nationaljournal.com/whitehouse/ what-a-week-afghan-deaths-s-p-and-debt-limit-debate-challenge-obama-20110806.

43. Zachary A. Goldfarb, "S&P Downgrades U.S. Credit Rating for First Time," *Washington Post*, August 5, 2011, http://www.washingtonpost.com/business/ economy/sandp-considering-first-downgrade-of-us-credit-rating/2011/08/05/ gIQAqKeIxI_story.html.

44. Ashe Schow, "Our Debt Has Reached 100% of GDP," *Heritage Action* (blog), Heritage Action for America, August 4, 2011, http://heritageaction.com/2011/08/ our-debt-has-reached-100-of-gdp/.

45. See Congressional Budget Office, *Federal Debt and Interest Costs: A CBO Study*, December 2010, p. 20, http://www.cbo.gov/ftpdocs/119xx/doc11999/12-14-FederalDebt.pdf; see also Brian Riedl, "CBO Baseline Shows Staggering Debt," National Review Online, January 26, 2011, http://www.nationalreview.com/ corner/258115/cbo-baseline-shows-staggering-debt-brian-riedl; see also Paul Ryan's comments on ABC News: "Look at these numbers. We are going to have a $25 trillion dollar debt in ten years." Jonathan Karl and Gregory Simmons, "ABC News Exclusive: eet the Budget Boss, Rep. Paul Ryan," ABC News, January 26,2011, http://paulryan.house.gov/News/DocumentSingle.aspx?DocumentID=221696.

46. Paul Ryan, "A Roadmap for America's Future," House Budget Committee, introduction, http://www.roadmap.republicans.budget.house.gov/Plan/#Intro.

47. Ibid.

48. These statistics come from the Board of Federal Old-Age and Survivors Insurance and Disability Insurance Trust Funds. See Wade Dokken, *New Century, New Deal: How to Turn Your Wages into Wealth through Social Security Choice* (Washington, DC: Regnery Publishing, 2000), p. 62.

49. "Abortion Statistics: United States Data and Trends," National Right to Life, January 27, 2011, http://www.nrlc.org/Factsheets/FS03_AbortionInTheUS.pdf.

50. See "Combined OASDI Trust Funds," Congressional Budget Office fact sheet, March 2010, http://www.cbo.gov/budget/factsheets/2010b/OASDI-TrustFunds. pdf. For more, see "A Summary of the 2011 Annual Reports," Social Security and Medicare Boards of Trustees, http://www.ssa.gov/oact/trsum/index.html.

51. Stuart Butler et al., "Saving the American Dream: The Heritage Plan to Fix the

Debt, Cut Spending, and Restore Prosperity," The Heritage Foundation, Special Report #91, May 10, 2011, chart 2, "Hiking Taxes to Pay for Entitlements Would Require Doubling Tax Rates," http://www.heritage.org/Research/Reports/2011/05/Saving-the-American-Dream-The-Heritage-Plan-to-Fix-the-Debt-Cut-Spending-and-Restore-Prosperity.

52. Ibid.
53. Ryan, "A Roadmap for America's Future," introduction, http://www.roadmap.republicans.budget.house.gov/Plan/#Intro.
54. Ryan, "A Roadmap for America's Future," "Reforming the Budget Process" section, http://www.roadmap.republicans.budget.house.gov/Plan/#budgetreform.
55. See Butler et al., "Saving the American Dream." The Heritage Plan quotes CBO projections extensively.
56. J. T. Young, "The Road to Greece," *Barron's*, January 22, 2011, http://online.barrons.com/article/SB50001424052970203676504575618561763058500.html.
57. Ibid.
58. Ibid.

CHAPTER TEN: THE WAR AND TERRORISM SCENARIOS
1. Cited by James Pethokoukis, "So How Goes Bin Laden's War on the U.S. Economy?" *U.S. News & World Report*, September 11, 2007.
2. Ibid.
3. Cited by Randall B. Hamud, *Osama bin Laden: America's Enemy in His Own Words*, (San Diego, CA: Nadeem Publishing, 2005), pp. 163–164.
4. Cited in "Ahmadinejad: Doom Will Befall U.S. Economy," Press TV, April 23, 2008.
5. Cited in "Iran Threatens to Close Strait of Hormuz if Attacked," MEMRI, Special Dispatch #2029, August 19, 2008.
6. I first heard these five vital interests defined clearly and effectively when I worked at the Heritage Foundation in the early 1990s. I'm grateful to my Heritage mentors on national security: Edwin Feulner Jr., Burton Yale Pines, Kim Holmes, and Jim Phillips. Along these lines, I would commend to your attention the following recent Heritage report outlining threats against the U.S. and how best to defend against them—"A Strong National Defense: The Armed Forces America Needs and What They Will Cost," April 5, 2011, http://www.heritage.org/research/reports/2011/04/a-strong-national-defense-the-armed-forces-america-needs-and-what-they-will-cost.
7. "Putin Threatens to Aim Rockets at U.S. Bases," Associated Press, February 14, 2008, http://www.msnbc.msn.com/id/23162722/ns/world_news-europe/t/putin-threatens-aim-rockets-us-bases/.
8. Alena Chechel et al., "Putin Denounces American Parasite While Russia Increases Treasuries 1,600%," Bloomberg, August 19, 2011, http://www.bloomberg.com/news/2011-08-18/putin-slams-u-s-parasite-after-1-600-jump-in-russia-holdings.html.
9. For more details, see my book *Epicenter* (Carol Stream, IL: Tyndale House Publishers, 2006, 2008).
10. Soviet premier Nikita Khrushchev famously vowed to the American people, "We will bury you." For more details, see the Pulitzer Prize–winning book by William Taubman, *Khrushchev: The Man and His Era* (New York: W. W. Norton & Company, 2004).

11. For more, see "Modernisation in Sheep's Clothing," *Banyan* (blog), *The Economist*, August 26, 2011, http://www.economist.com/blogs/banyan/2011/08/ chinas-military-power.

12. See Miles Yu, "Inside China: Spy Chief on Chinese Threat," *Washington Times*, June 8, 2011, http://www.washingtontimes.com/news/2011/jun/8/ inside-china-408425229/.

13. Patrick Tyler, "As China Threatens Taiwan, It Makes Sure U.S. Listens," *New York Times*, January 24, 1996, http://www.nytimes.com/1996/01/24/world/as-china-threatens-taiwan-it-makes-sure-us-listens.html?pagewanted=print&src=pm.

14. Joseph Kahn, "Chinese General Threatens Use of A-Bombs If U.S. Intrudes," *New York Times*, July 15, 2005, http://www.nytimes.com/2005/07/15/international/ asia/15china.html.

15. For more details on the Iranian threat, see my book *Inside the Revolution* (Carol Stream, IL: Tyndale House Publishers, 2009).

16. "Tehran Threatens West with Homicide Attacks," Fox News, April 16, 2006, http://www.foxnews.com/story/0,2933,191910,00.html. Marie Colvin et al., "Iran Suicide Bombers 'Ready to Hit Britain,'" *The Sunday Times of London*, April 16, 2006, http://www.timesonline.co.uk/tol/news/uk/ article706132.ece. "Iran: We Have 70,000 Suicide Bombers Ready to Strike Israel," Associated Press, January 5, 2009, http://www.haaretz.com/news/ iran-we-have-70-000-suicide-bombers-ready-to-strike-israel-1.267497.

17. John Esposito and Dalia Mogahed, *Who Speaks for Islam? What a Billion Muslims Really Think* (New York: Gallup Press, 2008), pp. x–xi.

18. According to a 2007 Pew Research Center poll, 28 percent of Egyptian Muslims say they believe suicide bombings against civilian targets are sometimes or often justified; 17 percent of Turkish Muslims agree, along with 10 percent of Indonesian Muslims, 14 percent of Pakistani Muslims, 29 percent of Jordanian Muslims, and 46 percent of Nigerian Muslims. See Andrew Kohut, "Muslims in America: Middle Class and Mostly Mainstream," Pew Research Center, May 22, 2007, http://pewresearch.org/ assets/pdf/muslim-americans.pdf, accessed June 24, 2008.

19. George Tenet, *At the Center of the Storm: My Years at the CIA* (New York: Harper Collins, 2007), p. 260, citing a *Time* article from December 24, 1998.

20. Ibid., p. 269.

21. See Sheikh Nasir bin Hamd al-Fahd, "A Treatise on the Legal Status of Using Weapons of Mass Destruction Against the Infidels," May 1, 2003; cited by Tenet, p. 274.

22. Tenet, pp. 259–260.

23. Porter Goss, interview with the author, February 12, 2008.

24. "Mullen: Debt Is Top National Security Issue," CNN, August 27, 2010, http://articles.cnn.com/2010-08-27/us/debt.security. mullen_1_pentagon-budget-national-debt-michael-mullen?_s=PM:US.

25. See Elizabeth MacDonald, "U.S. Debt a National Security Issue," Fox Business, October 11, 2010, http://www.foxbusiness.com/markets/2010/10/11/ debt-national-security-issue/.

26. See "Some Republicans Press for End to Afghan War after bin Laden's Death," FoxNews.com, May 24, 2011, http://www.foxnews.com/politics/2011/05/24/ republicans-press-end-afghan-war-bin-ladens-death/; see also Josh Rogin, "Grover

Norquist Calls for Discussion on Right about Leaving Afghanistan," *Foreign Policy*, January 12, 2011, http://thecable.foreignpolicy.com/posts/2011/01/12/grover_norquist_calls_for_discussion_on_right_about_leaving_afghanistan.

27. John McCain, interview by Chris Wallace, "9/11, Then and Now," *Fox News Sunday with Chris Wallace*, Fox News, September 11, 2011, http://www.foxnews.com/on-air/fox-news-sunday/2011/09/11/fox-news-sunday-911-then-and-now#ixzz1XyNsV8rt.

CHAPTER ELEVEN: THE NATURAL DISASTER SCENARIOS

1. Eric S. Blake et al., "The Deadliest, Costliest, and Most Intense United States Tropical Cyclones from 1851 to 2010," NOAA Technical Memorandum NWS NHC-6, National Weather Service/National Hurricane Center, August 2011, p. 9, http://www.nhc.noaa.gov/pdf/nws-nhc-6.pdf.

2. "2011 Record Year for Weather Disasters," UPI, August 19, 2011, http://www.upi.com/Top_News/US/2011/08/19/2011-record-year-for-weather-disasters/UPI-57581313783153/.

3. Marty Roney and Carolyn Pesce, "Dozens of Tornadoes Kill At Least 297 People in South," *USA Today*, April 29, 2011, http://www.usatoday.com/weather/storms/tornadoes/2011-04-28-deadly-tornado-south_n.htm?loc=interstitialskip.

4. See "Worst Fires on Record Ravage Texas," Voice of America, September 7, 2011, http://www.voanews.com/english/news/usa/Worst-Fires-on-Record-Ravage-Texas-129366213.html; see also "Worst Drought in Texas History Ravages Crops, Livestock," PBS *NewsHour*, August 31, 2011, http://www.pbs.org/newshour/bb/weather/july-dec11/texasdrought_08-31.html.

5. Katharine Q. Seeyle, "Above All Else, Eastern Quake Rattles Nerves," *New York Times*, August 23, 2011, http://www.nytimes.com/2011/08/24/us/24quake.html?_r=1&pagewanted=all.

6. John Wesley, "The Cause and Cure of Earthquakes," first published in 1750, included in a series of sermons of John Wesley posted on the Global Ministries of the United Methodist Church website, http://new.gbgm-umc.org/umhistory/wesley/sermons/129/.

7. "Rare 5.8-Magnitude Earthquake Jolts East Coast, Causing Various Disruptions," PBS *NewsHour*, August 23, 2011, http://www.pbs.org/newshour/rundown/2011/08/rare-59-earthquake-jolts-virginia.html.

8. Ker Than, "Rare Earthquake Hits Virginia, Rattles U.S. East Coast," *National Geographic*, August 23, 2011, http://news.nationalgeographic.com/news/2011/08/110824-earthquakes-today-washington-dc-richmond-virginia-science/.

9. Ibid.

10. Kirk Johnson, "Rare Strong Earthquake Hits Colorado," *New York Times*, August 23, 2011, http://www.nytimes.com/2011/08/24/us/24earthquake.html?_r=1&hpw.

11. Ben Tracy, "Haiti Revives Fears of 'Big One' in Calif.," CBS News, January 14, 2010, http://www.cbsnews.com/stories/2010/01/14/eveningnews/main6097974.shtml.

12. William M. Welch et al., "Chilean Earthquake Hints at Dangers of 'Big One' for USA," *USA Today*, March 1, 2010, http://www.usatoday.com/tech/science/2010-03-01-chile-quake-lessons_N.htm.

13. For more on the 1906 San Francisco quake, see "The Great 1906 San Francisco Earthquake," U.S. Geological Survey website, http://earthquake.usgs.gov/regional/nca/1906/18april/.

14. Wayne R. Thatcher, Peter L. Ward, David J. Wald, James W. Hendley II, and Peter H. Stauffer, "When Will the Next Great Quake Strike Northern California?" U.S. Geological Survey Fact Sheet 094-96, http://pubs.usgs.gov/fs/1996/fs094-96/.

15. Ibid.

16. "Significant Earthquakes and Faults: Northridge Earthquake," Southern California Earthquake Data Center, California Insititute of Technology, http://www.data.scec.org/significant/northridge1994.html.

17. "Forecasting California's Earthquakes—What Can We Expect in the Next Thirty Years?," U.S. Geological Survey fact sheet 2008-3027, 2008, http://pubs.usgs.gov/fs/2008/3027/fs2008-3027.pdf.

18. John Roach, "'Supercities' Vulnerable to Killer Quakes, Expert Warns," *National Geographic*, May 2, 2003, http://news.nationalgeographic.com/news/2003/05/0502_030502_killerquakes.html.

19. Ibid.

20. Ibid.

21. Stefan Lovgren, "Tsunamis More Likely to Hit U.S. than Asia," *National Geographic*, January 3, 2005, http://news.nationalgeographic.com/news/pf/66796484.html.

22. Ibid.

23. Ibid.

24. "Hurricane Irene Kills 10, Prompts Largest Mass Evacuation in U.S. History," *Haaretz*/Reuters, August 28, 2011, http://www.haaretz.com/news/international/hurricane-irene-kills-10-prompts-largest-mass-evacuation-in-u-s-history-1.381123.

25. "Over 5 Million Still without Power after Irene: DOE," Reuters, August 29, 2011, http://www.reuters.com/article/2011/08/29/us-storm-irene-outage-idUSTRE77S5TQ20110829.

26. Michael Cooper, "Hurricane Cost Seen as Ranking among Top Ten," *New York Times*, August 30, 2011, http://www.nytimes.com/2011/08/31/us/31floods.html?pagewanted=all.

27. Mike Wall, "Hurricane Irene vs. Hurricane Katrina: How They Stack Up," Live Science, August 29, 2011, http://www.livescience.com/15813-hurricane-katrina-irene-comparison.html?utm_source/feedburner&utm_medium/feed&utm_campaign/Feed%3A+Livesciencecom+%28LiveScience.com+Science+Headline+Feed%29.

28. Nate Silver, "A New York Hurricane Could Be a Multibillion-Dollar Disaster," *FiveThirtyEight* (blog), *New York Times*, August 26, 2011, http://fivethirtyeight.blogs.nytimes.com/2011/08/26/new-york-hurricane-could-be-multibillion-dollar-catastrophe/.

29. Ibid.

30. Ibid.

31. Ibid.

32. Ibid.

33. Eric Blake et al., pp. 7, 9.

34. Ibid., p. 6.

35. Wall.

36. Robert Lee Holtz, "Northern Landfall Puts Storm on Map," *Wall Street Journal*, August 29, 2011, http://online.wsj.com/article/SB10001424053111903352704576536790143615646.html?mod=WSJ_hp_LEFTTopStories.

37. Ibid.

38. See "Explore Mount St. Helens" history page, U.S. Department of Agriculture, Forest Service, http://www.fs.usda.gov/detail/mountsthelens/home/?cid=stelprdb5199437.

39. "Economic Impact of the May 18, 1980 Eruption," U.S. Geological Survey fact sheet, http://vulcan.wr.usgs.gov/Volcanoes/MSH/May18/description_economic_impact.html.

40. Natalie Wolchover, "Keeping an Eye on Yellowstone's Supervolcano," MSNBC, June 8, 2011, http://www.msnbc.msn.com/id/43329798/ns/technology_and_science-science/t/keeping-eye-yellowstones-supervolcano/.

41. Daniel Bates, "Could Yellowstone National Park's Caldera Super-Volcano Be Close to Eruption?" *Daily Mail*, January 25, 2011, http://www.dailymail.co.uk/travel/article-1350340/Super-volcano-Yellowstones-National-Park-soon-erupt.html.

42. See "Supervolcano Docudrama on Yellowstone Volcano—Questions and Answers on Supervolcanoes, Volcanic Hazards," Yellowstone Volcano Observatory, U.S. Geological Survey, http://volcanoes.usgs.gov/yvo/publications/2005/docudrama.php.

43. See "Steam Explosions, Earthquakes, and Volcanic Eruptions—What's in Yellowstone's Future?" U.S. Geological Survey Fact Sheet 2005-3024, 2005, http://pubs.usgs.gov/fs/2005/3024/.

CHAPTER TWELVE: THE RAPTURE SCENARIO

1. See *Strong's Concordance, harpazō* s.v., http://www.blueletterbible.org/lang/lexicon/lexicon.cfm?Strongs=G726&t=KJV.

2. Mark Hitchcock and Thomas Ice, *The Truth Behind Left Behind*, (Sisters, OR: Multnomah Publishers, 2004), pp. 22–23.

CHAPTER THIRTEEN: THE LAST BEST HOPE

1. For updated total population, see U.S. Population Clock, created by the U.S. Census Bureau, http://www.census.gov/main/www/popclock.html. For the figure 234 million people age 18 or older, see latest U.S. Census figures (2010) in U.S. Department of Commerce, "Age and Sex Composition: 2010," May 2011, http://www.census.gov/prod/cen2010/briefs/c2010br-03.pdf.

2. William J. Bennett, *The Index of Leading Cultural Indicators: American Society at the End of the Twentieth Century* (New York: WaterBrook Press, 1999), p. 4.

3. See Steven Ertelt, "New Zogby Poll: Americans Are Pro-Life on Numerous Abortion Issues," LifeNews.com, March 22, 2006, http://www.lifenews.com/2006/03/22/nat-2164/.

4. See Lydia Saad, "Doctor-Assisted Suicide Is Moral Issue Dividing Americans Most: Pornography, Gay Relations Produce Biggest Generational Gaps," Gallup, May 31, 2011, http://www.gallup.com/poll/147842/Doctor-Assisted-Suicide-Moral-Issue-Dividing-Americans.aspx. See also Steven Ertelt, "New Poll: 55% of Americans Say Abortion Morally Wrong," LifeNews.com, August 26, 2011, http://www.lifenews.com/2011/08/26/new-poll-55-of-americans-say-abortion-morally-wrong/.

5. "Abortion Statistics: United States Data and Trends," National Right to Life, January 27, 2011, http://www.nrlc.org/Factsheets/FS03_AbortionInTheUS.pdf.

6. Saad.

7. Jerry Ropelato, "Internet Pornography Statistics," Internet Filter Software Reviews, http://internet-filter-review.toptenreviews.com/internet-pornography-statistics-pg2.html.

8. Ibid.

9. Saad.

10. "Estimated Crime in the United States—Total," Uniform Crime Reporting Statistics, Federal Bureau of Investigation, U.S. Department of Justice, http://www.ucrdatatool.gov/Search/Crime/State/RunCrimeStatebyState.cfm. It should be noted that the number of forcible rapes in the U.S. peaked in the early- to mid-1990s, hitting a high of 109,062 in 1992 and remaining over 100,000 per year until 1994.

11. As of June 17, 2011, the National Center for Missing & Exploited Children listed 739,853 sexual predators in the U.S.; see "Map of Registered Sex Offenders in the United States," http://www.missingkids.com/en_US/documents/sex-offender-map.pdf. This is up from 603,000 in 2007. See John Gramlich, "The Ever-Growing Sex Offender Registry," Stateline, April 12, 2010, http://www.stateline.org/live/details/story?contentId=476264.

12. "Sex Offenders Getting Younger, More Violent," Associated Press, June 9, 2007, http://www.msnbc.msn.com/id/19143411/ns/us_news-crime_and_courts/t/sex-offenders-getting-younger-more-violent/.

13. Ibid.

14. Frank Newport, "For First Time, Majority of Americans Favor Legal Gay Marriage," Gallup, May 20, 2011, http://www.gallup.com/poll/147662/first-time-majority-americans-favor-legal-gay-marriage.aspx.

15. "Same-Sex Marriage, Civil Unions, and Domestic Partnerships: Quick Facts on Key Provisions," National Conference of State Legislatures, July 14, 2011, http://www.ncsl.org/default.aspx?tabid=16430.

16. George Barna, *Futurecast* (Carol Stream, IL: BarnaBooks/Tyndale House Publishers, 2011), p. 124.

17. Ibid., p. 132.

18. Ibid.

19. Ibid., p. 35.

20. These numbers were reported in the "Pastor's Family Bulletin," Focus on the Family, March 2000, cited in "Archive of Statistics on Internet Dangers," Enough Is Enough, http://www.enough.org/inside.php?tag=stat#9.

21. Ibid.

22. See editorial, "The Leadership Survey of Pastors and Internet Pornography," *Leadership Journal*, January 1, 2001, http://www.christianitytoday.com/le/2001/winter/12.89.html. Admittedly, these statistics are ten years out of date. I wonder if today they would be higher. However, I have not been able to find more recent data. Indeed, in an August 2010 article on "Protecting Churches from Porn," *Christianity Today* again cited the 2001 statistics: http://www.christianitytoday.com/le/2010/summer/protectingchurches.html.

23. Barna, *Futurecast*, p. 172.

24. George Barna, *Growing True Disciples* (Colorado Springs, CO: WaterBrook Press, 2001), pp. 35, 41.

25. George Barna, "The Year's Most Intriguing Findings, from Barna Research Studies,"

Barna Update, December 17, 2011, http://www.barna.org/barna-update/article/
5-barna-update/64-the-years-most-intriguing-findings-from-barna-research-studies.

CHAPTER FOURTEEN: A CAUSE FOR OPTIMISM: INSIDE AMERICA'S FIRST GREAT AWAKENING

1. Jill Lepore, *The Name of War: King Philip's War and the Origins of American Identity* (New York: Vintage Books/Random House, 1998), back cover and p. xi. See also Douglas Edward Leach, *Flintlock & Tomahawk: New England in King Philip's War* (Woodstock, VT: Countrymen Press, 2009).
2. Thomas Kidd, *The Great Awakening: The Roots of Evangelical Christianity in Colonial America* (New Haven, CT: Yale University Press, 2007), p. 2.
3. See Yale University's biography of Jonathan Edwards, http://edwards.yale.edu/research/about-edwards/biography.
4. Kidd, p. 10.
5. Ibid.
6. Jonathan Edwards, *A Faithful Narrative of the Surprising Work of God*, published in 1738, and available online at http://www.jonathan-edwards.org/Narrative.html.
7. Ibid.
8. Ibid.
9. Ibid.
10. To read the text of this famous sermon, go to http://www.jonathan-edwards.org/Sinners.html.
11. See biography of Jonathan Edwards, http://edwards.yale.edu/research/about-edwards/biography. See also Princeton University's biography of Edwards, http://www.princeton.edu/pr/facts/presidents/05.htm. Regarding the founding of Princeton University: "At Princeton, one of the founders (probably Ebenezer Pemberton) wrote in c. 1750, 'Though our great Intention was to erect a seminary for educating Ministers of the Gospel, yet we hope it will be useful in other learned professions— Ornaments of the State as well as the Church. Therefore we propose to make the plan of Education as extensive as our Circumstances will admit.'" Quoted in Alexander Leitch, *A Princeton Companion* (Princeton University Press, 1978). See also http://etcweb.princeton.edu/CampusWWW/Companion/founding_princeton.html.
12. See Kenneth P. Minkema, "Edwards' Family," Jonathan Edwards Center, Yale University, http://edwards.yale.edu/research/about-edwards/family-life.
13. See Diane Severance, "Jonathan Edwards, America's Humble Giant," Christianity.com, http://www.christianity.com/ChurchHistory/11630188/.
14. Arnold A. Dallimore, *George Whitefield: God's Anointed Servant in the Great Revival of the Eighteenth Century* (Wheaton, IL: Crossway, 1990), p. 17.
15. Ibid., p. 18.
16. Ibid., p. 21.
17. Ibid., p. 22.
18. Ibid., p. 46.
19. Collin Hansen and John Woodbridge, *A God-Sized Vision: Revival Stories That Stretch and Stir* (Grand Rapids, MI: Zondervan, 2010), p. 47.
20. Mark A. Noll, *A History of Christianity in the United States and Canada* (Grand Rapids, MI: Wm. B. Eerdmans Publishing Co., 1992), p. 91.

21. Bill Bright, "How to Introduce Others to Christ" (Orlando, FL: Cru Press, 2007). See http://www.centerfieldproductions.com/members/content/crucomm/brighthowtointroduceotherstochrist.pdf.

22. Richard L. Bushman, ed., *The Great Awakening: Documents on the Revival of Religion, 1740–1745* (Chapel Hill, NC: University of North Carolina Press, 1989), p. xii.

23. Dallimore, p. 76.

24. Ibid.

25. Ibid., p. 82.

26. Ibid., p. 141.

27. Noll, *History of Christianity*, p. 93.

28. Dallimore, p. 197.

29. Ibid., p. 201.

30. Bushman, pp. xi–xii.

31. Mark Noll, *The Rise of Evangelicalism: The Age of Edwards, Whitefield, and the Wesleys* (Downers Grove, IL: IVP Academic, 2003), p. 83.

32. Georgia Historical Society, "John Wesley," Today in Georgia History, http://www.todayingeorgiahistory.org/content/john-wesley. See also Noll, The Rise of Evangelicalism, pp. 83–84.

33. Noll, *The Rise of Evangelicalism*, p. 85.

34. Ibid., p. 95.

35. Ibid.

36. Cited in a profile of John Wesley, ChristianHistory.net, August 8, 2008, http://www.christianitytoday.com/ch/131christians/denominationalfounders/wesley.html?start=1. See also Noll, *The Rise of Evangelicalism*, p. 97.

37. Noll, *The Rise of Evangelicalism*, p. 84.

38. See Profile of Charles Wesley, ChristianHistory.net, August 8, 2008, http://www.christianitytoday.com/ch/131christians/poets/charleswesley.html.

39. Mark A. Noll, *Turning Points: Decisive Moments in the History of Christianity* (Grand Rapids, MI: Baker Academic, 2000), pp. 226–227.

40. Profile of John Wesley, ChristianHistory.net.

CHAPTER FIFTEEN: MORE CAUSE FOR OPTIMISM: INSIDE AMERICA'S SECOND GREAT AWAKENING

1. "The 25 Most Influential Evangelicals in America," *Time*, February 7, 2005, http://www.time.com/time/specials/packages/article/0,28804,1993235_1993243,00.html.

2. Mark A. Noll, *A History of Christianity in the United States and Canada* (Grand Rapids, MI: Wm. B. Eerdmans Publishing Co., 1992), p. 166. Noll was a highly acclaimed evangelical scholar and professor at Wheaton College for many years, then moved to the University of Notre Dame in 2006.

3. Steve Forbes, *A New Birth of Freedom* (Washington, DC: Regnery Publishing, 1999), p. 138. In the second paragraph of this excerpt, Steve quotes text from *Revival Signs* by Tom Phillips (Sisters, OR: Multnomah, 1995).

4. John Wigger, *American Saint: Francis Asbury and the Methodists* (New York: Oxford University Press USA, 2009), p. 3.

5. Noll, *History of Christianity*, p. 173.

6. Ibid., p. 171.

7. Wigger, p. 3. A 2008 article at ChristianHistory.net said the number of sermons was 16,500. See "Francis Asbury: Methodist on Horseback," ChristianHistory. net, August 8 2008, http://www.christianitytoday.com/ch/131christians/denominationalfounders/asbury.html.

8. Noll, *History of Christianity*, p. 173.

9. See General Commission on Archives & History, United Methodist Church, statistics posted online at http://www.gcah.org/site/c.ghKJIoPHIoE/b.3828783/.

10. Stephen J. Ahn, "Timothy Dwight and Yale: The Making of a University," *Yale Standard*, 2001, http://yalestandard.com/timothydwightandyale.aspx.

11. John R. Fitzmier, *New England's Moral Legislator: Timothy Dwight, 1752–1817* (Bloomington, IN: Indiana University Press, 1998), p. 15. The student cited was Lyman Beecher.

12. Ahn.

13. Brooks Mather Kelley, *Yale: A History* (New Haven, CT: Yale University Press, 1974), p. 123.

14. Collin Hansen and John Woodbridge, *A God-Sized Vision: Revival Stories That Stretch and Stir* (Grand Rapids, MI: Zondervan, 2010), p. 63.

15. Fitzmier, p. 53.

16. An article on Christianity.com stated that Dwight "fired all of the faculty members who favored the anti-Christian ideas of French rationalism. Subsequently, about one-third of the student body were converted to Christianity." See Dan Graves, "Yale Leader Timothy Dwight Died in Harness," Christianity.com, June 2007, http://www.christianity.com/ChurchHistory/11630378/. A biography published in the 1960s suggested that Dwight fired those with "infidel leanings" who did not fit into his vision for the college. See Kenneth Silverman, *Timothy Dwight* (New York: Twayne Publishers, 1969), p. 97.

17. Kelley, pp. 130–131.

18. Ahn.

19. Hansen and Woodbridge, pp. 65–66.

20. Ibid., p. 66.

21. Ibid., pp. 66–67.

22. Ahn.

23. Hansen and Woodbridge, p. 68.

24. Ahn.

25. Kelley, pp. 123–124.

26. See Noll, *A History of Christianity*, p. 169; see also profile of Lyman Beecher, resource for *God in America*, *American Experience*, PBS, 2010, http://www.pbs.org/godinamerica/people/lyman-beecher.html.

27. Hansen and Woodbridge, p. 73.

28. Charles Finney, *The Autobiography of Charles Finney*, ed. Helen Wessel (Minneapolis, MN: Bethany House Publishers, 1977), p. 6. This is an abridged version of Finney's original 1876 book.

29. Ibid., p. 11.

30. Ibid., p. 17.

31. Ibid., pp. 17–18.

32. Ibid., p. 31.

33. Ibid., p. 50.
34. Ibid., p. 38.
35. Noll, *History of Christianity*, p. 175.
36. Cited by Finney in *Autobiography*, pp. 164–165. In his book *Modern Revivalism: Charles Grandison Finney to Billy Graham* (Eugene, OR: Wipf and Stock Publishers, 2005; a republication of the original book published in 1959), historian William McLoughlin Jr. cited Presbyterian statistics from the Rochester area to argue that the number was not one hundred thousand but "more realistically" about sixty thousand. Still, he concurred that the revival had a huge impact on Rochester and beyond. See McLoughlin, pp. 57–58.
37. Finney, *Autobiography*, p. 164.
38. "Charles Finney: Father of American Revivalism," ChristianHistory.net, August 8, 2008, http://www.christianitytoday.com/ch/131christians/ evangelistsandapologists/finney.html.
39. McLoughlin, p. 57.
40. Charles G. Finney, *Lectures on Revival* (Minneapolis, MN: Bethany House Publishers, 1989, reprint of the original 1835 book), p. 15.
41. Noll, *History of Christianity*, p. 176.
42. Finney, *Lectures on Revival*, p. 13.
43. Finney, *Autobiography*, back cover.
44. Noll, *History of Christianity*, p. 170.
45. Thomas S. Kidd, *The Great Awakening: The Roots of Evangelical Christianity in Colonial America* (New Haven, CT: Yale University Press, 2007), p. 322.
46. Noll, *History of Christianity*, pp. 178–179.
47. Kidd, p. 322.
48. Ibid.
49. Noll, *History of Christianity*, pp. 178–179.
50. Ibid.

CHAPTER SIXTEEN: WILL AMERICA EXPERIENCE A THIRD GREAT AWAKENING?

1. We devoted the 2011 Epicenter Conference in Jerusalem to teaching through the book of Joel, chapter by chapter and verse by verse. The messages are available online for free at www.epicenterconference.com. I have also posted my notes on each chapter of Joel on my blog. Please go to www.joelrosenberg.com, click on the blog, and search for "Book of Joel."

CHAPTER SEVENTEEN: CAN AMERICA AGAIN BE A SHINING CITY ON A HILL?

1. Governor John Winthrop, "A Model of Christian Charity," address delivered in 1630 to passengers aboard the *Arbella*, redacted and introduced by John Beardsley, editor in chief, the *Winthrop Society Quarterly*, 1997, http://religiousfreedom.lib. virginia.edu/sacred/charity.html; for more, see Francis J. Bremer, *John Winthrop: America's Forgotten Founding Father* (New York: Oxford University Press USA, 2005).
2. John F. Kennedy, "Address to the Massachusetts General Court," January 9, 1961, transcript and audio at John F. Kennedy Presidential Library and Museum, http://www.jfklibrary.org/Asset-Viewer/OYhUZE2Qoo-ogdV70k900A.aspx; also see transcript at http://www.americanrhetoric.com/speeches/jfkcommonwealthmass.htm.

3. Ronald Reagan, "Farewell Address to the Nation," January 11, 1989, transcript and video at Miller Center, University of Virginia, http://millercenter.org/scripps/archive/speeches/detail/3418.

4. Cited by William J. Federer, *America's God and Country: Encyclopedia of Quotations* (Coppell, TX: Fame Publishing, 1994), p. 660.

5. Ibid., p. 12.

6. Ibid., p. 324.

7. Ibid., p. 323.

8. Cited by Tim LaHaye, *Faith of Our Founding Fathers* (Brentwood, TN: Wolgemuth & Hyatt Publishers, 1987), p. 127.

9. Cited by Walter Isaacson, *Benjamin Franklin: An American Life* (New York: Simon & Schuster, 2003), p. 30.

10. The rest of the citations came from Enlightenment sources, the Whigs, common law, classical literature, or other sources. Donald S. Lutz, *A Preface to American Political Theory* (Lawrence, KS: University Press of Kansas, 1992), pp. 134–135. Lutz cites a study he did several years earlier. See Donald S. Lutz, "The Relative Influence of European Writers on Late Eighteenth Century American Political Thought," *American Political Science Review* 78 (March 1984): 189–197.

11. See Thomas Jefferson et al., Declaration of Independence, July 4, 1776, transcription of the original document at the National Archives, http://www.archives.gov/exhibits/charters/declaration_transcript.html.

12. See the text of the United States Constitution at http://www.archives.gov/exhibits/charters/constitution.html and the Bill of Rights at http://www.archives.gov/exhibits/charters/bill_of_rights.html.

13. This number is cited here to describe a political reality, not a spiritual one. The number does not necessarily reflect how many Americans in 1976 truly understood the biblical meaning of the term *born again* found in John 3, believed every element of orthodox Christian teaching in the New Testament, and were fully devoted followers of Jesus Christ who had a personal relationship with him. Rather, it simply reflects a pollster asking a voter, "Do you consider yourself a born-again Christian?" and the voter saying yes. Also, it should be noted that these numbers (and those that follow in this section of the book) specifically refer to *white* born-again Christians, as this is the group the Gallup poll was tracking. See Albert L. Winseman, "'Born-Agains' Wield Political, Economic Influence," Gallup commentary, April 13, 2004, http://www.gallup.com/poll/11269/bornagains-wield-political-economic-influence.aspx.

14. See Doug Wead, "The History of the Evangelical Vote in Presidential Elections," *Doug Wead The Blog*, September 11, 2008, http://dougwead.wordpress.com/2008/09/11/the-history-of-the-evangelical-vote-in-presidential-elections/. Wead was a political advisor to Presidents George H. W. Bush and George W. Bush on evangelical political matters. He analyzed the numbers from numerous public and private exit polls, leaning most heavily on Gallup data.

15. The 39 percent figure comes from a December 7–10, 1979, poll. See Conrad Hackett and D. Michael Lindsay, "Measuring Evangelicalism: Consequences of Different Operationalization Strategies," *Journal for the Scientific Study of Religion* 47, (August 28, 2008): 502, Table 1, Gallup Poll Evangelical Questions.

16. See Sara Diamond, *Not by Politics Alone: The Enduring Influence of the Christian Right* (New York: Guilford Press, 1998), p. 62; see also Wead, "History of the

Evangelical Vote." The *New York Times* reported Reagan winning 56 percent of the born-again vote to 40 percent for Carter. See "National Exit Polls Table," *New York Times*, November 5, 2008, http://elections.nytimes.com/2008/results/president/national-exit-polls.html. The differences come from how pollsters define "born-again Christians," including whether they only include Protestants or also include Catholics.

17. Wead.

18. Ibid.

19. Ibid. The Ross Perot numbers come from the *New York Times* exit polls. See "National Exit Polls Table," http://elections.nytimes.com/2008/results/president/national-exit-polls.html.

20. "National Exit Polls Table."

21. Winseman.

22. Wead.

23. Ibid.

24. In March 2008, polls showed Senator McCain was losing the Christian vote to an unnamed Democratic nominee (Barack Obama and Hillary Clinton were still battling for the nomination), 36 percent to 45 percent, with 19 percent of Christian voters undecided. Among Protestants, McCain pulled even with the Democrats at 40 percent. But the Democrats had a strong 32-point lead over McCain among Catholics. Among white evangelical Protestants, McCain was doing better (51 percent to 28 percent) but had certainly not rallied born-again voters behind him at that point. For an analysis of Senator McCain's challenges among born-again Christians earlier in the campaign year, see Joel C. Rosenberg, "McCain's Evangelical Problem," National Review Online, March 26, 2008, http://www.nationalreview.com/blogs/print/224034. For final numbers, see "National Exit Polls Table," http://elections.nytimes.com/2008/results/president/national-exit-polls.html.

25. See CNN's national exit polls for the 2010 midterm congressional elections, posted online at "Exit Polls," Election Center, CNN Politics, http://www.cnn.com/ELECTION/2010/results/polls/#USH00p1.

26. Winthrop.

Index

How will we invest our time,
talent, and treasure now,
*before **revival** or **implosion** comes?*

★ ★ ★ ★ ★ ★ ★ ★

COMING FALL 2012:

THE INVESTED LIFE:
MAKING DISCIPLES OF ALL NATIONS
by Joel C. Rosenberg with Dr. T. E. Koshy

★ ★ ★ ★ ★ ★ ★ ★

Every follower of Jesus Christ should be
able to answer two simple questions:

★ *Who is investing in me?*
★ *Whom am I investing in?*

God wants to pour spiritual and emotional
capital into you. And he wants to use you to
pour spiritual and emotional capital into the
lives of others. Along the way, you'll
be changed. Others will change.
It's the heart of the Great Commission.

TYNDALE

CP0569

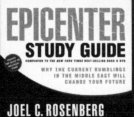

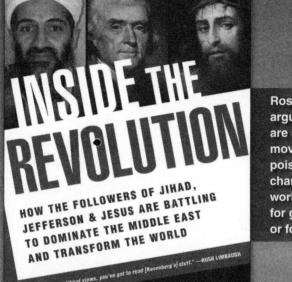

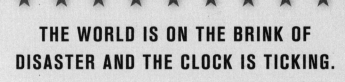